33.00

CORRUPTION IN CORPORATE AMERICA

Who Is Responsible?
Who Will Protect the Public Interest?

SECOND EDITION

Abraham L. Gitlow

University Press of America,® Inc.
Lanham · Boulder · New York · Toronto · Plymouth, UK

Copyright © 2007 by
University Press of America,® Inc.
4501 Forbes Boulevard
Suite 200
Lanham, Maryland 20706
UPA Acquisitions Department (301) 459-3366

Estover Road
Plymouth PL6 7PY
United Kingdom

Library of Congress Control Number: 2007929245
ISBN-13: 978-0-7618-3811-1 (clothbound : alk. paper)
ISBN-10: 0-7618-3811-2 (clothbound : alk. paper)
ISBN-13: 978-0-7618-3812-8 (paperback : alk. paper)
ISBN-10: 0-7618-3812-0 (paperback : alk. paper)

In memory of

My beloved Beatrice

Contents

Preface

Corruption in Corporate America evolved from a seminar I arranged and conducted in the Spring 2003 semester at New York University's Stern School of Business. The seminar itself resulted from my dismay over the disclosure of widespread corruption in major public corporations; corruption that spread like an evil virus and apparently infected many who came into contact with it. I had been a director of a number of public corporations, and was well aware of the fiduciary obligations and prudent business judgment responsibilities attendant on that position. Further, I had observed the growth of class action lawsuits by disgruntled shareholders in the merger and acquisition spree of the eighties, and thought that the behavior and independence of non-management directors had been improved as a consequence. And, the idea that leading auditing firms would compromise their audits under pressure from CEOs and CFOs seemed far fetched. After all, their professional reputations for integrity were at stake, and America boasted to the world that our accounting standards were a model that insured transparency and reliability. We were so concerned about the integrity of corporate behavior that we had even enacted a Foreign Corrupt Practices Act, to punish those who succumbed to the enticements of foreign misbehavior.

More important, I was deeply concerned that a loss of confidence in the integrity of corporate accounts would compromise confidence in the stability of our capital markets. I worried that such a loss of confidence could undermine the saving-investment process, which is the critical underpinning of future innovation, growth in productivity, and enlargement of society's well-being. Relevant to my distress and worry was the belief that America's business schools may have contributed to the problem, and have a responsibility to do something about it. I was and am convinced that the B schools have to exert every effort to make their graduates understand that as future business leaders they have to sustain the integrity of corporate accounts, because the effectiveness of the capital markets and the free market system itself rests upon that integrity. If the B schools produce only clever technicians, who seek profit and personal gain through malfeasance and tricky accounting and legal gimmicks, then they will have failed miserably in their mission to enhance economic and social well-being, for that is their true mission. It needed to be kept in mind that many of the leading corporate malefactors were the proud graduates of some of America's elite B schools, and, during their heyday, had often been honored guest lecturers.

It seemed a small step in the right direction to arrange a seminar at my own school. Dean Fred Choi was responsive to my suggestion, and we arranged for 20 select students to participate. I invited eight especially knowledgeable people to visit the seminar and discuss, in turn, the roles of executives, directors, accountants, lawyers, investment bankers, financial analysts, institutional investors, and government and nongovernment regulators as they interacted and influenced corporate behavior and accounts.

My guests were: Paul A. Volcker, former chairman of the Board of Governors of the Federal Reserve System; Harvey Golub, former CEO and board chairman of American Express; James Quigley, CEO (United States) of Deloitte & Touche; Dr. John Sexton, President of New York University and former dean of its law school; Martin Lipton, Wachtell, Lipton, Rosen & Katz; John C. Whitehead, former CEO of Goldman Sachs and Deputy Secretary of State; Arthur Levitt, former chairman of the Securities and Exchange Commission; and Muriel F. Siebert, CEO Muriel Siebert & Co. and the first woman member of the New York Stock Exchange.

The sessions were provocative and characterized by lively discussion. But, throughout the underlying questions were: What had brought about the corruption that besmirched Corporate America? What could be done to avoid repetition in the future? A light went on in my brain during John Sexton's session, when he used the phrase "speaking to power", while describing the role of lawyers in the corporate drama. The phrase was seminal, leading me finally to a unified perception of what had happened, and how it fit into the larger history and experience of the American political system. It led me also to an appreciation of how that system operates to contain such disasters.

The key is the idea of power, especially unchecked power. I realized that it was the development of such power in the hands of "imperial" executives that permitted those carried away with greed and a sense of entitlement to do wrong, and to compel or entice others to become complicit in their wrongdoing. Fear of confronting, i.e., speaking, to that power overcame all those who were presumably gatekeepers, and made possible the unhappy results. I realized also that, if the American political system is about anything, it is about the evil of unbridled power. The American Revolution was about that, and our famous Declaration of Independence speaks to it directly. In that experience and that document was born the idea of a nation ruled by law rather than by men. The further development of a tripartite political structure, characterized by checks and balances, was a brilliant means to achieve a distribution of power that sought to prevent concentration in any single person or group. The story of our recent corporate scandals fits neatly into that framework, and is elucidated by it. So it is that, in the wake of the scandals, comes the Sarbanes-Oxley Act, which, in its centrality, creates checks to executive power, and stiffens the spines of the gatekeepers so that they will speak to such power if it rears its head in the future. And that is what this small volume is about.

I would be grievously remiss if I failed to thank those who have been so helpful to me in completing this work. The list includes the seminar guests, who provided the students and me with an unforgettable experience. The seminar could not have been done without the support of Dean Fred Choi, and his able assistant, Mattie Kennedy. The students did their part, with provocative and constructive questions. Professor Ernest Kurnow, my dear friend and colleague of over a half century, gave me the invaluable benefit of his keen mind and editorial acuity. Also, Lauren Wohl was most helpful in sharpening the book's focus. Finally, a word of appreciation goes to Audrey Finkelstein. She encouraged me to act, when I complained about the scandals. They all have my profound thanks. Of course, as always, any deficiencies that remain are entirely my responsibility.

Abraham L. Gitlow
Miami Beach, Florida

This second, updated edition of the book results from: (1) the enthusiastic reception given to the original edition; (2) the continuing exposure of corporate misbehavior, in spite of the passage of the Sarbanes-Oxley Act of 2002 and its vigorous enforcement, evidenced most recently in backdating of stock options; and (3) the growing strength of complaints that regulatory enthusiasm has been overdone, and should be moderated. I hope that it receives a reception equal to that accorded to its predecessor, and proves as informative.

Abraham L. Gitlow

Chapter I

Introduction

The Context

The unifying and underlying theme of this work is the creation and encouragement of checks on the unrestrained exercise of power. Institutional arrangements that balance such power have been at the heart of the American political and economic system from its very beginning. It is a radical concept, overturning the millennia old order in which power was vested in a person, whether a king, an ayatollah, or a dictator, claiming that his (her) power derived from divine sources or from the mystical entity of the "volk." So it is that in America the concept of three co-equal branches of government was born; the legislative, the executive, and the judicial. The judicial branch provided the frame for the primacy of the rule of law against the power of a person. And, beneath it all lies the belief that the individual citizen is entitled *by right* to speak to power.

Restraints on power in America did not, and do not yet, function perfectly. But, they function better than the alternatives, and hold the hope of evolving into even better restraints on arbitrary power. The system encourages the correction of evils, as those evils manifest themselves. We have seen it in the removal of slavery, the establishment of anti-trust laws, the extension of suffrage to women and those previously denied access to the ballot box, and, most recently, in the legal and other reactions to the corporate accounting scandals of the late nineties. Those scandals occurred in the context of our free market capitalistic system.

Can Free Market Capitalism and Conscience Coexist?

Is it an oxymoron to speak of free market capitalism and conscience together? The answer resides in whether there are ethical values that underlie the system. In theory, capitalism can be considered an amoral system, since it relies on perfectly competitive markets, with knowledgeable, rational participants, to achieve the general welfare. Knowledgeable consumers and producers seek their self-interest, which, through the magic of Adam Smith's Invisible Hand, yields the greatest good for the greatest number. With that outcome, there would seem to be no need for anyone's conscience to be called upon in behalf of the general wellbeing.

But, the system is not perfect. Imperfect knowledge and inequality of bargaining power make it possible for some to exploit others. It is those shortcomings that require an exercise of conscience, and mechanisms through which conscience can be exercised. Personal freedom and political democracy, characterized by the rule of law and the existence of political checks and balances, provide the necessary mechanisms.

The corporate accounting scandals compromised the basic values that underlie the system; namely transparency, the honesty that is necessary to give transparency true and useful meaning, and the freedom to act and speak in the exercise of the knowledge yielded by transparency. In so doing, they undermined investor confidence and weakened capital markets. This is no small matter, because those markets are the mechanism through which our society accumulates the capital that advances technological innovation, productivity improvement, progress in living standards, and general welfare.

Transparency, honesty, and freedom are values requiring the exercise of conscience. They are critical to contemporary welfare capitalism. And it is no oxymoron to speak of capitalism and conscience as handmaidens.

Are Self-Interest and the Profit Motive Necessarily in Conflict with the Moral Claims of Conscience?

There is a notion that the self-interested pursuit of profit by privately owned business is necessarily in conflict with the basic moral values cited. That notion is often associated also with the idea that self-interest is a motive uniquely characteristic of the capitalistic market system. Yet history demonstrates that the pursuit of wealth, as well as power and fame, at the expense of and to the hurt of others is not so confined. It is easily discovered in alternative systems (monarchic, dictatorial, theocratic, any autocratic alternative.) It is easily discovered also among individuals in all the professions and organizational forms characteristic of complex economic, political, and social systems. What is truly unique of welfare capitalism (the form of capitalism characteristic of the United States and Western Europe) and the political democracy that is its partner is its built-in system of checks and balances to unrestrained power. This system is conductive to speaking to power, and enables the moral claims of conscience to exert themselves effectively.

Illustrations drawn from history abound. Ancient societies were characteristically hierarchical, with power concentrated in the higher orders. Yet, self-seeking behavior was well known. The Ten Commandments of the Old Testament, or the equivalent injunctions of the Muslim religion, were responses intended to subdue bad behavior. But, the emergence of the Judeo-Christian ethic did not end behavioral failures. In the Middle Ages in Europe, the Age of Faith, the Catholic Church introduced celibacy for the clergy, to a significant degree as a curb to bishops and other powerful clergymen siphoning church wealth to their families. And, in the Renaissance, Pope Leo X encouraged the wholesale selling of indulgences to raise funds to enable lavish and lascivious living. That abuse of papal power brought about the Lutheran Revolution, because Martin Luther could not speak to and curb that power within the structure of the church. Contests for political power led to the divisive Avignon papacy, which split the church in the early centuries of the second millennium. And, in today's America, the church has been deeply shaken by the immoral and destructive behavior of pedophile priests. Yet, if the church is about anything, it is about the self-sacrificing message of Christ.

In the supposedly ideal socialism of the Soviet Union, which became the dictatorship of the proletariat, black markets existed in currency exchanges as well as elsewhere, despite laws to the contrary. I observed it in 1935, as a teenager, on a lengthy train trip from Odessa to Moscow. And, Stalin's unbridled dictatorial power resulted in the deaths of millions of people, and the enslavement of millions more in the gulags. National Socialism, produced its own evils of genocide during its brief conquest of Europe. Throughout, in every system, some individuals engaged in unethical and self-seeking behavior that was not checked by institutional counterbalances that encourage challenges to the power behind that behavior.

It is not sufficient to rest support of the American system only on the failures of the alternatives. It is necessary to recognize that unethical self-seeking behavior also exists here. And, it is not confined to profit-seeking individuals and business organizations.

The legal profession has gotten a bad reputation, and is the object of derisive jokes. Politicians are regarded widely as being corrupted by contributions to their political campaigns. The so-called Ivory Tower of the academic world offers a plentiful supply of scandals, e.g., the evils of big-time college sports and its pampered athletes, whose supposed academic credentials are often a disgrace, as well as the excesses of grade inflation and undergraduate faculty staffing profiles that exploit graduate teaching assistants and part-time adjunct faculty. The media, which prides itself as the provider of the information necessary to an empowered citizenry, is another illustrative case, with serious lapses from its ideals. And so it goes. But, in America, the press is not an instrument of the State. Nor are any of the other parties to the body politic. In each case, in the long-run, excesses of power have been checked. What remains is the fact that the system of welfare capitalism and political democracy has produced well-being superior to that of any alternative.

Welfare Capitalism:
Capitalism With a Conscience[1]

When we move away from the construct of a pure, perfect capitalistic market system to the form of capitalism that is prevalent in the modern economic and political systems of the western industrialized world, we come to welfare capitalism. It is a fascinating evolution from the cruel nature of early industrialized capitalism. It reflects a societal exercise of conscience that is based on ethical values. Social conscience mediates the power of narrow self-interest to rule exclusively and in unlimited degree in the capitalist society.

Welfare capitalism is a particular form of capitalism, i.e., a free, competitive market economy, characterized by private property and the profit motive, and governed by the rule of law as interpreted and administered by an independent judiciary. This definition sets this brand of capitalism apart from systems also characterized by private property and profits, but subject to authoritarian governments led by dictators or other forms of an all powerful central authority, rather than the rule of law and an independent judiciary. Such an economy, unfettered by non-market institutions created by government, would, in theory, be directed by the preferences of free consumers as their purchases voted those preferences through the market. The owners of capital (plant and equipment) would direct their capital into producing the products and services demanded by consumers, because that would be where profits were to be found. And so the system would achieve resource allocation consistent with consumer preferences, without any obvious central authority controlling the economy's direction and priorities. Since everyone is a consumer, the system distributes voting power among all consumers, and is inherently democratic. Of course, to the degree there is inequality in the distribution of income and wealth, there is also inequality in its voting power. But, depending on the degree of inequality, this limitation is far less than in other systems that human history provided as comparatives.

Welfare capitalism introduces major qualifications into the free market capitalism of pure theory. One example is a free public education system supported by taxation. Relevant also is the creation of far reaching social security systems, providing pension protection for older retired citizens, and extensive or all inclusive medical provision programs. These systems, created by legislative (government) action and supported by taxation, allocate productive resources in accordance with the decision of central government authority. They are responsive to the will of the people through the political institutions, and are subject to change based on political considerations rather than market directives. The political mechanism is one through which a social conscience can direct society's energies and resources to the well-being of those who are otherwise powerless. It mediates and softens the harshness that might otherwise characterize a purely self-interested market economy.

While welfare capitalism enables a sense of social conscience to operate and influence the use of resources, it does not eliminate bad behavior, which can be found in the life of every society, but, hopefully, it is constrained and inhibited in our society by the rule of law. How does the rule of law operate to inhibit unethical and harmful behavior in business? To find the answer, we need to understand the nature of corporate America and its governance, within the context of the entire body politic. We need to look into the interactions of those involved in the management of organizations with the professions and agencies that they influence, as well as the reverse influence of those professions and agencies on them. Our system of checks and balances provides the central mechanism, as it encourages and even mandates speaking to power.

Welfare Capitalism and Checks and Balances at Work

But, an objection can be made immediately. There was an elaborate system of checks and balances in place before the current corporate scandals broke open; a system designed following the stock market collapse of 1929, and during the Great Depression that ensued, but having its origins in the closing years of the 19th century.

Business in America was essentially unregulated in the 19th century. Yet, as the nation spread across the continent and railroads were constructed to tie it together, large scale industry and the capital necessary to finance it stimulated the emergence of corporate combinations designed to curb competition and control market prices. Privately held economic power attended these developments, and its excesses inspired legislation designed to curb it. The infamous trusts developed in the oil, sugar, and whiskey industries inspired the Sherman and Clayton Anti-trust Acts of 1890 and 1914, as well as the Federal Trade Commission Act of the latter year. The Anti-trust division was established in the Department of Justice to enforce the Sherman and Clayton Acts, while the Federal Trade Commission (FTC) was created to enforce the Federal Trade Commission Act. Other agencies with enforcement powers evolved over time, e.g., the Interstate Commerce Commission (ICC), the Civil Aeronautics Board (CAB), the Federal Communications Commission (FCC), and the Secretaries of Agriculture, Treasury, and Interior. Violators were subject to significant punishments, most notably treble damages to those injured. These checks and balances to concentrations of economic power reflected a basic characteristic of our system at work.

A period of relative rest followed 1914, which was broken by the stock market collapse of 1929, and the Great Depression that followed. A series of laws were enacted, to check business excesses and malpractices that became evident in the crisis. Those laws included the Securities Act of 1933, the Securities Exchange Act of 1934, the Public Utility Holding Company Act of 1935, the Trust Indenture Act of 1939, the Investment Company Act of 1940, and the Investment Advisers Act of 1940. Perhaps most notably, the Security Exchange Act of 1934 created the Security and Exchange Commission, to regulate public corporations, and require public disclosure of financial data for the investing public. Unfortunately, these checks, as well as those contained in the other laws, failed ultimately to prevent "cooking" the books and other corporate malpractices.

The stock exchanges, as self-regulating organizations, were supposed to monitor listed companies and check malefactors. Other self-regulating organizations, i.e., the American Institute of Certified Public Accountants (AICPA) and the American Bar Association (ABA) promulgated rules of professional conduct for CPAs and attorneys, intended to check misbehavior. All failed, breaking down before a tsunami of greed in the intoxicating climate of the nineties.

Now, we have the Sarbanes-Oxley Act of 2002, the current effort to restore vigor to our system of checks and balances. Evidently, there are cycles in the eternal struggle between good and evil in the behavior of corporate executives and the professionals who work with them. In later chapters, we will revisit the Act in detail. At this point, we simply note the Act's central purpose of limiting the unbridled power of corporate executives (management), through certain new requirements placed directly upon them, as well as through new and more powerful strictures placed upon boards of directors, accountants, attorneys, investment bankers, financial analysts, and regulatory agencies, as well as others. The Act encourages, indeed mandates, that management's power be challenged when it is inclined to bad behavior, i.e., the other professions and agencies must "speak to power."

The checks and balances that existed prior to Sarbanes-Oxley proved inadequate to rein in the excessive executive power in the hands of management, which allowed the scandalous surge of corporate chicanery that occurred in the economic bubble of the nineties. The outcome was enabled by a combination of causes that coalesced at that moment of time. Those causes, in summary, were: (1) a speculative bubble that was based on an expanding economy and an exploding securities market; (2) an avalanche of greed that fed the bubble; (3) the unleashing of executive power, unchecked by existing institutional mechanisms; (4) a consequent explosion of executive compensation (fixed price stock options, rich pension plans, lavish personal perquisites such as corporate jets and multiple mansions, etc.), often unrelated to managerial performance; and (5) a suspension of public distrust of huge short-run gains in the market values of corporate stock that were unrelated to the underlying financial realities beneath that stock.

Management and the related professions which advise them and/or certify their financial statements are now subject to new and enlarged checks and balances. The essence of the matter is to stimulate the professions and the regulatory agencies to speak to and check the unrestrained exercise of executive power by management. The chapters that follow will examine the incentives and conflicts of interest that contributed to the economic bubble of the nineties, and led to its collapse amid revelations of corporate malfeasance. Those chapters will also attempt to show how the new and additional checks and balances encourage speaking to executive power.

Note

1. This section rests heavily on my paper "Welfare Capitalism and Democracy: Handmaidens Forever or a Coming Conflict?" *Rivista Internazionale di Scienze Economiche e Commerciale* (International Review of Economics and Business), Vol. L, No. 1, March 2003, 1-14.

Chapter II

Management

Management as the Repository of Organizational Power in Public Corporations

Chapter I limned the nature of the American polity. It described the marriage of welfare capitalism and political freedom that rested on concepts of conscience and morality, and that abhorred concentrations of unbridled power. It described further how the system developed mechanisms designed to check and balance such power. Despite those mechanisms, corporate America developed an unhealthy number of imperial chief executives, who, possessing such power, abused it in a rapacious pursuit of personal wealth and perquisites. How did it happen? How did the system respond? We start with management, because it is the locus of executive power in the modern public corporation.

The Historical Development of the Joint Stock Company. The root of the problem lies in the separation of ownership and control that came about when the joint stock company, the progenitor of the modern public corporation, came into being. In emergent modern capitalism, ownership and control were not separated; they were united in the person of the owner-manager. Society was mainly agricultural, and land was held by the nobility and the church. There was no large scale industrial or manufacturing aggregation of capital. What there was, was small scale, and generally comprised of craftsmen and their apprentices, usually organized in guilds. The guilds set "just prices" for their products, and "just wages" for labor. Markets, in the modern sense, did not rule. Their appearance waited on the development of cities and the burghers who became the bourgeoisie who constituted a newly emergent middle class of businessmen.

As trade grew, first, with the construction of canals and turnpikes that expanded the trading area inland, and, second, with the adventurous sailing vessels that opened the Age of Exploration and transoceanic empires, the scale of activity expanded enormously, and stimulated the need for increasingly larger aggregations of capital to support that trade.

Markets expanded and became national and international. Then, in the latter part of the 18th century, when James Watt invented the steam engine, the age of railroads and steamships was born. It destroyed the traditional cottage based production of textiles, and replaced it with large factories. Railroad networks tied together and expanded national markets and trade. And, on the high seas, trade came to be carried in the holds of fleets of large, expensive steamers.

John Stuart Mill, a prescient intellectual in a nineteenth century England well-populated by outstanding thinkers, wrote that the joint stock form of corporate organization had important advantages. Among them, these appeared pre-eminent: (1) the ability to aggregate large amounts of capital; and (2) transparency (in his words, "publicity"). Mill explained them briefly in his encyclopedic *Principles of Political Economy*, first published in 1848 and subsequently revised through a 7th edition by Mill in 1871, and later reissued well into the 20th century.[1]

Mill illustrated the first advantage by pointing to steamship companies, with fleets of large and expensive vessels that could maintain scheduled, frequent, and reliable service. It was the sheer size, the scale, of such an operation that moved it beyond the capital raising ability of an individual or partnership. Mill's second major advantage, publicity or transparency, referred to the requirement that public companies publish periodic statements of their accounts. He believed that this requirement set some boundaries on the ability of the managers of a company to mislead the public as to the financial state of affairs of the firm. Mill was not unsophisticated; far from it. He recognized that managers might try to cheat, but he wrote that ". . . this cannot so easily happen in the case of a joint stock company, whose accounts are published periodically. The accounts, even if cooked, still exercise some check; . . ."[2] His choice of words is delicious, for his reference to "cooked accounts" has a contemporary flavor.

Mill saw disadvantages, as well as advantages, in the public company form of organization. The major disadvantage was the separation that occurred between ownership and control (management). In his words:

> The administration of a joint stock association is, in the main, administration by hired servants . . . But experience shows, . . . how inferior is the quality of hired servants, compared with the ministration of those personally interested in the work, and how indispensable, when hired service must be employed, is the "master's eye" to watch over it.[3]

Mill pointed out also that the successful conduct of an enterprise required these two qualifications: fidelity and zeal. By fidelity, Mill meant responsibility. He thought that this quality could be gotten through careful specification of the duties to be performed, and the risk to the employee of being discharged in the event of a failure to perform to those specifications. Zeal was a different matter. It related to the ability of the "hired servant" to meet the intellectual challenges of managing a complex organization, as well as the intensity of effort the hired manager would expend in his work.

Mill did not believe that the required intensity could be expected from a "hired servant," who was working for another person's profit.[4] He maintained that there were "experiments in human affairs which are conclusive on the point." But, Mill did not feel that the problem was intractable. Compensation arrangements did not have to be bound by any limited pattern of payment by the hour or the week. Specifically, he pointed to the "common enough" practice of giving senior managers a percentage of the profits, and thereby aligning their interests with those of the owners. Although Mill thought that manager and owner interests would thereby be aligned, time and experience showed that that outcome did not necessarily follow.

The Separation of Shareholder Ownership and Management Control: The Relocation of Power

Separation of ownership and management control involves a separation of interests between the two. While the pursuit of corporate profit may seem common to both parties, it is not joined as it is when ownership and control are combined. Self-enrichment becomes the objective of a self-interested management, and it can be achieved at the expense of ownership. "Cooking" the corporate accounts is an obvious management means to the accomplishment of its objective.

Separation of ownership and control did not command major attention until the Great Depression of the 1930s, when Adolf A. Berle and Gardiner C. Means produced their *magnum opus, The Modern Corporation and Private Property*.[5] Published by Macmillan in 1932, it attracted great attention among publicists and politicians, as well as the wider public, and seemed to exert significant influence on public policy, although some have challenged that claim.

Robert Hessen, of the Hoover Institution at Stanford University, was enthusiastic in his recognition of the durability and prominence of *The Modern Corporation*.[6] But, having made initial bows to Berle and Means, he went on, and, at the end, disagreed sharply with their conclusions, arguing that the separation of ownership and management control are not inimical to the interests of the former. In fact, he argued that owner-shareholders, through their ability to buy and sell a corporation's stock in the market, are both active and responsible with regard to their investment.

Hessen did not envisage the corporate accounting scandals that rocked corporate America at the turn of the century. The books were cooked. The earnings data were not truthful, and too often did not depict the real financial condition of the corporation. Stock values, therefore, were easily inflated and misled investors. This chicanery could and did make fortunes for executives, thereby enriching management at the expense of shareholders. Chief executive officers and chief financial officers received rich compensation packages based on performance data that were illusory. The fact that investors eagerly bought into the shares of high-flying corporations, even when the earnings data showed losses rather than profits, is an indication of the degree to which they had succumbed to the prevailing speculative frenzy. Unquestioning reliance on the market and its valuation of stocks as an indicator of managerial competence and a reliable guide for investment decisions is an exercise for a fool. *Caveat emptor!* Investors must be prudent, and study corporate financial data carefully, if they are to minimize the danger of severe losses due to management control coupled to cupidity.

Seven decades after the publication of *The Modern Corporation and Private Property*, Berle and Means's warnings about the dangers of the separation of ownership and control still resonate. The collapse of the stock market bubble harmed so many so grievously that their alarm about the separation of ownership and control must still command our attention.

The Centralization of Power in the Imperial Executive

The corporate accounting scandals that exploded on the American scene at the end of the 20th century involved more than the separation of ownership and management control. They involved a massive concentration of management control in the hands of the chief executive officer. Many CEOs achieved complete dominance over their boards, thereby neutralizing the board's power over them. Once that domination was achieved, it was not too difficult to extend it over the professional people retained by the corporation to do its audits and perform other services (lawyers, investment bankers, financial analysts, etc.). And, in a feedback symbiosis, significant numbers of those professionals became, with time, active initiators of schemes that helped misbehaving executives achieve unethical ends.

The means by which control came to be concentrated in the hands of the CEO were both blatant and subtle. The simplest and most obvious was the joining of the positions of CEO and chairman of the board. In England, the positions are typically separate, but in America they have typically been joined. The board chairmanship enhances the power of the CEO by giving him/her direct influence over the venue and agenda of board meetings, as well as their timing and frequency. The nature and amount of supportive information provided to the board is also under the CEO's influence. The organization of the board, i.e., its committee structure, can be steered by the chairman-CEO. Will there be executive, nominating, compensation, and audit committees? What will be the composition of the board and its committees in terms of independent and inside (management) directors? Will the CEO's family and friends become members of the board?

More subtle means of exercising control would include corporate contributions to the favorite charities of presumably independent board members, such as university presidents, deans, and professors. An endowed professorship or scholarship program will always elicit their gratitude, and bring subtle pressure on them to approve the CEO's plans and proposals. There is also a wide range of pleasant perks that independent board members can enjoy, e.g., travel on the corporate jet, meetings at luxurious resorts, and meals in the executive dining rooms (the chefs are almost always excellent). A cozy, club-like atmosphere is created, and board meetings become more social and less business-like. If, in addition, the meetings are infrequent and relatively brief, the board becomes a rubber-stamping instrument for the CEO.

A board thus diverted from serious inquiry into the financial affairs of the corporation is not likely to be undertaking any independent meetings minus the participation of the CEO, or soliciting information or opinions from members of management other than the CEO, or contacting the auditors or outside counsel regarding the affairs of the company. Under those circumstances, auditors and other professional people retained by the corporation will be looking to the CEO as the final arbiter of their services and fees. And, the ability of the CEO to engage in wrongful conduct that enriches him/her at the expense of the shareholders is magnified manifold.

A meaningful vignette is relevant to the state of mind that is thereby engendered in the CEO. It involved the SureBeam Corporation, a firm with a technology for irradiating food to make it safer. SureBeam's CEO, John C. Arme, formerly a partner with the now defunct accounting firm of Arthur Andersen, had hired KPMG as auditor after the collapse of Arthur Andersen. He fired that firm after 14 months, on the grounds that their fees were too high. He then retained Deloitte & Touche as auditor. Unhappily, Deloitte & Touche's partner in charge of the account differed from Mr. Arme on the company's policy for booking revenue on the basis of the percentage of a contract that was completed, rather than after the work was done. Mr. Arme, who was a former partner at Arthur Andersen and an accountant, was not about to have his judgment on an accounting method questioned, and he fired Deloitte & Touche. In its report of the incident, the *New York Times* concluded: "It is refreshing to see an auditor walk away rather than sign off on old accounting it doubts."[7]

Ralph Windle, an English management consultant with a fine sense of humor, captured the attitude of imperial executives in this little poem, which one can imagine set to the music of Gilbert and Sullivan:

Directors are the firm's elite;
They fall, but mainly on their feet;
For once they have their board regalia
Most seem impervious to failure;
And changes, when the critics frown,
Are mainly somewhat lower down.
They come in two quite separate blends,
Professionals, and Chairman's friends;
The former tested by survival,
The latter non-executival;
The first have offices and functions,
The second don't, except for luncheons.
We love our board, and hold them dear,
So long as they don't interfere.[8]

It should be clear that, with separation of ownership and control, the governance structure of the corporation becomes a vital matter. Does it concentrate management power in the hands of the CEO, or does it provide checks to that power, without compromising the ability of the CEO to provide leadership to the organization? If it does the former, then the opportunity for chicanery is multiplied. If it does the latter, then it diminishes that opportunity. It should be clear also that the board of directors is a key element in the corporation's governance structure, if only because it has the final power to hire and fire the CEO. Even when the CEO appears to possess complete power, the board is like a sleeping lion. It can awaken, and, in a display of that power, fire the CEO. It need not awaken of its own volition. Centers of power external to the company, like governmental or non-governmental regulatory agencies, can exert their power and awaken the board to action. More will be said on this matter in the next chapter, when we consider the Grasso case, which involved the New York Stock Exchange and the SEC, the Eisner case, which involved the Disney company, and the Cawley case, which involved MBNA. The WorldCom and Enron cases are also noteworthy, because in both instances ex-directors agreed to settlements of suits against them under which they paid substantial penalties out of their own pockets. More will be said about these cases in chapter V.

Power and the Self-Perception
of the Imperial CEO

There is a significant contradiction between the apparent greed and rapaciousness of many CEOs in their corporate behavior, and the generosity of spirit so often shown in their public and charitable behavior. They are frequently community leaders and major patrons of the arts, universities, and charitable organizations. One can wonder: Are these people moral schizophrenics?

I think not. I believe they have a sense of entitlement in their business behavior. The key is their conviction that they are creating wealth for shareholders, and for the community, as they build corporate empires and stock values soar. The belief is fed like a gas fueled fire by the "irrational exuberance" of a market bubble. Accounting adjustments that help the process seem validated by stockholder behavior that bids the market value of corporate securities up into the economic stratosphere. Given such a context, it seems easy for the CEO to convince himself that the creation of vast wealth, even if it is only on paper at the moment, entitles a goodly share to go to the creator. If 50 million shares of a stock are outstanding, and the stock goes up $10 per share, then $500 million of new value is created. Why shouldn't its creator get a cut of 5 or 10 percent ($25-$50 million)? The logic is most seductive, and so pleasant to the CEO's psyche and sense of self-worth. And, ultimately, a large sense of entitlement can swell an eager ego and cover substantial behavioral lapses. There is no taint of any sort of impropriety that attaches to Harvey Golub, former CEO of American Express (1993-2000), so his rationale re large executive compensation is worthy of particular attention. Quoted in the *Wall Street Journal*, he said: "I made a lot of money. I became wealthy. My shareholders became even wealthier." Noting that American Express's shares increased more than sixfold and its market capitalization rose from $10 billion to $65 billion during his tenure, he asked: "How much of that $55 billion should I get?"[9]

The sense of entitlement takes on added importance, after the bubble is pricked, when these CEOs are prosecuted, and the paper house collapses. The Tyco case is a perfect illustration. The prosecution of Dennis Kozlowski and Mark Swartz, its CEO and CFO, ended in a mistrial. One juror, Ruth B. Jordan, a former teacher and attorney, held out against conviction. When her name became public, the publicity subjected her to pressure, and the judge then declared the mistrial. The relevant point is that Ms. Jordan had a problem finding Kozlowski and Swartz guilty of "criminal intent," the basic finding necessary for a guilty verdict. The difficulty she faced was her belief that both defendants believed they were entitled to the huge sums they took from the company. If that belief was genuine, and she seemed to think it was, then how could they be guilty of "criminal intent"? This kind of legal subtlety is a prosecutorial "mare's nest."

Consider further that Kozlowski, whose picture was on the cover of *Business Week* in May 2001, must have seen himself as one of America's leading executives, and a model for others who aspired to equal or exceed his success. At the time, he boasted that he was disinterested in lavish corporate offices and personal perks, noting that Tyco could be viewed as the "leanest" company in America. Note also that he advised graduates at a college commencement to "Think carefully, and for your sake, do the right thing, not the easy thing." Also, he pointed out that his primary residence was a modest 3,500 square foot home in Rye, N.H. Yet, concurrently, he occupied an opulent Manhattan apartment, furnished with valuable art and fixtures. And, he arranged a $2 million birthday party for his wife in Sardinia, half of which he billed to Tyco.[10]

In the end, Kozlowski and Swartz were retried, convicted, and sentenced to prison time plus large monetary payments. The same fate met other formerly high flying executives. More will be said about them later.

B-School Education and Business Behavior

Possession of power is one thing. The ends to which it is applied are another. It is precisely at the nexus where those two elements are joined that a set of values and a sense of morality become critically important. And, it is there also that the influence of B-School education can be applied either for good or evil ends.

B-Schools seek to educate managers, and they pride themselves on the number of their alumni who become CEOs and members of top management. To emphasize techniques aimed at achieving maximum profitability while ignoring ethical considerations would be a travesty of the mission, and a gross disservice to students and society. Yet there is a substantial disagreement among B-school professors and deans about the matter.

Some think student character is already formed by the time students get to the school and cannot be changed by ethics courses or discussions of ethics. They believe family, church, and earlier educational experiences have been the critical forces. Then, there are those deans and professors who, while agreeing that family, church, and earlier experience are of great importance, think the B-school can be a significant factor—and should try. I belong to the second group.

In spite of the introduction of courses on ethics, I fear that the B-school curricula and course content have tended to focus too heavily on sophisticated and mathematically complex techniques, and their application to the several functional areas of study. Finance is perhaps a case in point, although that field does not deserve to receive more attention than Accounting, or Management, or Marketing. Each area is keen on modeling, with heavy reliance on computer simulations. The heavy emphasis on mathematical techniques tends to lend an air of quantification and precision to business decision making that belies the reality of the estimations and the judgments that they rest on. The influence of greed and a lust for power to vitally influence those estimates are difficult, if not impossible, to include in a model. Yet, they are of critical importance.

To be more specific, B-schools emphasize planning and budgeting, with clear objectives and target goals for revenues, costs, and profits, as being essential to rational management. These are vital processes, and deserve to be emphasized, but they should not lose sight of the pitfalls that lurk in the processes themselves.

Consider for a moment the budgeting process. It can be done top down or bottom up. In the first case, top management, with board approval, can set very ambitious profit goals, in a desire to get the corporation's lower management levels and workers to stretch their efforts to the utmost, to achieve a result unsupported by any prior experience. If an authoritarian climate pervades the organization, fear of being fired can cause lower management levels to fudge financial data for their segments of the business, and to take actions that produce paper results that hide operational problems, e.g., shifting bills or revenues from one time period to another, not facing problems in bad inventories or receivables, etc. More competent members of management, rebelling at the cultural climate of fear and chicanery that it can induce, leave the firm for better employers, with the weaker managers remaining to face the ultimate reckoning. On the other hand, bottom up budgeting may leave a slack management setting targets that are below what the firm should be producing.

Students need to be aware of these pitfalls. They should understand that unrealistic goals set in a climate of fear can, and likely will, produce chicanery and efforts to cover up problems. Or, an unhealthy fixation on short term earnings and stock values can induce financial manipulation, to achieve desired results that are not sustainable over time. A corollary, seemingly making perfect sense and not involving stealing, would be a desire by management to smooth earnings over time, to lend them an aura of predictability that is false, but that may impact favorably on the value of the company's stock. Useful techniques need to be clothed in garments of integrity.

There is a further dimension to the relevance of ethics to business behavior. It is the implicit assumption that the overriding, if not sole, goal of management should, indeed by law must, be the maximization of sustainable profits for the shareholder. But, that seems to set aside the well-being of other stakeholders, e.g., employees, consumers, and the community at large. Of course, market theory holds that under perfect competition profit maximization works to everyone's long-term benefit. Unfortunately, as one wag has said, "In the long-run, we are all dead." And, in the short-term, there is imperfect competition. Given that, is there not room for consideration of other stakeholders? Is there not also room for that consideration to include ethical values?

Some decades ago (the sixties and seventies), there was a spate of discussion of the importance of stakeholder interests to responsible corporate conduct. It died out, being over-run by the merger wave of the eighties and the speculative enthusiasm of the nineties. With shareholder class action suits against management and directors who were charged with insensitivity to their fiduciary obligations to shareholders, enthusiasm for other stakeholders faded. It may be time to revive stakeholder considerations. Much of the current concern over ethics involves them, as well as management's honesty and faithfulness in its relationship with shareholders.

One thing is certain. The business schools have a responsibility to make the moral dimensions of business decisions clear to their students. Not only because it is right, but because it may save them from disgrace, or even prison.

Are Shareholder Interests and Management Incentives Aligned Through Performance-Based Compensation Plans?

John Stuart Mill thought that shareholder interests and management incentives could be aligned, making specific reference to offering management a percentage of the profits. Contemporary arrangements feature bonus plans and fixed price stock option plans. Many observers have expressed confidence in those plans. Yet, none of those arrangements insure the sought-after alignment of interests. In the case of a percentage of the profits, management, with a short-term time frame in mind, can "cook the books" and achieve some profit target to collect fat bonuses, which may not have to be regurgitated at a later date, when the fraud is ultimately revealed. The false profit figures can also temporarily swell the stock's value, sucking in unwary shareholders while management quietly unloads its own stock holdings.

Fixed price stock options require more than a passing glance; for they have become a large and popular part of executive compensation plans. Most popular initially in the burgeoning high tech companies in Silicon Valley, they were seen as a vital recruiting tool to attract smart, ambitious, highly qualified employees with many other attractive employment alternatives. The stock option offered such prospective employees the promise of large financial gains, should the company live up to its promise and prosper. The resultant capital gains inherent in the stock options constituted a reward that was an incentive to maximum effort, which promised also to benefit all shareholders, thereby wedding the interests of management and shareholder-owners. Unfortunately, there was a reverse side to the coin. If the market value of the stock fell after the date of issue of the stock option, then the promised gain would be replaced by a loss. This downside stimulated a variety of arrangements designed to offset the danger, but those arrangements eventually turned out to involve, too frequently, fraudulent accounting and other unlawful actions.

The "gaming" that occurred usually involved timing the stock option grants, and the fixed price at which they were issued, through: (1) backdating; (2) a variation of backdating that involved a so-called 30 day window; (3) forward dating; and (4) spring-loading. Backdating involves retroactively picking a grant date prior to the approval date of the option, with the latter date having a known market price higher than the option price. Clearly, this arrangement has a gain built-in, and there is no direct tie to any future performance of the company's stock. The alleged incentive effect is undermined. In the 30 day window, the backdating occurs at the end of a 30 day period after the option grant is approved, allowing the choice of a date within that period when the stock's price was lower than it was on the approval date. Forward dating involves choosing a grant date after the approval date, in the event that the stock's market value has been declining, but after the stock has reversed course and begun to rise. The grant date chosen would be one on which the stock's value was less than the option price. In this case, the grant must be reported within two business days, in order for it to meet the requirements of the Sarbanes-Oxley Act. Spring-loading involves choosing a grant date, or sometimes an approval date, a little before the issuance of favorable corporate news.

In its heady early days, the fixed price stock option won the approval of corporate boards, compliant accountants, and attorneys. But, the honeymoon began to run into trouble as the halcyon high-tech prosperity of the late nineties came to an end. Today, it is apparent that many of the companies that favored the stock option are in trouble with the IRS, the Justice Department, and the SEC. Investigations, indictments, and prosecutions are increasingly in the news, and litigation among and between companies, accountants, lawyers, and regulatory agencies are rife. Indeed, it is clear that the magnitude of the manipulations committed in stock option grants exceeds greatly any early expectations; taking on the aspect of a major scandal. As of October 2006, over 100 corporations were reported to be subject to investigations, and dozens more were engaged in internal examinations. In November 2006, the *New York Times* reported that a number of studies indicated "broad manipulation of options." One study indicated that over 2,000 companies (29.2 percent of the companies in the study) backdated options. Another study estimated the figure at 12 percent; still a significant number. The differences in the estimates were probably due, in part, to differences in the nature of the studies.[11] The "dating" game also has tax implications, because the exercise and sale dates can be selected with an eye to bringing any gains under the capital gains tax rate, rather than the higher income tax rate. Such manipulation can be fraudulent, illegal, and subject to stiff tax penalties when uncovered.[12]

One of the most egregious cases involved Brocade Communications Systems, and its former CEO, Gregory L. Reyes. Mr. Reyes made some

$500 million from stock options, while his company, according to the *New York Times*, "was overstating its profit by more than $1 billion as a result of accounting errors connected to backdated options."[13] Another case, notable because of the prominence of the company and its CEO, involved United Healthcare Group and its former chief executive, Dr. William W. McGuire as well as his successor, Stephen J. Hemsley. Dr. McGuire had built the company up to a market capitalization of some $66 billion, making it one of the giants of the health care industry. At the same time, he had accumulated some $1.78 billion of stock options, a significant part of which appeared to involve backdating. As a consequence, he was compelled to leave his positions as CEO and chairman, and return part of his options The ultimate decision required Dr. McGuire to forfeit $200 million in stock options, while Hemsley had to give back $190 million. The company's general counsel and a board member were also forced out.[14]

The foregoing manipulations were fraudulent, but equally unhappy results can come about through completely legal accounting actions. Perhaps the best example is provided by the case of defined benefit pension plans, which were widely popular with American corporations, as well as governmental entities (State, Local, and Federal). Although profit seeking organizations have replaced them in part by defined contribution plans, they are still significant; especially among public employees.

Defined benefit plans specify the benefits to be received by plan participants, with the annual corporate contributions required to support those benefits varying with the value of the accumulated pension fund and the estimated annual income produced by the investment of the fund. During an economic bubble, with stock values driven to artificially high levels by speculative fever and interest rates high, the estimated annual contribution becomes artificially low. The reverse situation prevails during a severe bear market, with annual contributions skyrocketing because of the double impact of a sharply reduced fund value and lower interest rates that reduce the income flow from the fund. This description of events appears to apply exactly to the conditions encountered during the nineties and the early years of the following decade.

The foregoing realities demonstrate that corporate financial statements, even when they are scrupulously legal and honest in intent, inexorably involve estimates that are, by their nature, not precise. Yet, the profit figures derived from them impact on stock values, and on the interests of shareholders and management. As management realizes, as it must, that estimates are unavoidable, the temptation to manipulate them to management's advantage and shareholder disadvantage can become very great, which emphasizes the importance of behaving ethically, as well as having checks on the power of the CEO.

The volatility in pension fund values and annual contributions just noted has major adverse effects on corporations that are suffering financially, and may even threaten them with bankruptcy. Northwest Airlines is a case in point, as are other airlines and other industries with under-funded pension plans (auto manufacturing, steel manufacturing, etc.). Normally, a company with an under-funded plan must contribute cash or "qualified securities," e.g., U.S. Treasury notes or bonds, to bring the fund up to the level required to meet the pension plan retirement obligations. Northwest could not meet that obligation, and requested that it be allowed to contribute stock it owned in a subsidiary airline (Pinnacle). That stock was not "qualified," but it was used with the permission of the U.S. Labor Department, under the provisions of the Employee Retirement Income Security Act (ERISA). While not fraudulent, it did "cover up" the serious and unpleasant financial realities of the situation. Companies facing funding problems can also receive waivers, allowing them to postpone contributions to their pension funds, another lawful way around unpleasant financial facts.[15] A striking illustration of the point is provided by a House-Senate agreement on a pending pension bill that was reached on April 1, 2004.[16] The major provision would change the interest rate computation used to calculate the size of annual contributions to a pension fund, by raising it. The effect would be to reduce the amount of the contribution, with a positive further effect on corporate earnings. Another provision would provide temporary relief to aircraft companies and steel companies, by reducing their required contributions by 80 percent in the next two years. Opponents of the bill were concerned that it would seriously weaken the financial stability of the pension plans affected by the proposed legislation. They were upset also by the fact that the measure covered only some firms and industries, and was inequitable.

A further point should be made. In 1974, the Congress created the Pension Benefit Guaranty Corporation, to insure covered pension plans that defaulted. In the ebullient economy of the nineties, the PBGC reached a peak surplus of some $9 billion. But, following the collapse in 2000-2001, that surplus turned into a deficit of over $23 billion, and rising as airlines and other failing companies became bankrupt and defaulted on their pension plans. In mid 2005, the SEC reported that a study of a sample group of corporations reported to their shareholders that they had an aggregate surplus of $91 billion in their pension funds (under existing accounting rules). The SEC reported also that, under more realistic accounting rules, they would have shown an aggregate deficit of some $86 billion. That's a breathtaking swing of $177 billion. Recognizing the magnitude of the problem, the Financial Accounting Standards Board, late in 2005, initiated a year long study of the rules used in reporting the value of pension funds. The aim is to develop more realistic actuarial and financial assumptions, before we are overcome by an economic disaster.[17]

Arthur Levitt, former SEC chairman, writing about the situation, observed that the present system of pension accounting is a "shell game, misleading taxpayers and investors about the true fiscal health of their cities and companies—and allowing management to make promises to workers and saddle future generations with huge costs." He cited an estimate by Credit Suisse First Boston that unfunded pension liabilities of companies in the S&P 500 could hit $218 billion by the end of 2005, and upwards of $700 billion for State and Local governments.[18] Take note of Levitt's reference to government funded pension plans. Those plans appear to be grossly under-funded; perhaps not all, but far too many. One of the most extreme examples is provided by the city of San Diego, in California, which was in a financial crisis due to the failure of city officials and their advisers to adhere to proper funding decisions. In fact, they engaged in allegedly fraudulent acts to cover up their failure. And, Levitt led an investigation into the San Diego crisis that was scalding in its report. Speaking about the report's findings, Levitt was quoted in the *New York Times* as saying "The city's pension system was not brought to a crisis merely as a result of abnormally low investment returns. . . . Nor was the system brought to a crisis as a result of a 'perfect storm' of unpredictable catastrophies." Instead, he said: "San Diego officials fell prey to the same type of corruption of financial management and reporting that afflicted municipalities such as Orange County, and such private sector companies as Enron, HealthSouth and any number of public corporations." Using incorrect and complicated calculations, coupled with other devious devices, they made the pension fund look healthy when, in fact, it was developing some $1.4 billion of promises in excess of the actual funding available to pay them. In the case of government, we have elected public officials, always seeking reelection, defrauding taxpayers in much the same way that corrupt managements defraud shareholders. In both cases, those managing the contents of the purse fail in their fiduciary duty to its owners.[19] Hopefully, the adequacy of government pension funds will improve; as of year end 2006, accounting rules makers were proposing changes that would tighten the estimates being used. Also, the Governmental Accounting Standards Board was proposing that state and local governments be required to use outside (independent) auditors to pass on the adequacy of their pension fund financial estimates.

Take heed! Overly optimistic assumptions, while they may appear legal, can produce hugely misleading financial statements and economic disaster.[20]

The Impact of the Sarbanes-Oxley Act

The Sarbanes-Oxley Act treated white collar crimes more seriously than had earlier been the case. Substantial fines and imprisonment became real results that could follow on egregious examples of fraud. Rules were multiplied, and responsibilities spelled out, perhaps overly so, but on a scale that could not be overlooked by CEOs, other top members of management, boards of directors, accountants, attorneys, and other professionals and agencies involved in corporate affairs. One thing is certain. The attention of executives, directors, and everyone else concerned was gotten. Even the most dim-witted among them became aware of the trend of the time.

Sarbanes-Oxley was a full-employment act for consultants. Lawyers, accountants, management consultants, anyone and everyone who could claim some expertise in the meaning and the requirements of the act came to life, and offered their services. And, corporate America appeared eager to retain them, to insure that violations of the letter, and often the spirit, of the law did not occur.

The Act's impact on management needs to be viewed from the angle of its effect on the power of the CEO. To discern that effect, we must examine: (1) the Act's impact on the CEO's state of mind, i.e., his/her sense of personal exposure to severe financial and criminal penalties in the event of malfeasance; (2) the CEO's relationship with the board of directors, i.e., the power balance between the two; and (3) the CEO's sense of the power balance in his/her relationship with the professions and agencies that interact with the corporation.

In every case, the Act had very large effects. While only the further implementation of the law, and probable actions to ease its more onerous provisions, will show its long-term consequences, the short-term effects were great. At the time of this writing, more than four years have elapsed since the law was passed, and hardly a day has gone by without multiple stories in the press about widespread and substantial changes in corporate governance, as well as investigations, prosecutions, and settlements of cases of malfeasance.

While some people complain about the slowness of these activities, their pace reflects the complexity of the legal issues they involve. Nonetheless, by late 2006, trials of major corporate culprits were far advanced and had almost always resulted in guilty findings, accompanied by severe jail sentences and substantial fines. Early on, Andrew Fastow, former CFO of Enron and a key figure in its corruption and collapse, agreed to a plea deal that subjected him to a 10 year prison term and a monetary penalty of some $29 million. Subsequently, based on his cooperation in the prosecution of other Enron executives, his sentence was reduced to 6 years imprisonment, plus 2 additional years at home under court supervision.[21] His wife, Lea, a former assistant treasurer at Enron, was also enmeshed in the scandal. She agreed to a companion plea deal, with a limited prison term (5 months, plus 5 months home detention or in a halfway house), but U.S. District Court Judge David Hittner subsequently rejected the plea deal. The judge's action was unusual, and upsetting to both prosecuting and defending attorneys. A new deal, somewhat more severe but satisfactory to the judge, was arranged. Lower level Enron executives were also sentenced in November 2006, receiving reduced prison terms based on their cooperation in the prosecution of higher ranking executives. Richard A. Causey, Enron's former chief accounting officer, was sentenced to serve five and a half years, reduced from 7 years, plus $1.25 million to the government as well as forfeiting $250,000 of deferred compensation. Also, Michael Kopper, a former aide to Andrew Fastow, was sentenced to three years and a month in prison, while Mark Koening, former Enron chief of investor relations, was sentenced to 18 months imprisonment. Both men were also fined $50,000.[22]

The indictments and prosecutions of Kenneth Lay and Jeffrey Skilling, former CEOs of Enron, finally ended with guilty verdicts in late May 2006. Both men had taken the stand in their own defense, a move usually considered hazardous because it opens the defendant to harsh cross-examination, but the jury did not find them credible. In the end, the jury convicted Jeffrey Skilling on 19 out of 22 counts of conspiracy, fraud, and insider trading, while finding Kenneth Lay guilty on 6 counts of conspiracy and fraud. Sentencing by Judge Simeon T. Lake III was scheduled for September 2006, with maximum possible jail sentences of 5 to 10 years on each count, plus likely substantial financial penalties. On the personal side, we witness the tragedy of individual lives brought low from great social and economic standing. In Kenneth Lay's case, death came before sentencing, on July 5, 2006, from coronary artery disease. It seems clear that the tension associated with Enron's collapse, and his subsequent trial and conviction, was not good for his health. And, while other defendants have not died, their fall from grace and personal humiliation are not minor aspects of their punishment. It is worth noting that, since Lay's death, prosecutors have moved to hold Skilling liable for Lay's monetary penalties. They based this action on an alleged conspiracy in which both men were presumably participants, and asked Judge Lake to enter a $182.8 million judgment against Skilling. The action also reflected concern that Lay's estate might escape any judgment against him; a possibility that turned out to be the reality when Judge Lake undid Lay's conspiracy and fraud conviction on October 17, 2006 (a ruling based on the legal requirement that a conviction must be voided when it is under appeal, if the appeal cannot go forward—in this case due to Lay's death) The financial impact of these claims are to be seen against the estimate of prosecutors that Skilling has $55 million of assets, mostly in municipal bonds that are frozen under a federal order. But, Skilling's legal fees are eating up his assets at a rapid pace; he had already paid his lawyers $23 million before his trial opened in January 2006. As of July 2006, he faced a further legal bill of $30 million.[23]

Executives were not the only parties to be punished in the Enron debacle. The board of directors failed in its duty to properly oversee management. As a result, 10 directors agreed to a plea agreement in 2005, without admitting or denying guilt, under which they paid $13 million out of their personal assets to Enron shareholders. They suffered further personal humiliation because, as a result, they were forced off the corporate boards of 21 other companies. It warrants note that 2 other Enron directors were not part of the plea deal. They did not have to pay any part of the $13 million settlement, and they continued to hold other corporate board seats (Herbert S. Winokus and Frank Savage).[24]

Enron's management and directors were not the only parties blamed and punished in its collapse. The banks that helped hide its financial abuses, in a civil settlement approved by a federal judge, agreed to pay a total of $7.6 billion to the company's shareholders ($2.4 billion by Canadian Imperial Bank of Canada, $2.2 billion by J.P. Morgan Chase, $2 billion by Citigroup, and the remainder by Bank of America, Lehman Brothers, and others).[25] And, Arthur Andersen, Enron's auditor, was destroyed; thereby bringing down America's largest and once most prestigious accounting firm.

Bernard Ebbers of WorldCom (now MCI), convicted of fraud, conspiracy, and making false filings, was sentenced to 25 years in prison; a probable life sentence given his age of 63 years. He appealed the severity of the sentence, but the appellate court upheld it on July 28, 2006. In addition, he agreed to a financial penalty of $5 million in cash, plus a transfer of all his assets to a liquidation trust estimated to be worth $25-$40 million (a cash tax refund, his home plus 800 acres of land, 300,000 acres of timberland in Mississippi, a sawmill and lumber company, 28,000 acres of farmland in Louisiana, a refrigerated trucking company, a marina in Jackson, Mississippi, a Marriott Courtyard Inn, and a country club). He was left only with money for his legal bills, a modest living allowance, and a small house for his wife. CFO Scott Sullivan cooperated with the prosecutors and testified against Ebbers. Like Lay and Skilling, Ebbers took the stand in his own defense, and, like them, his defense failed to achieve credibility with the jury.(he claimed ignorance of what had been done).[26] In the WorldCom case, the banks that were involved settled a class action suit for an aggregate somewhat more than $6 billion. Of that sum, Citigroup paid $2.58 billion, J.P. Morgan Chase paid $2 billion, and other Wall Street firms put up the rest. And, 12 former directors, again out of personal assets, had to pay a total of $25 million.[27]

The prosecution of L. Dennis Kozlowski and Mark H. Swartz, of Tyco, which ended in a mistrial, in April 2004, ended in a conviction upon retrial in 2005. Both men were found guilty of grand larceny, conspiracy, securities fraud, and falsifying business records. Each was sentenced to 8½-25 years in prison. Kozlowski was ordered to pay $97 million to Tyco in restitution, and $70 million in fines. Swartz was ordered to pay $38 million to Tyco in restitution, and $35 million in fines. Tyco itself settled with the SEC for $50 million, to go to the firm's shareholders.[28] Putting a more personal note on matters, monetary and jail time were not the only travails visited on Kozlowski. In 2001, he married a much younger woman, and, perhaps in celebration, threw a highly publicized birthday party for her that cost some $2 million; $1 million of which was charged to Tyco. Following his conviction and imprisonment, his bride, a former waitress, filed for divorce; claiming alimony and a share of certain assets. One can safely assume that Kozlowski has ample matter for meditation in the years ahead about the fickleness of fate.[29] A remote alternative interpretation would view the wife's actions as designed to rescue a significant portion of Kozlowski's remaining assets, to be held by her for his future release from prison. But, such a scheme seems very far-fetched; requiring, as it does, an unusual sense of loyalty and abiding affection for her erstwhile spouse.

Other cases involved Adelphia, Cendant, Qwest, and Rite Aid. The Adelphia prosecution resulted in the conviction of John J. Rigas, the aged founder of the firm, and his son Timothy, its CFO. Both received lengthy prison sentences; tantamount to a life sentence for John Rigas. And, Adelphia's auditor (Deloitte & Touche) and banks (Bank of America, Citigroup, J.P. Morgan Chase, Wachovia, et al) agreed to pay $455 million to the firm's investors in a confidential settlement approved by Judge Lawrence McKenna on November 10, 2006. The investors claimed that the auditor and banks had aided and abetted Adephia in its fraudulent behavior.[30] The Cendant prosecution resulted in guilty verdicts for E. Kirk Shelton, vice-chairman, and Cosmo Corigliano, CFO. Walter A. Forbes, chairman, who was being retried a third time after two mistrials, was finally convicted on the third go-round, on October 31, 2006. In the Qwest case, Joseph P. Nachio, chairman and CEO, was found guilty of insider trading, selling his own stock while touting the company's shares to the public. In the Rite Aid case, Martin L. Grass, chairman and CEO, pled guilty to conspiracy and obstruction of justice. Franklin C. Brown, vice-chairman, pled guilty to conspiracy and witness tampering, plus other charges. Grass was sentenced to 8 years in prison. Brown was sentenced to 10 years in prison.[31]

Executives, directors, bankers, et al would have to be deaf, dumb, and blind not to get the message! Of more than passing interest is a *Business Week* report that there is a sharp rise in proxy resolutions requiring directors to receive a majority of shareholder votes cast, rather than a plurality as is now usual. The number of such resolutions rose from 12 in 2004, to 62 in 2005, and more than double that (over 140) as of early March 2006. This development probably reflected pressure from the trustees of union pension funds, as well as others.[32] Also of interest, a Booz, Allen, Hamilton international survey of CEO turnover in 2004, still early in measuring the change in attitude and climate in corporate board rooms, showed 355 CEOs, of the world's 2,500 largest public companies (14 percent of the total) left office. Of that number, 111 were forced out due to disagreement with their boards, or due to poor performance. Not a large number, but perhaps a portent of what is coming.[33]

Executive accountability is becoming more robust than it was; which wasn't much. There does appear to be a significant increase in board activism and the assertiveness of regulatory authorities, as well as other gatekeepers and investors. Arthur Levitt, a former SEC chairman, believes a cultural change is occurring; one that is larger than simply reflecting the impact of Sarbanes-Oxley. He feels that the humiliation and embarrassment attendant on the prosecutions and punishments being meted out in so many high profile cases is overwhelming the hubris which had become the too frequent characteristic of too many executives. Presumably, pressure from institutional investors, regulators, and the media will reinforce the willingness of gatekeepers to speak to the power of executives. In Levitt's words, "The imperial CEO is no more." Such a sweeping judgment may be premature, as illustrated in the case of Robert Nardelli, long time CEO of Home Depot, a company that he brought to leadership in its industry. He has been receiving large compensation packages from a passive, apparently supine board, probably reflecting his long term record, although the company's recent stock performance is poor. In that context and with media attention focused on him and the company, he orchestrated an annual stockholder meeting minus any board members in attendance, and not allowing any questions from shareholders. A large outcry followed, stimulated in part by CalPers, a large public employee pension fund investor, which evidently compelled him to promise that future meetings would have board members in attendance, and would allow questions from stockholders. Nardelli's promise became hollow. He was forced to resign as CEO by his previously passive board, taking a severance package worth some $210 million. That package caused outrage, and helped fuel SEC changes in the requirements for reporting the values of stock options in executive compensation. Although eased somewhat from the reporting requirements originally adopted in July 2006, the December 2006 changes still represented a major advance over the rules that previously prevailed.[34]

The trial of Frank Quattrone, a onetime high-flying investment banker with Credit Suisse First Boston, which had ended in a mistrial, proved an exception. He was retried, found guilty, and sentenced to a prison term of 18 months. Subsequently, however, his conviction was overturned on appeal. And, under the terms of a deferred prosecution deal, consummated in late August 2006, he was relieved of the threat of a third trial, providing he avoided any new legal problems for one year. As a consequence, he became eligible to receive his 2003 compensation of $120 million from Credit Suisse First Boston, his former employer. That sum ($100 million, plus $20 million of restricted stock and other items) must be seen coupled with his restored ability to pick up his career in investment banking at the still young age of 50 (because his banning from the securities industry, by the SEC, was also reversed). But, for several years, his life was in limbo, and he suffered the stress associated with his defense. The legal cost of his defense amounted to at least $20 million, but that was covered by Credit Suisse.[35]

Probably, the most notable exception to the roster of executive convictions was the case of Richard M. Scrushy, former CEO of HealthSouth. In the primary prosecution of him, in which he was charged with fraudulent activities in the company's operation, he was acquitted by a Birmingham jury of 7 Afro-American and 5 white jurors. The acquittal followed a well orchestrated campaign in that city to create an image of Scrushy as a religious man with powerful sentiments of interracial harmony. Perhaps to that end, he made "regular appearances on early morning Bible study programs on local television," and joined a predominantly Afro-American church. In addition, he preached at Afro-American churches in and around Birmingham. Significantly, his acquittal came despite guilty pleas by 14 other HealthSouth executives, including a former CFO, William T. Owens. Those defendants received prison terms of 5 years. Scrushy did not walk away Scot free. In a separate shareholder suit against him, a judge ordered Scrushy to pay HealthSouth $47.8 million of unjustly received bonuses. There is also a civil case against Scrushy by the SEC, which is to be tried in April 2007. Further, Scrushy was convicted in a bribery case involving the former Governor of Alabama, in mid-2006. Finally, he is involved in countersuits with HealthSouth, in which he is suing the company for wrongful termination and the firm is suing him for fraud. People facing prosecution for corporate wrongdoing are not finding life easy.[36]

Perhaps of most immediate concern to CEOs is the requirement of section 302 that the chief executive officer and the chief financial officer certify that the financial statements and disclosures fairly represent, in all material respects, the operations and financial condition of the company. A "knowing and intentional" violation exposes the violator to a maximum fine of $5 million and up to 20 years imprisonment. I do not pretend to readily understand the difference between knowing and intentional, but assume that the latter condition requires some positive action in pursuit of the violation. Alternatively, an intentional act must also be "knowing," i.e., the executive knows that it is illegal. In any case, CEOs and CFOs must view these certifications seriously. Section 302 also requires CEOs and CFOs to "establish and maintain internal (financial) controls." Section 404, as indicated below, requires them to assess those controls annually. Even if they push the responsibility down to lower levels of management, by requiring subordinate divisional heads to sign off on their segments of the company, they cannot avoid scrutiny. And, those subordinates will now have their own "hides" to look out for, so they may well be encouraged to speak to the power of the CEO or the CFO.

Section 404 requires an annual management assessment of internal controls. Further, the assessment must be attested to by an outside auditor. The importance of the requirement is its pressure on management to pay attention to and certify the quality of the corporation's internal financial controls. Presumably, the outcome will be greater accuracy and reliability in the financial statements. In short, laxness will be sharply reduced, if not eliminated, and wiggle room for chicanery made more difficult. The significance of the section is indicated also in the reaction to it. Specifically, objections have been raised about the costliness of the provision. But, the provision is having a salutary effect, especially in firms with multiple and disparate divisions, e.g., conglomerates.[37] The reporting requirements of section 404, which became effective November 15, 2004 (with some exceptions), was related to a substantial uptick in reported disclosures of internal control problems at year end. Citing *Compliance Week*, a business newsletter, *Fortune* magazine reported a total of 550 public company internal control disclosures for the 11 month period January-November 2004. *Fortune* also cited a report by Financial Executives International indicating an expectation that compliance with section 404 would cost an average of $3.14 million.[38] And *Business Week* magazine cited a report that indicated that public companies with at least $4 billion in annual revenues were spending an average of $35 million to comply with Sarbanes-Oxley.[39] Appendix III presents a more detailed and recent discussion of the costs of compliance with Sarbanes-Oxley, especially section 404.

Section 402 (a) of the Sarbanes-Oxley Act touched another sensitive nerve-ending in the bodies of corporate executives, when it made it generally unlawful for companies to make personal loans to them. Such loans had become so large and common place in a number of firms that the executives involved seemed to treat the firm as though it was a personal bank account. Perhaps the most egregious case involved Adelphia, where the founder of the firm and members of his family used corporate funds for personal ventures in excess of a billion dollars.

The power of the CEO was being peeled away, like the layers of an onion. With or without tears, checks and balances were being introduced to encourage directors and others to speak to the remaining power of the CEO. Of course, there is a danger in all this regulatory machinery. If it destroyed the ability of the CEO to provide organizational leadership, then it would be severely counter-productive. But, if it encouraged a more open and collegial style of management, without compromising the ability to achieve decisions and to act, then it would serve us all well.

What is the CEO Required to Know: The Cendant Case

Most, if not all, CEO defendants have stoutly maintained their innocence of charges of fraud by pleading ignorance; arguing that any wrongdoing was perpetrated by lower managerial levels engaged either alone or in conspiracies to achieve attractive but dishonest earnings results. The usual target of their accusatory fingers was the CFO and his key staff members, perhaps with the connivance of in house legal counsel, as well as outside consultants retained at their suggestion. Of course there is a lack of symmetry in that argument, because the same CEOs, in the flush and exuberant days of illusory earnings, did not usually credit their underlings for the achievements. Rather, they were usually quick to accept credit, as well as rich compensation packages, for their presumed vision and managerial brilliance as the basis for the results. But, in adversity, acceptance of responsibility was an orphan. However, the law usually requires "knowledge' and "intent" as necessary for a conviction, so the claim of ignorance is understandable as a defense argument, requiring prosecutors to prove guilt.

Sarbanes-Oxley changed the picture, especially in the sections requiring the CEO to sign off on the financial statements, as well as sharing responsibility for the adequacy of internal controls (section 404). The CEO, if lacking expertise in these areas, is now well advised to become knowledgeable; certainly, to make sure he/she knows the accounting rules being applied in handling reserves, receivables, inventories, etc. If reserves are being manipulated to smooth earnings, or to make earnings look better than they are, then ignorance will no longer be as effective a defense as it once was.

The Cendant case is a fascinating case in point. Walter A. Forbes, former CEO of the company escaped conviction in two trials for accounting fraud and securities fraud, when two juries, after deliberating respectively for 33 days and 27 days were deadlocked. But, in a third trial he was found guilty of accounting fraud, after that jury deliberated for two and a half days. Throughout, Forbes adamantly maintained his innocence, arguing that he wasn't involved in the daily management of the business, and was ignorant of the fraudulent activities of his managerial colleagues. It may be of passing interest that Forbes has an MBA degree from Harvard's Business School. In any case, the defense worked in the first trial, when his co-defendant E. Kirk Shelton, former vice-chairman of Cendant, was found guilty and sentenced to 10 years in prison, while the jury was deadlocked over Forbes. Shelton, while his conviction was on appeal, was free on bond, with some travel restrictions. Subsequently, on December 6, 2006, Judge Alvin W. Thompson ordered him to be under house confinement, with some minor exceptions. Shelton's original conviction also required him to pay restitution to Cendant in the amount of $3.27 billion; which seems ridiculous in light of the accompanying specification that the payment consist of an initial amount of $15 million, plus installments of $2,000 per month following his release from prison. It seems clear that the intent was, in light of Shelton's actual resources, to keep him under financial pressure for the rest of his life.[40] All the while, Cosmo Corigliano, Cendant's CFO, testified that he worked closely with Forbes, cooking the books at the direction of Forbes.

The key elements in the third trial appear to be: (1) the prosecution's simplification of the charge of accounting fraud; and (2) the appearance as a witness and the testimony of Henry Silverman, former CEO of

HFS. Silverman had merged his company with CUC International, Forbes' original company, to form Cendant. Silverman, considering himself knowledgeable in accounting and financial matters, was apparently furious when he discovered, after the merger, that he had been fooled and embarrassed. Silverman, in his testimony, said: "CEOs are paid to know . . . CEOs are not paid to not know." Pending any easing of the impact of Sarbanes-Oxley, CEOs will be well advised to keep Silverman's words clearly in mind.[41]

Notes

1. John Stuart Mill, *Principles of Political Economy*, Longmans Green & Co., 1871. The edition cited here is the 7th, with an Introduction by Sir W. J. Ashley, reprinted in 1961 by Augustus M. Kelley, New York, 137-141.

2. J. S. Mill, *Principles*, 138.

3. J. S. Mill, *Principles*, 138-139.

4. J. S. Mill, *Principles*, 139.

5. Adolf A. Berle and Gardiner C. Means. *The Modern Corporation and Private Property*, revised edition, 1968, Harcourt, Brace and World, Inc. New York, 4-5, 114.

6. Robert Hessen, "The Modern Corporation and Private Property," *Journal of Law and Economics*, Vol. XXVI, June 1983, University of Chicago, 273-289.

7. Floyd Norris, "They Fired Two Auditing Firms. Anyone Want to be No. 3?" *New York Times*, August 22, 2003, C1.

8. *Fortune*, February 25, 1991, p. 100. See also: Bertie Ramsbottom (Ralph Windle), *The Bottom Line, A Book of Business Ballads*, Century Publishing, London, 1985, 18.

9. *Wall Street Journal*, October 12, 2006, p. A16.

10. Alex Berenson, "Kozlowski's Words Versus His Actions," *New York Times*, April 3, 2004, B5.

11. *New York Times*, November 17, 2006, p. C2.

12. *Wall Street Journal*, December 12, 2006, pp. A1, A13.

13. *New York Times*, June 19, 2006, pp.C1, C7; *New York Times*, July 21, 2006, pp. A1, C5; *New York Times*, July 25,2006, pp. C1, C8; *New York Times*, October 12, 2006, pp. A1, A16.

14. *New York Times*, October 16, 2006, p. A1; *Wall Street Journal*, October 16, 2006, p. A1; *Wall Street Journal*, November 9, 2006, pp. B1, B6.

15. Ellen E. Schultz and Susan Carey, "Northwest Airlines Can Use Stock of Unit to Fund Retirement Plans," *Wall Street Journal*, August 19, 2003, A1.

16. Mary Williams Walsh, "Agreement is Reached on Pension Bill," *New York Times*, April 2, 2004, C1, C2.

17. *New York Times*, November 8, 2005, pp.C1, C2; *New York Times*, November 11, 2005, p. C3.

18. *Wall Street Journal*, November 10, 2005, p. A16.

19. *New York Times*, August 9, 2006, p. C3.

20. Mary Williams Walsh, "Deficit Soars At Agency That Insures Pension Plans," *New York Times*, November 16, 2004, C1.

21. *New York Times*, September 27, 2006, pp. C1, C4.

22. *New York Times*, November 16, 2006, p.C3; *New York Times*, November 18, 2006, p. B4.

23. *Wall Street Journal*, May 26, 2006, pp. A1, A9; *New York Times*, May 26, 2006, pp. C1, C4, C5, C6; *New York Times*, August 15, 2006, p. C3; *New York Times*, October 18, 2006, p. C3.

24. *New York Times*, January 29, 2006, section 3, pp. 1, 9.

25. *New York Times*, May 25, 2006, p. C2.

26. *New York Times*, July 1, 2005, pp. C1, C6.; *Wall Street Journal*, July 14, 2005, pp. A1, A8.

27. *New York Times*, March 19, 2005, pp. B1, B4.

28. *Wall Street Journal*, September 20, 2005, pp. C1, C4.; *New York Times*, April 18, 2006, p. C3.

29. *New York Times*, August 27, 2006, section 3, p. C3.

30. *New York Times*, December 9, 2006, p. B4.

31. *New York Times*, January 5, 2006, p. C4; *New York Times*, February 10, 2006, pp. C1, C6; *New York Times*, February 15, 2006, p. C15.

32. *Business Week*, March 6, 2006, p. 37.

33. *New York Times*, July 16, 2005, p. C5.

34. *Wall Street Journal*, March 17, 2005, p. A16; *Business Week*, April 25, 2005, pp. 88-96.

35. *Wall Street Journal*, August 24, 2006, pp. C1, C3.

36. *New York Times*, June 29, 2005, pp. A1, C4; *New York Times*, July 6, 2005, p. C5; *New York Times*, December 10, 2005, p. B13; *New York Times*, December 17, 2005, p. B4; *New York Times*, January 4, 2006, p. C3; *Wall Street Journal*, May 31, 2006, pp. C1, C4.

37. *New York Times*, "Too Much Regulation? Corporate Bosses Sing the Sarbanes-Oxley Blues," Jan. 23, 2004, C1.

38. Ellen Florian Katz, "by the numbers," *Fortune*, January 10, 2005, 22.

39. *Business Week*, January 17, 2005, 30.

40. *New York Times*, December 7, 2006, p. C5.

41. *New York Times*, November 1, 2006, pp. C1, C4.

Chapter III

The Board of Directors

Who Holds the Power?

The board possesses the ultimate authority to hire and fire the CEO. Yet, we saw in the last chapter that the imperial CEO subverted that power by achieving operational control over the board. The merger of the CEO and board chairman positions was a critical piece of the picture. With effective control over agendas and venues, as well as frequency of meetings, the CEO-chairman was able to steer matters to his/her wishes. In addition, the ability to direct the selection of board members enabled packing that body with other members of management, who were subservient to the CEO, or with family and friends, or with others who would be pliable and responsive to subtle and not so subtle perks and favors.

We saw, also in the last chapter, that Sarbanes-Oxley directly and indirectly stimulated major changes in the power relationship between the CEO and the board. A non-quantifiable, but most important, part of the picture is the state of mind of the players. And, an important influence on the state of mind is the sense of serious exposure to personal liability, both financially and in terms of possible imprisonment, felt by the players. In the chummy, club-like atmosphere that formerly characterized corporate boards, the sense of such exposure seemed remote. In the current climate, that is no longer the case, and the sense of exposure is very real. For example, on March 15, 2004, Federal and State officials announced a tentative agreement with Bank of America requiring 8 directors of Nation's Funds, a subsidiary, to resign within a year, because of their roles in allowing trading violations. As we will see later in the case of the New York Stock Exchange, there is the additional possibility, even probability, that individual directors may be held personally liable for their actions. And, ten former WorldCom directors agreed to pay personal penalties of $18 million, while ten former Enron directors agreed to pay personal penalties of $13 million.

It is instructive to begin with consideration of the legal responsibility of the board member. What is the nature of that responsibility, and to whom is it owed? Berle and Means had some useful observations about those questions seven decades ago. They noted that board members were subject legally to three main rules of conduct: (1) a decent amount of attention to business; (2) fidelity to the interests of the corporation; and (3) at least reasonable business prudence.[1]

The first and the last are usually referred to now as the duty of care and business judgment, i.e., the commitment of time and attention to the affairs of the business and the use of knowledge and appropriate experience in its behalf. The meaning of fidelity to the corporation has evolved and changed since Berle and Means wrote. In 1932, it was clear that a board member was in violation of that requirement if he/she took an action that was personally profitable, but caused a loss to the corporation.

They cite an example. The director owns a piece of property and uses his position to sell the property to the company at an inflated price. The director gains, but the company loses by the amount of excess in the price paid. The transaction is a blatant violation of the director's obligation of fidelity to the corporation.

They cite a second example, involving the relationship and obligation of the director to a stockholder. In that case, the director has information, not yet public, that the company is about to enjoy a major windfall. In anticipation of the future run-up in the value of the firm's stock, the director locates a stockholder who is ignorant of the good news, and buys that person's stock. The director gains, and the duped stockholder loses, but the corporation is unaffected by any loss.

When Berle and Means presented that case, the law was not clear, although some courts had held that the director did have a fiduciary obligation to the shareholders, as well as to the corporation. Berle and Means believed that the view that a director had a fiduciary obligation to both the corporation and the shareholders would prevail. They were right, and that is the legal situation today. However, rapacious CEOs, with effective control over their boards, were able to compromise their boards' sense of fiduciary obligation to the shareholders, and produce the scandalous consequences of their greedy malfeasance that shocked the nation when exposed. Their behavior was facilitated by the celebrity status that many of them acquired. And, that status was enlarged by the attention and praise of the media. Indeed, many of them were prized guest speakers at America's elite business schools, as well as sought after donors by universities, museums, and other worthy institutions and causes.

The state of mind has changed radically! Yesterday's heroes are today's objects of scorn. Many are under investigation for alleged malfeasance, and, while convictions may not be easy because of claims of lack of knowledge or reliance on professional accounting or legal advice, disgrace is a blanket that darkens their lives. Also, the costs of defending oneself in legal proceedings can be horrendous, as well as imposing severe psychological strain, so even non-imprisonment doesn't spare them painful scars. Most important is the rise of a sense of serious responsibility among directors. The position is no longer a cushy, comfortable, and non-demanding one. Sarbanes-Oxley is an important part of the reason. But, it is not all. Attitudes are different. Regulatory bodies are demanding. And directors are responding. Perhaps equally important is the fact that CEOs and other members of management have also undergone a change of attitude. They are less inclined to seek dominance, and more interested in achieving power of leadership, which they must have, through cooperative and participatory management. It would be unfortunate if the outcome of all this was an inability to make effective decisions.

A cautionary note is in order. The conclusion that Sarbanes-Oxley and other measures have profoundly altered the power relationship between the CEO and the board may be premature. Memory makes me realize that I wrote about such a change having already occurred in the late eighties, more than a decade ago. The huge merger-acquisition wave in the decade of the eighties, accompanied by a powerful bull market prior to October, 1987, was associated with many of the excesses observed a decade later. Class action suits in behalf of shareholder plaintiffs were common in the face of management led buy-out efforts. A Korn/Ferry International study of boards of directors said:

> Clearly, the balance of power between the CEO and the board has shifted. The CEO no longer reigns as an absolute monarch, expecting corporate policy to be rubber-stamped. Rather, directors have become stronger and more independent partners in corporate leadership.[2]

I believed that was true at the time, and thought my own experience as a director confirmed the fact. So, what is different today? The corporate accounting scandals and the discovery of management malfeasance on a large scale are different, as is the passage of the Sarbanes-Oxley Act and its direct and indirect impact on corporate governance. They have altered the state of mind, and the attitudes of CEOs and directors.

Clouding the Picture: Majority Control

The foregoing discussion has assumed implicitly public corporations in which the separation of ownership and control is essentially complete; i.e., the managers own only small amounts of stock relative to the total outstanding, while the mass of the stock ownership is distributed across a large number of shareholders. Consequently, control is concentrated, while ownership is widely dispersed.

The picture is more complicated. There are public corporations in which the managers who possess executive power also hold a majority of the stock, or, alternatively, a large enough minority to be able to outvote the other stockholders. Put differently, the ownership stake is sufficiently large to guarantee to its possessors control of the board of directors and the executives who are the company's managers. The heretofore heralded separation of interests between owners and managers is no longer clear. Indeed, it is clouded. But, the existence of significant numbers of minority shareholders still leaves us with the troubling problem that the majority owners may enrich themselves at the expense of the minority. Does the fiduciary responsibility of the directors then require them to look to the protection of the minority against the majority, when the majority has the power to vote opposition directors out? Do the managers, who are also the majority shareholders, have a fiduciary responsibility to look after the interests of the minority?

Until 2004, the answers to those questions seemed to favor the majority shareholder-owners. But, change appears to be underway, and there are some interesting and important cases that point the way. One case involves Spiegel Inc. (a firm specializing in catalog retailing) and its subsidiary Eddie Bauer Inc. (an apparel company). Spiegel is 89 percent owned by a German billionaire, Michael Otto, and his family, while a modest 11 percent is held by the public. Further, Mr. Otto holds 100 percent of the voting stock in the company. Possessing that voting power and that degree of ownership, Mr. Otto, facing adverse financial developments in Spiegel and Bauer, kept them from filing quarterly financial reports for a period of 15 months in 2002 and 2003. Then, belatedly, he filed for bankruptcy protection. Now, after struggling to come to some agreement with creditors, being subjected to an 18 month investigation by the SEC, followed by a severely critical report, he is facing the probability of heavy fines. Obviously, any explanation based on the view that Spiegel and Bauer were part of his personal domain and property, to do with as he wished, will not wash. The same outlook likely applies to his explanation that his American legal advisers failed to explain clearly the potential penalties. Apparently, he expected only moderate fines. He did not figure on the impact on his reputation as one of Germany's outstanding business leaders, a consequence that is apparently more painful than monetary penalties. More important, his power is clearly shown not to be exclusive and unassailable. He is subject to SEC review and sanction, because, in spite of the small size of the minority ownership by the public, Spiegel and Bauer are public companies. And, they are subject to the full coverage and protection of shareholders that pertain to such companies.[3]

A second case, probably of even greater significance, involves Hollinger International, a giant media company that owned over 100 newspapers, including *The Daily Telegraph* of London, *The Chicago Sun Times*, and *The Jerusalem Post* in Israel. The company was built by Conrad M. Black, originally a Canadian but now Lord Black of England. Hollinger International had a two tier stock structure, consisting of non-voting and voting stock. While Lord Black, who was CEO, controlled some 30 percent of the non-voting stock, he controlled 73 percent of the voting stock. He was long viewed as, and was in fact, the undisputed boss of Hollinger, even though his board included a number of internationally famous people, e.g., Henry Kissinger and Richard N. Perle.

In 2002, allegations arose that Lord Black and some other executives had taken millions of dollars out of the company for personal loans and other reasons; all unauthorized by the board. Public shareholders called for investigations, but it took some two years for those calls to bear results. Finally, as an outcome of a law suit by the disgruntled shareholders, Lord Black surrendered his position as CEO, and agreed to restitution of the moneys improperly taken. Then, the board undertook to liquidate the firm's assets, hoping thereby to maximize the funds due the shareholders following liquidation.

Lord Black, however, having recovered some degree of feistiness, made other plans. He decided to use his 73 percent voting power, to alter the company's by-laws so as to block the asset sales by the board. The issue of his power versus the board's power then went to the Chancery Court of the State of Delaware, where Hollinger was incorporated. In February 2004, Vice Chancellor Leo E. Strine, Jr. ruled against Lord Black. That ruling did not finally settle the issue, because Lord Black subsequently challenged the board of directors' decision to sell the Telegraph Group of British newspapers to David and Frederick Barclay. The prospective purchasers, prominent British publishers, offered $1.2 billion for the newspapers comprising the Group (The Daily Telegraph of London, The Sunday Telegraph, and The Spectator). Lord Black's challenge claimed that the board of directors lacked the power to consummate the sale without a shareholder vote of approval. Since Lord Black had a large majority of the voting shares in his control, he could have then blocked the sale. But Vice Chancellor Strine denied Lord Black's challenge, reinforcing his earlier decision in favor of the board and the public shareholders. Clearly, the court held that the board's primary obligation was to the public shareholders. No less significant is the fact that a board that had not manifested much independence in the past, was awakened sharply to the locus of its responsibility, and went head to head with its long time leader.[4]

The distance traveled by the Hollinger board, as it increasingly manifested its independence from Lord Black, became clear when a report by a special committee, chaired by Gordon A. Paris (an independent director, who later became Hollinger International's CEO), charged that Black and F. David Radler, former COO of Hollinger and Black's closest "partner" in running the company, had diverted some $400 million of the firm's earnings to their use and benefit between 1996 and 2003. More immediate were blistering criticisms of the board during that period for either blindly signing off on transactions, or not paying attention to what was transpiring. Singled out for particular criticism was Richard Perle, who had been an Assistant Secretary of Defense in the Reagan administration, and who allegedly engaged in transactions between Trireme Partners, an investment firm he helped found, and a Hollinger investment subsidiary that he chaired; from which he collected some $3.1 million. In fact, the committee report called on Perle to return $5.4 million to

Hollinger. Other prominent members of the board at the time, who were scolded for passivity, were Henry Kissinger, Robert S. Strauss, a former chairman of the Democratic National Committee and U.S. Ambassador to Russia, and Richard R. Burt, former U.S. Ambassador to Germany. The board failures were bipartisan, politically speaking.[5] Shortly after the issuance of the committee report, Perle issued an outraged response alleging factual errors and lies in the report. In addition, he put space between himself and Lord Black, maintaining that the latter had misled him; all of which may have had an eye on his future defense in a personal liability case that might be filed against him by Hollinger.[6] More telling is the fact that in May 2005 the Hollinger directors agreed to pay the company $50 million to settle charges of laxness; a sum which was covered by a directors and officers insurance policy.[7] A little later in 2005, in May, F. David Radler pled guilty to criminal fraud charges involving payments of $32 million to executives of Hollinger and its parent company (Ravelston Corporation). Radler agreed also, apparently in exchange for a reduction in his prison sentence to 29 months, to cooperate with authorities in upcoming proceedings against Black and Hollinger.[8]

The Special Committee noted above was unsparing in the language it used to describe the malefactions of Black and Radler. It said: "The Report . . . is about how Hollinger was systematically manipulated and used by its controlling shareholders for their sole benefit, and in a manner that violated every concept of fiduciary duty. Not once or twice, but on dozens of occasions Hollinger was victimized by its controlling shareholders as they transferred to themselves and their affiliates more than $400 million in the last seven years. The aggregate cash taken by Hollinger's former CEO Conrad M. Black and its former COO F. David Radler and their associates represented 95.2% of Hollinger's entire adjusted net income during 1997-2003. . . . Behind a constant stream of bombast regarding their accomplishments as self-described 'proprietors,' Black and Radler made it their business to line their pockets at the expense of Hollinger almost every day, in almost every way they could devise. The Special committee knows of few parallels to Black and Radler's brand of self-righteous, and aggressive looting of Hollinger to the exclusion of all other concerns or interests, and irrespective of whether their actions were remotely fair to shareholders . . . the evidence reviewed by the Committee establishes an overwhelming record of abuse, overreaching, and violations of fiduciary duties by Black and Radler."[9]

To escape the confusion caused by suits between Hollinger International and Hollinger, as well as Ravelston (the other member of the triumvirate of companies that Black used to carry out his financial manipulations), the shareholders of Hollinger International voted to change the name of the company to Sun-Times Media Group, effective in July 2006.[10] And, in August 2006, Judge Colin Campbell of the Ontario Superior Court (Canada) froze the assets of Black and his wife, permitting them to receive only some $23,000 per month as an allowance.[11] The financial impact of this ruling, if it stands up, is to be judged against Black's claim, made in the summer of 2006, that his monthly expenses amount to some $200,000; probably too low a figure if the monthly mortgage payment on his Toronto home of $114,000, plus $9,000 for gardeners and $8,000 for taxes, are taken into consideration. Remember! The foregoing figures do not consider the millions being spent on legal fees. And that is after he sold his homes in London and New York, and became delinquent on monthly payments related to the mortgage on his Palm Beach estate. Further, he no longer enjoys the use of the company's Gulfstream jet, or the lake cruiser, Rolls Royce, antique Toronto office furniture, and art work. One is almost, but not quite, moved to crocodile tears at his current misfortunes.[12]

The Spiegel-Bauer and Hollinger cases seem to indicate that majority control of a public corporation does not carry with it the power to control the board's independence and fiduciary obligation to protect the interests of minority shareholders. That conclusion would be incorrect, for there is a loophole that has been approved by the SEC. The loophole involves an exemption to the independence requirements for boards of directors in public corporations controlled by a small group of shareholders, i.e., an individual, a family, or other group with over 50 percent of the voting stock, and voting their shares as a bloc. In such a case, the company can declare itself a "controlled company," and register for the exemption. A number of firms have taken advantage of the loophole, and filed for the exemption. They include MGM, Viacom, Tyson Foods, Dillard's, Kraft Foods, and others.[13]

The SEC approved the exemption on the assumption that the inherent conflict of interests between management and shareholders disappears when there is majority control of the corporation. Since a majority of shareholder votes controls management, the conflict seems to vanish. Unhappily, that is a large assumption that may have to be revisited. After all, it is still possible for the majority to direct the management to do things that enrich them at the expense of the minority. It is interesting and significant that a number of public corporations, characterized by majority control of a block of stock, have not chosen to file for the exemption. In that case, they are treated as all other public corporations are, and must meet the independence requirements for their boards. Prominent among them are the *New York Times* and the *Washington Post* (except for a nominating committee, which does not exist at that paper), as well as Hershey Foods. Both the SEC and the corporations that have not filed for the exemption may believe that the stock markets themselves may provide the necessary discipline on the firms that do file. The reason is simple; there must be disclosure, so that the firms that file are known to investors, and may be considered riskier investments than those firms that do not file.

Google, the exciting internet search engine company founded in 1999 by two Ph.D. computer science students at Stanford University (Sergey Brin and Larry Paige), may be a relevant case to watch. In the half decade prior to its going public in August, 2004, it enjoyed phenomenal growth and a growing aura of being special. For one thing, its founders projected a personal philosophy that seemed to eschew maximizing profit as a principal goal. In public statements, they promoted goals such as "doing right" and widely sharing gains with employees. Pursuant to these goals, they distributed stock options generously, as a major means of sharing corporate success. They made plain also their scorn for short-term profits or emphasizing quarterly financial results. And they were clear that they did not intend to surrender power and control when they took the firm public. None of those beliefs and intentions were hidden. All were freely disclosed. In fact, the prospectus accompanying Google's initial public offering (IPO) disclosed that the position of board chairman would be held by an "independent" non-employee of the firm, but his/her identity and qualifications (if known to the founders) were not revealed. Also, the IPO, as was noted in an earlier section, used a Dutch auction procedure, apparently in an effort to hold down the influence of the investment banking firms handling it, and to preclude any preferential distribution of stock prior to public sale. The IPO was successful, i.e., the demand for the stock was strong, and its price following the opening remained above the issuing price. Indeed, Google's market price has risen far above the IPO level. The relevant long-term issue is how the public reacts to a stock in a firm meant to be firmly under the continuing control of its founders, although the founders have not used a stock structure (non-voting stock, as well as voting stock) that would enable them to declare the company a controlled corporation. No less relevant, and equally interesting, will be the ability of the founders to retain control with a presumably independent board and chairman, coupled with an increasingly wide distribution of stock in future years.

Board Composition: Impact of Sarbanes-Oxley

Majority voting power carries with it the power to determine the composition of the board of directors, i.e., the proportion of inside (management) directors to independent (non-management) directors. Plainly, as we have already seen, that proportion has historically been vital to management and its ability to control the board. Control of the board brought with it the power to prevent challenges to management's decisions and actions. But, we have seen that the trend of events is running counter to insider (management) control of the board of directors. It is clear also that the trend of events reflects the impact of the Sarbanes-Oxley Act.

The Act affects the issue of board composition in two ways: first, by requiring that a majority of the directors be independent of management: i.e., outside directors minus direct or indirect ties to management; and, second, that there be audit, compensation, and nominating committees of the board, with the composition of those committees being dominated by independent directors. Independent board power over executive compensation, board membership, and corporate auditing was thereby intended to be secured.

Implementation will be the final arbiter. While independent members of the board must predominate, there is disagreement as to degree. Some feel that a simple majority of independent directors will be sufficient, and allow them to have the benefit of the experience and inside knowledge of the company provided by the presence of management directors. Others feel that the CEO alone should be the only insider member of the board. Of course, holders of the latter view tend to believe that management directors, in addition to the CEO, will not feel free to express any adverse opinions in the presence of the CEO.

None of the above will guarantee meaningful fulfillment of the fiduciary responsibility of the board of directors unless the directors possess these two characteristics: independence and competence. Independence is not insured simply due to a director not being a member of corporate management. A truly independent director can have no ties to the CEO or other members of management that would inhibit free expression and voting of the director's honest judgment. The director should not be a family member, social friend, consultant, or recipient of valuable considerations from the corporation or members of its management, apart from the fees paid for service as a director. The prohibition includes relationships with other firms or consultants who do business with the corporation or its management. Judging by the amount of attention being given to the matter, as the end of 2006 approached, executive compensation appeared to growing as a test and indicator of board independence. I do not want to overstate the point, but such prominent business voices as Warren Buffet's were being quoted as strongly opposed to the current level of executive compensation, as being greatly out-of-line with historical relationships with the pay of average workers. Buffet, who attributed part of the blame to the influence of so-called executive compensation experts acting as consultants to boards of directors, with the eager encouragement of CEOs, referred to such consulting firms as "Ratchet, Ratchet, and Bingo."[14]

Competence is a necessary mate of independence. The director must have knowledge and experience. They are necessary ingredients, if the director is to be able to understand and to judge the corporation's financial statements and operations. There cannot be prudent business judgment without them. Given those characteristics, the director is well positioned to render competent oversight to the corporation's affairs, and to bring beneficial results to its shareholders.

Given independence and competence, how does one become a director? The short and overly simple answer is; by being nominated and elected through a shareholder vote at the company's annual meeting. Formerly, the CEO, i.e., management, pretty much controlled the nomination process. Now, the nominating committee, while dominated by independent directors, will usually obtain input from the CEO with respect to nominees. The result is a slate of director nominees that is presented to shareholders for approval. But, can shareholders influence the outcome, except by withholding their approval? Actually, the shareholder vote is controlled pretty much by two other parties; brokerage firms that hold their clients' shares and vote them without consulting the clients; and mutual funds, who, while owned by their customers, are themselves the owners of corporate shares. These two intermediaries control the shareholder vote, and the record shows that they overwhelmingly vote the shares in favor of the nominees put forward by the existing board and management. The resulting situation has been subject to considerable criticism from advocates of reform in corporate governance. Proponents of the existing pattern argue that brokerage firms and mutual fund managers are more knowledgeable than the average shareholder, so no significant change is called for. Reform advocates reject that argument, insisting that shareholders be able to exert some influence on the nominating process; a position feared by those defending the status quo as likely to lead to chaos in governance.

Voting client shares by brokerage firms, minus any instructions or prior approval by the clients, was considered by NYSE in June 2006, when it announced a plan to halt the practice, effective for the Spring 2007 season of annual stockholder meetings. Since it is estimated that some 80 percent of public corporations' shares are held in "street name," i.e., by the brokerage firms, the change was significant as a potential factor affecting corporate governance (through its possible impact on the nomination and selection of directors). But, by early October 2006, the NYSE, without fanfare, delayed the implementation of the plan. The ultimate outcome of the proposed plan warrants watching, for the delay in implementation indicates substantial opposition.[15]

The mutual fund part of the picture is illustrated by the example of Fidelity Management and Research, which is reported to manage over $1 trillion in investor assets. Fidelity's size gives it great power to influence boards of directors, through its voting of the shares of corporations in which it has invested. Gretchen Morgensen, a *New York Times* columnist, reported that "Fidelity sided with corporate management and directors in 92.5 percent of its votes and supported 99 percent of the directors whom management nominated."[16] Fidelity makes no apologies for that record, pointing out that it rests on Fidelity's confidence in its investment decisions, i.e., its judgment that the companies comprising its portfolio of stocks are well managed, and well served by their directors. Ms. Morgensen shows some skepticism, especially when it comes to executive compensation at those firms. She draws attention also to the proposal that directors be required to win their seats on boards by majority, rather than plurality, votes; a proposal that Fidelity opposes. Displaying a diametrically different attitude, the American Federation of State, County, and Municipal Employees, representing its members' interests in AIG, the insurance giant, wanted to put forward a stockholder proposal that would change the process through which AIG's directors would be elected (so that AFSCME could nominate their own candidates, and have their names appear on AIG's proxy forms). In September 2006, an appeals court upheld AFSCME's position. Subsequently, the SEC undertook a re-examination of the issue, and is scheduled to render its decision in December 2006.[17]

One other aspect of director choice warrants mention. Once elected, is their individual performance as a director ever evaluated, and become a factor in their continuance in the position? In the cozy atmosphere that formerly prevailed in America's boardrooms, the answer to that question rested mainly on the director's congeniality, and willingness to go along with the wishes of the CEO-Chairman. I believe the evidence indicates that is no longer true; witness the trend toward peer evaluation of director performance by other board members. In October 2006, the *Wall Street Journal* reported that: "In a survey of more than 1,100 directors serving on the boards of the 2,000 biggest public companies in the U.S., conducted last year by Corporate Board Member magazine and PricewaterhouseCoopers, 77% of respondents agreed that individual directors should be appraised regularly on their performance—while only 37% said they had actually done so."[18] Of course, this is a most sensitive issue, as is indicated by the difference between the percentage of directors thinking it to be a good idea, and the percentage actually doing such evaluations. But, in earlier times, the very idea was generally unthinkable. In any case, director evaluations go directly to the critical matters of judging director independence and competence.

Board Structure: Impact of Sarbanes-Oxley

Sarbanes-Oxley diminished the power of the CEO also by requiring that; either the CEO and chairman positions be separated, or, alternatively, that a lead director be designated. The lead director, or independent chairman, would have the power, by virtue of the position, to call meetings of the independent directors, set meeting agendas, and order the conduct of the board's affairs and its committees. This is a major structural change in the board. Sarbanes-Oxley required additionally that the independent members of the board meet at least once per year in executive session, to guarantee its ability to discuss any matters of company interest and concern privately and not subject to the influence that might be exercised by the presence of the CEO.

When the board chairmanship is put into the hands of an independent lead director, the independent directors have a mechanism through which they can discuss and explore corporate matters of concern. In England, a non-executive board chairman is common. But, in the United States it has been relatively rare, and CEOs typically have fought the separation. Consequently, in the U.S. the stock exchange has gone mostly in the direction of the lead director arrangement. That requirement is a significant change, and encourages independent directors to become more active in their oversight role. I remember well the concern evidenced by CEOs of public companies where I served as a director, when the independent directors indicated a desire to meet without them. It is an interesting and possibly significant fact that the very same concern was evidenced by a university president when the deans indicated a desire to meet independently. The "boss" knows that such arrangements facilitate initiatives and inquiries outside of his/her control. The implicit and real diminution of power is well understood by everyone.

Although boards have long had committees to meet and consider particular facets of corporate operations, e.g., executive, audit, compensation, and nominating, they were not specifically required by stock exchange regulations, and their composition was not specified by any such regulations. Now, the stock exchanges, being subject to the regulatory requirements of the Securities and Exchange Commission, require at least audit, compensation, and nominating committees. They require also that these committees be comprised only of independent directors. Further, in addition to a code of ethics for the entire board, each committee must have a charter that describes its function, and how it is to operate.

The audit committee is charged with the responsibility of dealing with the corporation's auditor, and the auditor is responsible to the committee (Title II of Sarbanes-Oxley—Auditor Independence). The arrangement is designed to enlarge the knowledge and involvement of the independent directors with the financial facts of the company's operations. Also, the chairman of the audit committee must meet especially stringent requirements of independence and professional competence as an auditor (must possess the CPA and have substantial experience in the profession, and must have been free of any professional practice relationships for at least two years). The nominating committee is responsible for vetting new members of the board, and for reviewing the performance of board members. The compensation committee is charged with reviewing and recommending management's compensation arrangements, hopefully to get a handle on extremely generous packages. All these requirements reflect the impact of Sarbanes-Oxley.

The exchange does not now mandate an executive committee, probably assuming that the board itself and its committees will be meeting frequently enough to make that committee unnecessary. When board meetings were held infrequently, not unusual in the past, the executive committee would meet between board meetings to authorize important actions by management. The arrangement could work to neutralize too close attention by independent board members to company affairs, especially if the executive committee was "packed" by buddies of the CEO.

The requirement that the audit committee's chairman have special professional qualifications raises a highly significant question: Will that person now have a higher level of personal liability than fellow directors, who presumably will rely on his special expertise and competence to catch abuses? The issue has already been raised in a case before a Delaware Chancery Court judge.[19]

Board committees increase the effectiveness of the board because they: (1) increase the time directors spend on corporate business; (2) increase the information in the hands of directors, and, consequently, their knowledge and expertise; (3) increase a sense of social interaction among the independent directors, and their readiness to discuss sensitive issues; and (4) encourage a sense of solidarity in the committee and in the board. All these factors operate to bring balance into the relationship between the CEO and the board.[20]

There is considerable public misunderstanding of the role of the board of directors and its committees. The misunderstanding attributes to the board responsibilities and functions that it is not able to carry out; namely, to guarantee that management will not commit fraud, to design a corporate strategy and implement it, to insure profitability, and/or to insure the quality of the company's products or services. Those responsibilities and functions belong to management, for they require diligent, thoughtful daily attention to the company's strategy and operations. The board's responsibility and function is to provide an oversight of management's effectiveness in achieving profitability, while producing quality products and services. The board is there to spot problems early, and to get management's attention directed to their solution. Failing solution, the board has the responsibility to replace management.

The Director's Job: Then and Now

The American Society of Corporate Secretaries conducted a survey of *Current Board Practices* in 1997, and published the results in March 1998.[21] An earlier survey had been done two years before, and the full report contains some comparisons. Our initial emphasis is on the 1998 report. The results clearly reflect some early stirring in the direction of increased director independence, but several of the responses reflect the tendency to concentrate power in the hands of the CEO.[22]

Practices notable for their unpopularity were: (1) separating the CEO and board chairmanship positions; (2) setting up a procedure for formal evaluation of individual directors; and (3) scheduling regular meetings of independent directors separate from the CEO and other management directors. Despite some stirring in the direction of greater board independence, the key indicators of concentration of power in the hands of the CEO show the real nature of the governance situation.

In the foregoing context, the typical pattern of board meetings would include an executive summary of the financial situation, with back-up material that might or might not be distributed to the directors prior to the meeting. Generally, the material would not highlight problems. Since many directors did not devote much time to study of the material, it was more show than substance. Also, the material that was distributed was usually too detailed, too long, and too technical for most independent directors to analyze meaningfully. To make the director's job less onerous, it was common for the committees to meet on the same day as the board did. The committees could meet at 7:30 or 8:00 in the morning, concluding at 9:00 or 9:30, and then the entire board could convene immediately after. The board as a whole would then meet until noon, with lunch scheduled in the executive dining room thereafter.

The board meeting was usually well choreographed, with presentations by members of management reporting on the various divisions. Also, requests for board approval of capital expenditures and projects would take up time. With most everyone sensitive to the time dimension, since directors were generally scheduled for return flights home in mid-afternoon, in depth discussion of difficult issues was not frequent. In fact, many directors would not even stay for lunch, unless they lived in the area. The pattern could and would be disrupted if a crisis arose, but the pattern was not conducive to early warning signals showing themselves.

The pattern has changed. Today, the truncated half-day board sessions have often been replaced by multi-day arrangements. Committee meetings may be held on the day before the full board meeting, probably in the afternoon, and lasting until dinner time. Then, the committee members (remember—audit, compensation, and nominating committees now consist entirely of independent directors) can have dinner together, and discuss freely the management of the company, or any other topic.

The entire board meets the following day, starting in the morning, going through lunch, and winding up before dinner. There is time for full discussion of issues and plans, and directors come away with a real understanding of the business. Finally, it is becoming common for the full board to now schedule an annual meeting lasting three or four days, for a full strategic review of the corporation's business, with attention to its divisions as well as to the entity. These meetings give the independent directors a good opportunity to assess the management of the company, and to get some insight into possible successors to the CEO.

The Business Roundtable, comprised of 150 leading corporations, conducted a survey of its members in June 2003, and another in early 2004, to measure the corporate governance reforms undertaken by them in the wake of the Sarbanes-Oxley Act and the new standards of the New York Stock Exchange. The Roundtable is an association of the CEOs of corporations with a combined workforce of over 10 million employees in the United States and $3.7 trillion in annual revenues. The highlights of the survey were reported by the Roundtable in July 2003, and again in March 2004.[23]

Most notable were: (1) a tremendous increase in the percentage of independent directors (99 percent of the boards reported that at least 60 percent of their members were independent); (2) 71 percent of the companies have an independent chairman, independent lead director, or presiding outside director; (3) formal director education programs are now a prevalent practice—89 percent of the companies, and director evaluation arrangements are also prevalent; (4) 100 percent of the companies surveyed now meet in executive sessions of the independent directors at least twice a year, and 61 percent expect to do so at every board meeting; and (5) increased awareness of the need for improved shareholder communication is reported by the Roundtable companies (87 percent of the companies have adopted a procedure to communicate with shareholders). Korn /Ferry International's 31st annual survey of directors, released on November 22, 2004, buttressed these findings, in part, reporting for

American corporate directors that: (1) 93 percent said they held executive sessions during regular meetings that did not include the CEO, an increase from 41 percent two years before; and (2) since enactment of Sarbanes-Oxley, the percentage of directors reporting that their boards had formalized the lead director role grew from 32 percent to 80 percent. The Korn/Ferry survey reported also that prospective board members were increasingly declining invitations to join boards, because of concern over increased personal liability exposure; the percentage of turndowns growing from 13 percent in 2002 to 29 percent in 2004.

Significant controversy exists relative to board and management responsiveness to shareholder concerns; especially in connection with elections of board members. Typically, a single slate of board nominees is presented to shareholders; who can either approve or oppose. But, alternative board nominees are not presented simultaneously for shareholder consideration. As a consequence, to unseat board members who have lost significant shareholder support, or who are opposed when originally nominated for a board seat, it has been necessary for dissatisfied shareholders to mount a complex and expensive campaign to revamp the membership of the board. Typically, also, the existing arrangement was conducive to management control of board nominations and membership. From a legal standpoint, the arrangement was supported by SEC interpretations of its rule 14a-8, which dealt with board elections. The matter was opened up for reconsideration by the SEC, as a consequence of a decision by the U.S. Court of Appeals for the Second Circuit (as of early September 2006) that disagreed with the current SEC interpretation of rule 14a-8. SEC chairman Cox thereupon announced that the Commission would revisit rule 14a-8, and make changes in time for the 2007 proxy season.[24]

Turning to the substance of board activity, the McKinsley Quarterly reported in April 2006 that "Boards of directors are becoming much more knowledgeable about and actively involved in their companies' core performance and value creating activities, according to the executives who responded to the latest McKinsley Quarterly survey. However, in one controversial area of corporate governance—compensating executives with stock options and bonuses tied to earnings growth—these more active board members have effected relatively little change." Specifically, the executives of publicly held companies reported that, comparing how actively directors were involved in the areas of company performance and value creation as contrasted with five years ago, 75 percent were more active. Greater involvement appeared more commonly in larger public companies than in smaller ones; the survey noted that 72 percent of the companies with annual revenues of $1 billion or more reported greater board activity.[25] I believe that, given current regulatory, media, and public attention being given to back-dating and other manipulations of stock options, board attention to these matters can be expected to rise significantly.

The changes outlined above involve costs, and the Roundtable member companies attempted some estimates. Of course these estimates are imprecise, but they are indicative of seriousness of purpose. The companies that provided estimates indicated provision of $1 million to over $10 million to achieve implementation of the provisions of the Sarbanes-Oxley Act and the proposed New York Stock Exchange listing standards (22 percent estimated costs of more than $10 million, 31 percent estimated costs of $6-$10 million, and 46 percent estimated costs between $1 million and $5 million). The 2004 Korn/Ferry survey, referred to above, reported that the average cost of Sarbanes-Oxley compliance amounted to $5.1 million, and that 99 percent of the boards said that they were in compliance. The 99 percent figure may overstate actual full compliance, because board members may construe current efforts to come into compliance as being in compliance. Considering current problems with stock options and restatement of earnings by a number of public companies, that hypothesis seems reasonable. A more recent and more complete consideration of compliance costs is found in Appendix II.

An especially interesting example of the shift that has taken place in the state of mind of corporate boards and managements is provided by WorldCom, a corporation that emerged from bankruptcy in April 2004. WorldCom is an outstanding illustration of the scandal ridden corporations that attracted so much opprobrium when the bubble of the nineties burst. It is a huge telecommunications organization, hoping to have a post-bankruptcy life as MCI with a new board, new management, and new governance arrangement.

The company's transformation was reported in the *New York Times*.[26] The report noted that Michael D. Capellas, who replaced Bernard Ebbers as CEO, supported all 78 recommendations contained in a 149 page report that had been submitted to the new MCI board. Among the recommendations, designed to enhance board independence, are a limitation on directors serving more than ten years, and a requirement that at least one director leave the board each year, evidently to insure rotation and fresh blood. Large shareholders are to be given a voice in nominating directors. This idea has gotten some traction, because the SEC is moving in the direction of opening up the proxy used at annual meetings to elect directors to greater shareholder participation.[27] Also, the report suggested that outside auditors would have to be switched every ten years. Finally, a court appointed monitor, Richard C. Breeden, will continue to function in that capacity for at least two years after the new MCI emerged from bankruptcy.

Capellas, and many others, are enthusiastic over the direction of events, especially over the empowerment of independent directors. While I favor significant checks on unbridled CEO power, I have indicated already that there can also be danger in compromising the ability of management to lead an organization. Peter J. Wallison, a resident fellow at the American Enterprise Institute, is more worried than I am. He expressed his concern in the *Wall Street Journal*.

> Sarbanes-Oxley was adopted hastily, and without adequate consideration by a Congress panicked about the possibility that the Enron and WorldCom cases had seriously weakened investor confidence. Most lawmakers probably thought they were voting for a harmless piece of legislation that would simply give the Securities and Exchange Commission more authority. But the act went much further than that. Among other things, it placed new emphasis on the role of independent directors on corporate boards, . . . Although many who supported the act viewed this as a healthy reform, it may have had unintended consequences—a reluctance of managements to take the risks and make the investments that had previously brought the economy roaring back from periods of stagnation or recession.[28]

Wallison's worry is excessive, although there is a chance that we may overshoot in our efforts to balance management's power. We need to be conscious of that possibility. One way of dealing with that hazard may be to emphasize the proper role of the board in sessions devoted to developing sound board-management relationships. Such sessions must emphasize the importance of management's role to lead and to implement policy, and the further importance of a sense of unity of authority in an organization, if it is to carry forward a strategic vision. In any case, it seems clear that Sarbanes-Oxley has brought about profound changes in board structure and composition, which enhanced the power and effectiveness of independent directors vis-à-vis management. Their role and effectiveness in dealing with such substantive matters as corporate goals and strategy, both short and long range, remain to be seen.

Examples of External Pressure: NYSE, Disney, and MBNA

For a time, the board of directors of the New York Stock Exchange appeared to be in a contest with the Securities and Exchange Commission. On the surface, the issue seemed to be a compensation arrangement between the NYSE directors and its chairman, Richard Grasso. Grasso was an executive of the stock exchange for many years, and, under the terms of his employment contract, received compensation that exceeded $10 million for a number of years. The contractual arrangement also allowed Grasso to defer part of his compensation each year, and accumulate the deferred amounts at a guaranteed 8 percent annual return beginning in 1998 (the rate was less before that year).

In 2003, the NYSE board and its compensation committee renegotiated the Grasso agreement, which was due to expire shortly, and replaced it with a new one that extended his employment to 2007. While the new agreement was reported to save the stock exchange $3.5 million in 2003, it resulted in Grasso being able to collect in cash the entire amount that had accumulated under the old agreement. That sum amounted to $139.5 million, a breathtaking bundle of money.

The amount shocked many people, but most notable among them was William H. Donaldson, chairman of the Securities and Exchange Commission. It turned out subsequently that Grasso was entitled to an additional $48 million, but, faced with the fury already aroused, he decided that he would forego that sum, a decision that he subsequently altered. If anything, that action got lost in the continuing uproar, and the issue blossomed more and more into inquiries into the governance of the NYSE.[29]

Donaldson's surprise and shock could in itself occasion some surprise, because he had been the chairman of the NYSE before Grasso assumed the position, and the latter man had served as his number 2 during that time. It is probable that Donaldson was not aware of the fact that Grasso was deferring most of his annual compensation, allowing it to accumulate at an attractive yet riskless rate. In any case, Donaldson, who was called by Grasso the night before the stock exchange announced the payout publicly, reacted strongly and most critically. Parenthetically, it may be worth noting that Donaldson had been, before being chairman of the NYSE, a very successful investment banker and founding dean of the Yale University graduate business school. Also, he may well have viewed the chairmanship of the NYSE as being a quasi-public task, and so possessed of a *pro bono* element.

Donaldson reacted to the news of Grasso's payout by questioning the governance of the stock exchange. It must be kept in mind that the NYSE was, at that time, a non-profit and non-governmental self-regulatory agency, owned by its member firms, but operating under the broad jurisdiction of the SEC.

Pursuant to provisions of the Sarbanes-Oxley Act, the SEC had earlier asked the several securities exchanges (the American Exchange and the NASDAQ, as well as the NYSE) to draw up governance standards for their member firms that would reform them and increase the power of independent directors and key committees. The NYSE had distributed a list of such standards, but had not yet brought them to adoption. The delay may well have upset the SEC and its chairman, and aroused in them suspicion that the NYSE was deliberately delaying. If so, the flap over Grasso's payout provided a convenient basis for pressing the governance issue.

Donaldson demanded that the compensation committee and the board of the NYSE provide relevant minutes of committee and board meetings relating to the details of Grasso's compensation agreement. The point of the demand was probably to see if the board was fully informed on the matter. While Ms. Dale B. Bernstein, an executive vice president of NYSE, said that she hid data regarding Grasso's total compensation from the compensation committee during 1999, 2000, and 2001, both Grasso and Langone denied the accuracy of her testimony. They claimed that the committee and the board were fully informed. Langone, in particular, was outraged, and, in a separate and later proceeding against him by Eliot Spitzer, argued strongly that the board of the NYSE was made up of top Wall Street executives, who were very sophisticated financial experts. The implication that they could be misled or uninformed on a significant financial matter seemed ludicrous.[30] In any case, Donaldson expressed his demand with specific reference to the delay in the governance matter. He said: "I am especially concerned that the pay package was awarded before the exchange completed its governance review, which has been pending since March."[31] The publicity served Donaldson's purpose of jawboning executive compensation packages down to significantly lower levels than had become common during the economic bubble of the nineties; an outcome that remains elusive.

There is another aspect to the Grasso affair, ancillary to the issue just discussed. It involves the matter of disclosure, i.e., transparency in corporate affairs. The directors of the NYSE seemed to believe that their disclosure of the Grasso arrangement satisfied their obligations as directors. H. Carl McCall, chairman of the stock exchange's compensation committee and a former controller of New York State, was cited as follows: "Mr. McCall said in an interview that he was 'surprised' by Mr. Donaldson's questioning of the exchange's self-oversight. The SEC chairman 'was given a heads-up that this (news) was coming,' said Mr. McCall. 'I don't see the relevance between this and our new corporate-governance initiatives, except in a positive way, that is the . . . principle that there will be full disclosure of compensation. And we did that.'"[32] John Stuart Mill, over a century and a half ago, thought that transparency was one of the advantages of the public corporation, even though "cooking the books" was possible. We see now that disclosure, by itself, is not sufficient to afford the protection desired in behalf of the public weal.

Although Grasso is out, the matter of his compensation package did not go away, despite disclosure. For a time following its initial disclosure, it seemed that the compensation package, no matter how outrageous it might appear, could not be challenged legally. The constant furor has changed that idea. John Reed, who followed Grasso as NYSE's interim chairman, initiated an investigation of the matter by Dan Webb, who had been a federal prosecutor. His investigation raised legal issues, and stimulated further investigations by both the SEC and Attorney General Spitzer's office. Spitzer's investigation led him to initiate legal action against both Grasso and Langone seeking the return of some $100 million from Grasso. The basis of the suit was a New York State law that required that the compensation of executives of not-for-profit organizations must be "reasonable," and Spitzer argued that Grasso's compensation package did not meet that test. As for Langone, the suit alleged that he had a conflict of interest, since he was also the CEO of a major financial firm subject to regulation by the NYSE, of which Grasso was CEO. Although the suit was filed in May 2004, the actual trial was scheduled for October 16, 2006. Spitzer won a procedural point on August 8, 2006, when Justice Charles E. Ramos, of the New York State Supreme Court, ruled that the core issue in the case (the reasonableness of Grasso's compensation) could heard by a judge rather than a jury.[33] Langone's attitude is summed up in his comment that the suit is a "boondoggle of a case."[34] The *Wall Street Journal* opined on its editorial page that the Webb report did not provide conclusive support for Spitzer's suit, because the final report omitted some 1,000 pages of interviews which suggested conclusions contrary to those alleged.[35] As a side note, Grasso sued McCall, who was chairman of the NYSE board's compensation committee when the compensation package was approved, holding that, if his compensation was held to be unreasonable, then McCall should share some of the repayment burden. It is reasonable to assume that there was a bit of political animus involved, because both McCall and Spitzer are prominent leaders of the New York State Democratic party. But, Judge Ramos dismissed this suit in August 2006.[36]

In any case, Langone made clear his intention to fight Spitzer's suit. In a column in the *Wall Street Journal*, entitled "Let's Bring on the Jury, Mr. Spitzer," he argued that all members of the NYSE Compensation committee had complete information about Grasso's compensation. He referred specifically to H. Carl McCall, a former New York State Comptroller and prominent member of the Democratic Party, and Henry Paulson, former chairman of Goldman Sachs and a new Secretary of the Treasury as of July 2006. Both men were not charged by Spitzer, although McCall had also been chairman of the NYSE Compensation committee and Paulson a member. Actually, Paulson questioned "the propriety" of Grasso's cashing out his accumulated $140 million in one lump sum at a time when there was a public furor over outsize executive compensation deals. He suggested that Grasso get legal advice, and Grasso sought such advice from Martin Lipton, a leading authority on corporate governance. While the payout was eventually authorized by the board, there was substantial internal debate about it. And, eventually the board forced Grasso's retirement as CEO of NYSE.[37] Langone's column in the *Wall Street Journal* implied that McCall's absence from the legal action might be related to Spitzer's political ambitions.[38]

As of October 19, 2006, Judge Ramos ruled against Grasso's contention that the NYSE board was fully informed about the facts of his compensation package, holding that, as a director and board chairman, Grasso had a fiduciary obligation to make sure that his fellow directors were so informed, yet failed to fulfill that obligation. The judge was also severely critical of other board members, observing that they had not fulfilled their duty of care to make themselves properly informed of a matter involving some $100 million. Such criticism of directors in connection with a compensation case is most unusual, and may have significance down the road as a precedent. The "reasonableness" of Grasso's compensation remains to be decided, presumably before the end of 2006. Despite the judicial setbacks he has suffered, Grasso shows no sign of a willingness to settle, and is appealing Judge Ramos's rulings.[39]

The conflict of interest issue arose in another case, in which Spitzer was embroiled with Maurice "Hank" Greenberg and AIG, the insurance giant that Greenberg formerly headed. Greenberg was concurrently a director of the NYSE board and a member of its compensation committee, while Grasso was the CEO of NYSE and negotiating his compensation package. The allegation appeared to be that Greenberg had attempted to use his board position to influence Grasso to help improve the market's perception of AIG stock. Presumably, Grasso would get that result by influencing NYSE specialists trading AIG stock through Spear, Leeds, & Kellogg (a Goldman Sachs subsidiary) to take a more favorable view of the value of AIG stock. Unfortunately, when Grasso was deposed before the SEC about the matter in June 2005, he "repeatedly" invoked his 5th amendment rights against self-incrimination. This fact was disclosed on June 14, 2006, when relevant government documents were released. In a subsequent deposition, Grasso said that he had not exerted any influence in behalf of AIG stock, although he knew that Greenberg was unhappy with the market value of the stock, thought that it was undervalued, and had spoken about this with the specialists. It's a neat trick to discern the dividing line where generalized griping about something mutates into an effort to use pressure to achieve a desired outcome. The ugly implication in this case was that Greenberg would go along with Grasso's compensation package if Grasso was helpful in raising the market value of AIG stock. Of course, that implication has yet to be proved.[40]

The outcome, no matter the feelings of observers, is not ordained to go in favor of Spitzer. While public and press animus against Grasso is strong, the legal case has some weak points. The basic charge, that Grasso sought favorable NYSE treatment of the firms of NYSE directors, to influence those directors in his favor, must overcome the possibility that directors were misled about Grasso's compensation.[41] Also, the charge that Grasso's compensation exceeded what was "reasonable" for an executive of a non-profit organization, under New York State law, may prove difficult to prove, if a comparison with top Wall Street executives holds up in the eyes of a jury.

Another high profile illustration of the present effectiveness of external pressure on corporate governance involves the Disney Company, and its long-time CEO and board chairman, Michael D. Eisner. Eisner has been regarded by many observers as an imperious chief executive, who brooked little or no dissent. Unfortunately for him, in recent years the performance of Disney stock has been unsatisfactory to important and increasingly numerous shareholders.

Matters came to a head in 2003, when two especially prominent board members resigned angrily, after confronting Eisner and calling for his resignation. The two board members were Roy Disney, a nephew of company founder Walt Disney and long-time executive with Disney, and Stanley P. Gold, a well-known investor. After leaving the board, they mounted a widely publicized campaign calling for the ouster of Eisner and soliciting shareholder support, especially among large institutional shareholders like Calpers (the California State Employees Pension Plan).[42]

Roy Disney and Stanley Gold achieved a significant measure of success at Disney's annual meeting in Philadelphia on March 3, 2004. Their opposition to Eisner had finally attracted the support of both large and small shareholders, who amassed a 43 percent vote against the re-election of Eisner to the Disney board. Several independent board members, most prominently George J. Mitchell (well known former U.S. Senator and negotiator of peace in Ireland), as well as Judith L. Estrin and John E. Bryson, were rejected by 24, 23, and 22 percent of the shareholder's vote. This was a large and unprecedented rejection.

The shareholder revolt was followed immediately by board action transferring the title of board chairman from Eisner to Mitchell, who had been designated before as lead director. And, Mitchell had, only a day or two earlier, explained in a *Wall Street Journal* column that that separation was unnecessary and unlikely because of his designation as lead director. In a real sense, George Mitchell is placing his own very solid reputation on the line. Michael Eisner's future, which seemed to depend on a near term major transformation in his managerial style and in Disney's financial results, is now moot, since he announced his intention to retire as CEO in September 2006.[43] Some days later, he announced also that he would not continue as a board member. And, Mitchell, Estrin, and Bryson's future as directors is doubtful, although Mitchell's may depend on his leadership as chairman of the board during the transition period until a new CEO is installed. In fact, Mitchell indicated that he would likely give up the chairman's role in 2006.

MBNA is a major credit card company, having created the concept of affinity cards, i.e., credit cards that are identified with an organization or group (university, airline, charity, team, professional association, bank, etc.).[44] The concept was the brainchild of Charles M. Cawley, a co-founder of the company with Alfred Lerner. His first tie-in was with his alma mater, Georgetown University, and the promotion of the credit card was directed to the school's alumni. From that humble beginning, the company grew to its present giant size, with an estimated 85 percent of the affinity credit card business and with over 5,400 organizations and groups. It is one of America's 50 most profitable companies, earning a net of $2.34 billion in 2003. Founded in 1983, it went public in 1991, and the value of its shares increased an average of 28 percent per annum since.

Mr. Cawley ran the company after January 1991, its IPO date, as though it was still his private domain. And he was a lavish, even flamboyant spender. A fleet of jet aircraft was acquired, as was 2 yachts, a multi-million dollar collection of paintings by Andrew Wyeth and other famous artists, and a beautiful campus in Maine that was used as a summer retreat for management. When Alfred Lerner died in October, 2002, Mr. Cawley arranged for the company to pay $160,000 for an antique rug for his widow's office in Manhattan. Also, a new Mercedes was made available for her use. And, she was made a member of the board, while Alfred Lerner's son was elected by the board to be chairman (Cawley was CEO). Finally, the company made substantial contributions to causes dear to Mr. Cawley's heart.

In 2003, seeing the public reaction to Grasso's compensation package, and the regulatory initiatives investigating and prosecuting companies and boards that were lax in overseeing and controlling free-wheeling corporate spending and lavish perks, the MBNA board became restive and began to challenge Mr. Cawley's compensation arrangements for himself and his management team. They turned their attention also to the jets, yachts, and other lavish expenditures paid for by the company, even though the record seems to indicate that Cawley and other recipients of company largess did make modest payments to the company for personal items and usage.

The issue came to a head at a board meeting on November 12, 2003. Months earlier the board's compensation committee had retained a consultant to review MBNA's executive compensation arrangements, a move that Mr. Cawley strongly opposed, especially since he was poised to propose substantial increases for the next four years. The November 12 meeting must have been a bruising affair, because on the 22nd of the month Mr. Cawley notified the board chairman that he had decided to retire. He was out of the office by year-end, and was succeeded by Bruce L. Hammonds.

Under Mr. Hammonds' direction, cutbacks of major proportions have occurred, with further ones in prospect. The company's six top executives, who received compensation of $150 million in 2002, would be cut 22 percent from 2003 to 2004, and that was subject to producing specified financial goals. Two corporate jets and the two yachts were sold, as was a recently acquired Andrew Wyeth at $3.5 million and a number of real estate assets.

We see once again that corporate governance has changed, with boards becoming more responsive to the external pressure of regulatory agencies and public opinion. Still, my memory that I mistakenly came to that same conclusion some dozen years ago gives me pause. In any case, independent directors now have a clear legal responsibility to do what ethics and fiduciary duty always required. The WorldCom and Enron cases, discussed in chapter V, have particular relevance because individual directors paid significant sums out of their personal funds to settle suits against them.

Notes

1. Berle and Means, *The Modern Corporation*, 107.

2. Korn/Ferry International, *Seventeenth Annual Study of Boards of Directors*, 1990, New York, 1.

3. Mitchell Pacelle and Matthew Karnitschnig, "Spiegel's European Owner Gets a Hard Lesson in U.S. Business," *Wall Street Journal*, March 2, 2004, pp. A1, A6. Mark Landler, "For Spiegel Investor, a Hard Lesson in Securities Law," *New York Times*, September 11, 2004, B1, B14.

4. Jacques Steinberg and Geraldine Fabrikant, "Executive Testifies for 6 Hours on Woes With Hollinger Board," *New York Times*, February 21, 2004, B1, B14. Jacques Steinberg and Geraldine Fabrikant, "A Deal to Sell Hollinger Stake is Blocked," *New York Times*, February 27, 2004, C1, C2. Rita K. Farrall, "Court Allows Hollinger to Sell Paper Without Investor Vote," *New York Times*, July 30, 2004, C4.

5. Floyd Norris, "Misdirected: The Trouble With Hollinger's Board," *New York Times*, September 1, 2004, C1, C6. Geraldine Fabrikant, "Hollinger Files Stinging Report on Ex-Officials," *New York Times*, September 1, 2004, A1, C6.

6. Stephen Labaton, "Under Attack, Director Say's Hollinger's Black Misled Him," *New York Times*, September 6, 2004, C1, C4.

7. *New York Times*, May 4, 2005, p. C2.

8. *New York Times*, August 19, 2005, pp. C1, C4; *New York Times*, August 22, 2005, pp. C1, C4; *Wall Street Journal*, November 18, 2005, p. A3.

9. Report of Investigation by the Special Committee of the Board of Directors of Hollinger International, Inc., Gordon A. Paris, chairman, Counsel and Advisors, Richard C. Breeden & Co., O'Melveny & Myers LLP, August 30, 2004, pp. 1-4.

10. *New York Times*, July 7, 2006, p. C7.

11. *New York Times*, August 31, 2006, p. C3.

12. *New York Times*, September 4, 2006, pp. C1, C3.

13. Deborah Solomon, "Loophole Limits Independence," *Wall Street Journal*, April 28, 2004, C1, C4.

14. *New York Times*, October 15, 2006, section 3, pp. 1, 7.

15. *New York Times*, October 3, 2006, pp. C1, C6.

16. *New York Times*, October 8, 2006, section 3, pp. 1, 4.

17. *Wall Street Journal*, October 27, 2006, p. A14.

18. *Wall Street Journal*, October 9, 2006, p. R5.

19. Kara Scannell, "Judge Decides Some Directors Are More Liable," *Wall Street Journal*, October 12, 2004, C1, C3.

20. Abraham L. Gitlow, *Being the Boss, The Importance of Leadership and Power*, Business One Irwin, Homewood, Illinois, 1992, 143-144.

21. ASCS, *Current Board Practices*, March 1998, 521 Fifth Avenue, New York.

22. ASCS, *Current Board Practices*, 2-4.

23. The Business Roundtable, *Corporate Governance Survey Highlights*, July 2003, 2 pages; and *Corporate Governance Survey Highlights*, March 2004, 2 pages.

24. *New York Times*, September 8, 2006, p. C5.

25. *McKinsley Quarterly*, premium edition, "What directors know about their companies: A McKinsey Survey," April 6, 2006, p. 1.

26. Barnaby J. Feder, "WorldCom Report Recommends Sweeping Changes for its Board," *New York Times*, August 26, 2003, C1, C2.

27. *Business Week*, October 13, 2003, 114.

28. Peter J. Wallison, *Wall Street Journal*, September 3, 2003, A16.

29. Joann S. Lublin, "Where Was the NYSE Board?" *Wall Street Journal*, Sept. 11, 2003, C1.

30. *Wall Street Journal*, September 30, 2005, p. A10; *New York Times*, April 7, 2006, p. C3.

31. Landon Thomas, Jr., "S.E.C. Chairman Wants Details of Compensation Paid to Grasso," *New York Times*, September 3, 2003, C1, C8.

32. Deborah Solomon and Kate Kelly, "SEC Head Demands Details on Pay Deal for NYSE's Grasso," *Wall Street Journal*, September 3, 2003, C1, C11.

33. *New York Times*, August 9, 2006, p. C3.

34. *New York Times*, April 7, 2006, p. C3.

35. *Wall Street Journal*, June 14, 2005, p. A14.

36. *New York Times*, August 29, 2006, p. C3.

37. *New York Times*, June 25, 2006, section 3, pp. 1, 3.

38. *Wall Street Journal*, June 10, 2004, A 12.

39. *Wall Street Journal*, October 20, 2006, pp. A1, A10; *New York Times*, October 20, 2006, pp. A1, C7.

40. *New York Times*, June 15, 2006, pp. C1, C4.

41. *New York Times*, May 25, 2004, C1-C4; May 26, 2004, C1-C2.

42. Floyd Norris, "Corporate Democracy and the Power to Embarrass," *New York Times*, March 4, 2004, C1, C4. Bruce Orwall, Brian Steinberg, and Joann S. Lublin, "Eisner Loses 43% of Disney Vote," *Wall Street Journal*, March 4, 2004, A1, A13.

43. *Wall Street Journal*, September 10, 2004, A1.

44. Lowell Bergman and Patrick McGeehan, "Expired: How a Credit King Was Cut Off," *New York Times*, March 7, 2004, Section 3, 1, 10.

Chapter IV

The Accountants

The preceding chapters showed how unchecked executive power developed in public corporations, and overwhelmed the inherent power of the board of directors to contain and control it. But, what about the check represented by the requirement that the financial records of those corporations be subject to independent audits by CPAs? How did the imperial CEOs manage to suborn the accountants? More, why did the corruption of auditors succeed so well that numbers of them became themselves producers of schemes to cook the books, or push the parameters of the tax codes? This chapter attempts to provide answers.

The Nature of the Profession

There is a grotesque, but widely held, view of the accounting profession as inherently boring. That view has been depicted popularly in cartoons by a figure of a man, usually in shirt sleeves and with a green eyeshade, hunched over pages of numbers. His pencil is poised, as he inscribes additional numbers, or makes alterations in those already inscribed. Apparently, his exercise is devoid of any meaningful aspect that would impart significance to those numbers, let alone high dramatic impact. How strange it is then that financial statements comprised of those numbers have been at the center of the corporate accounting scandals. Huge corporations collapsed into bankruptcy, amid charges of fraud and manipulation of their accounting procedures. Investigations proliferated, and eventual indictments of a number of the alleged malefactors were forthcoming. And Arthur Andersen, the most prominent and respected firm in the accounting profession, was crushed out of existence by the Enron scandal. Plainly, such high drama and human trauma proclaims the importance of the accounting profession. It is boring only to those who do not comprehend the meaning of the numbers, and the ease with which they can be manipulated.

Charles Waldo Haskins, a pioneer in the profession, played a major part in elevating it beyond simple bookkeeping. Haskins was a well-educated and well-traveled man who established, with his partner Elijah Sells, the firm of Haskins and Sells, long one of America's leading accounting firms. That was not long before the beginning of the twentieth century. Haskins was, more importantly, a leader in getting New York State to enact a law in 1896 creating the title "certified public accountant," and limiting it to those practitioners who passed a state examination and met certain prescribed standards of experience and knowledge. That law was the first of its kind in the United States, and it was, in time, followed by others adopted by all the states.

Haskins was no numbers cruncher. He saw accounting as the language of business, the means through which understanding of the financial affairs of those complex organizations could be obtained and communicated to others. Seen in that light, it assumed great importance in facilitating the flow of savings into investment and the accumulation of capital. Having that perception of the profession, it is no mystery that Haskins was the leading figure in the establishment of the School of Commerce, Accounts, and Finance at New York University in 1900. He was also the founding dean. In short, Haskins believed that the higher accountancy warranted formal education at the university level, although he did not view it as a substitute for a well-founded general education at that level as well.

A century later, the corporate accounting scandals sullied the profession's status, despite a code of professional conduct that would seem to have made such an outcome impossible, if only it had been followed in both spirit and letter. It is instructive to take a look at the code, for it serves to emphasize the susceptibility of such pronouncements of ethical standards for professional behavior to fail in the face of greed and a fear of speaking to the power that greed may command.

The code referred to here was issued by the American Institute of Certified Public Accountants (AICPA) in January 1988, having been adopted by the membership of the organization. The AICPA is the national society of certified public accountants, and is the premier voice of the profession in the United States. There are two main sections of the code: (1) the principles, which set forth the ethical values considered central to professional conduct; and (2) the rules, which set forth the technical auditing standards applicable to the practice of accounting. The Council of the AICPA, its governing body, has designated the Financial Accounting Standards Board to promulgate the standards. We focus on the principles, the ethical body of values adopted in 1988.

The preamble to the principles notes that each AICPA member "assumes an obligation of self-discipline above and beyond the requirements of laws and regulations." It adds that "The Principles call for an unswerving commitment to honorable behavior, even at the sacrifice of personal advantage." The principles require that members: (1) exercise sensitive professional and moral judgments in all their activities; (2) act in a way that will serve the public interest, honor the public trust, and demonstrate commitment to professionalism (where conflicting pressures arise members should act with integrity, i.e., do what is right and just); (3) avoid subordination of service and the public trust to personal gain and advantage; (4) maintain objectivity and be free of conflicts of interest in discharging professional responsibilities; and (5) observe the profession's technical and ethical standards, striving continually to improve competence and the quality of services, and discharging professional responsibility to the best of their ability. Finally, members should: (a) practice in firms that have internal quality control procedures; and (b) determine whether the scope and nature of other services provided to an audit client would create a conflict of interest in the performance of the audit function. This final injunction appears to address directly the issue of the inherent conflict between auditing and consulting services provided to the same client at the same time.

Adherence to the principles of the code would have prevented the corporate accounting scandals from happening. But the promise of the principles was aborted by the pursuit of personal gain. Writing about the Enron scandal and the associated collapse of Arthur Andersen, Professors Paul M. Healy and Krishna G. Palepu, of Harvard's Business School, emphasized that Andersen's large consulting relationship with Enron, amounting to some $27 million in 2000, was the basis for charges that it was consequently lax in its audit of that firm (the audit was $25 million in 2000). Andersen's Houston office, which handled the Enron account, was presumably influenced by the fact that the Enron audit represented 27 per cent of its total audit fees for the year. One thing is clear. The

Houston office overruled the opinion of Andersen's national office questioning Enron's accounting practices.[1]

Plainly, and despite the specific warning in the code against conflicts of interest, the profession entered whole hog into concurrent auditing and consulting arrangements with clients. The consulting activity put the accounting firm into intimate contact with corporate management, making it easy for the resulting cordiality to engender joint scheming and manipulation of the financial accounts to enhance earnings and inflate stock values. When the auditing side of the firm came in to perform their function and discovered signs of such manipulation, they could, and would, be put under pressure from the consultants to close their eyes to the manipulation. The fees would be the hammer that drove the nail into the heart of professional integrity. Before we turn to the importance of estimation in the financial statements and the ample opportunities it affords for manipulation, we should take a brief look at the Financial Accounting Standards Board (FASB).

The Financial Accounting Standards Board

The FASB is the body that establishes standards for financial accounting and reporting. The standards govern the preparation of the financial statements of public corporations. They are given official standing and authority by virtue of being recognized by the SEC (via the PCAOB) and the AICPA.

The standards set the parameters within which CPAs determine the correctness of management's estimates of critical financial "facts." It should occasion no wonder that the Board is subject to many pressures to set standards that are more, rather than less, flexible. And, flexibility provides the room for playing the estimation game so that the corporate financial picture is clouded and opaque rather than clear and correct.

The FASB also develops broad accounting concepts. It conducts research, is open to public participation, and actively solicits input from various constituencies on accounting issues. Its guiding precepts are: (1) objectivity; (2) the views of its constituents; (3) examination and weighing of costs as well as benefits in the promulgation of standards; (4) minimization of disruption to the continuity of reporting practice when making needed changes to standards; and (5) continuing review of the effects of past decisions.

The FASB is an independent body, but it has a number of constituent organizations. They are: the American Accounting Association; the AICPA; the Association for Investment Management and Research; the Financial Executives International; the Government Finance Officers Association; the Institute of Management Accountants; the National Association of State Auditors, Comptrollers, and Treasurers; and the Securities Industry Association. These organizations are represented on the FASB's Board of Trustees.

The FASB came into being in 1973, as a successor to the Accounting Principles Board of the AICPA (1959-1973), which, in turn, had succeeded the AICPA's Committee on Accounting Procedure (1936-1959). The separation of the standard setting authority from the exclusive control of the AICPA in 1973 probably reflected a demand for more input into the standards from the groups that now comprise the constituent organizations.

One problem, with so many cooks in the kitchen, is the difficulty of arriving at a consensus in establishing or revising standards. On top of that, there is now the new reality that any standards that relate to public corporations are subject to the oversight of the Public Company Accounting Oversight Board that was created by the Sarbanes-Oxley Act. That relationship may engender some tension. At least, when the PCAOB was formed, the FASB hastened to submit a body of standards to it, but they were put on hold, which may have been a signal.

The initial action by the PCAOB was temporary. By late July 2004, it was clear that FASB remained the major originator of accounting standards in the United States. A significant indicator of that fact was its action calling for public corporations to expense the value of stock options that they issued. That action was strongly opposed by a number of the covered corporations. They pressed Congress to enact a law that would negate the action of the FASB. The House of Representatives accommodated the pressure by adopting the Stock Option Accounting Reform Act, by a vote of 312 to 111. The proposed law overruled the FASB action, but the Senate did not go along. The incident reveals starkly the working of opposition to regulatory actions that have bite, and leave the imprint of teeth on those who are bitten.[2] Subsequently, the FASB did go forward with the rule to expense stock options.

The Importance of Estimation

Baruch Lev, Professor of Accounting and Finance at New York University's Stern School of Business, wrote:

> Earnings manipulation is prevalent; but, except for egregious cases, it is hard to detect and prosecute. Most of these manipulations are perpetrated by misestimating the multitude of provisions and reserves underlying earnings computations and by exploiting the vulnerabilities inherent in the accepted accounting framework. While the adverse social consequences of manipulations are difficult to measure, they may well be substantial. Trying to regulate earnings manipulation out of existence with ever-more-detailed rules seems unlikely either to produce more informative financial reporting or, ultimately, to reduce the extent of earnings manipulation, which actually thrives in a thicket of rules. Thus, we must think seriously about reforms that will change the incentives for earnings manipulations and will make corporate financial reports more truthful and revealing.[3]

One thing that might be helpful would be to change the public's perception of the accounting profession and the financial statements that are its output. To start, the importance of estimation in arriving at earnings figures must be recognized; exactly the point made by Lev. Perhaps a fallacious syllogism will indicate the nature of the problem: financial statements consist of numbers; numbers are factual; therefore, financial statements are factual, implying that they represent the truth. Lev refers to reserves and provisions in the financial statements, as bases for inaccurate estimation. Let us take note of some more specific examples.

We already considered defined benefit plans in chapter II, and learned there that estimates involving future interest rates and the value of the pension fund affect the annual contributions needed to sustain those plans. In turn, the annual contributions directly affect the earnings of the corporations making them. This was true when management and auditors involved with the corporations used legally accepted accounting standards. In short, estimation can be both honest and legal, yet result in misleading earnings data. The fact is that estimation can't be avoided in dealing with certain items in the financial statements.

A taste of the difficulties encountered in estimating certain items can be grasped readily by considering accounting for the cost involved in redeeming credit card points accumulated when using a credit card to pay for a purchase. A credit card company has millions of credit cards issued and in use. As they are used, the cardholders accumulate points, which can be redeemed some time in the future for goods or services having value. When redeemed, those goods or services will involve some cost to the credit card company, and that cost is an obligation (liability) to the company that must be shown in its financial statements. The cost is not, at the present time, a precise and known amount, nor is it known at what rate and over what time period the points will be redeemed. The amounts must be estimated. Understand that, if a high figure for the redemption cost is used, it will impact directly on corporate earnings, by reducing them, and vice versa.

The estimation process is not completely blind. There are statistical techniques for analyzing past experience that can be used to project future experience. But, again, they are estimates, and can vary, perhaps widely, from actual events, no matter how honestly and carefully done. It should be obvious that, given dishonest intent, it is easy to manipulate the numbers. More subtle is the ease with which an honest executive and auditor can slip into favoring the figure that is on the edge of deliberate manipulation, but just happens to help the bottom line when it is under pressure from various other unfavorable economic events. The same problem would apply to frequent flyer miles issued by airlines, a disquieting thought in light of the severe financial problems that industry has been facing since 9/11.

Estimation is involved also in recording receivables, although it may not be plain at first sight. Presumably, when goods or services are sold, the customer pays, and the facts of the transaction are clear and known. But the presumption is not correct. Many sales are essentially on credit, with payment to be made after billing. Unfortunately, not all customers pay their bills promptly, or at all, making it necessary to allow for some bad receivables. Once again, we face estimation. But there is more, because many managers are unwilling to accept the fact of non-payment, and will carry the amounts involved on their books as real revenue, when they should set aside some reserves as an offset. In a private corporation, management is deluding only itself. But in a public corporation it is misleading the shareholders. Another aspect of the receivables matter involves reporting revenues for goods in the hands of distributors, where the goods can be returned for credit. Unsavory games have been played with that item. Consider also a contract covering an extended time period, where goods or services are to be delivered over a number of months. Is the stream of income reported immediately, or as received over the time period? Some managements have done it one way and some the other.

Other accounting items that provide room for judgment involve inventories and depreciation. If sales fall short of forecasts, inventories can accumulate, and become out-dated. If they cannot be returned, they must be written off, or sold at a loss for whatever they will bring. But managers are often unwilling to recognize the implicit error they have made in their forecasts, don't want to take the loss, and continue to carry the bad inventories at full value on their books. Depreciation recognizes that capital goods wear out over time, and eventually have to be replaced. Although there are accounting conventions that apply, there is also room for judgment as to the time period that will be used. If shorter, the depreciation is larger, and the earnings smaller. And vice versa. Some bad cases of accounting manipulation involved treating current expenditures as though they were capital, and so stretching out the time period over which they were recognized. The objective is to falsely reduce costs, and inflate reportable profits.

The foregoing cases are illustrative, and do not in any way exhaust the possibilities open for accounting estimation to be misused. Piling up detailed rules will not solve the problem. A likelier approach (while not ruling out the usefulness of accounting principles, regulation, and punishment for malefactors) would try to strike at the incentives that often induce misbehavior, e.g., realistic pricing of stock options, reducing as far as possible conflicts of interest, and stimulating those with oversight responsibility to speak to the power of misbehaving managements. Also, so-called Chinese walls can be erected, to separate those with power from being able to exercise their power over those with a need to be independent, e.g., investment bankers over financial analysts.

The Auditing-Consulting Conflict

This chapter began with a delineation of a cartoon figure of an accountant. It implied a bean-counter whose counting was essentially devoid of any profound or substantive meaning. It then decried the cartoon as grotesque and wrong, claiming that the numbers involved told a story to anyone with the insight to read the language of business. In that claim may lay the seed that grows into the auditing-consulting conflict. The auditor examines the numbers, but, if he/she is competent, then they have meaning. They reveal the financial condition of an enterprise, and, in that revelation, they become a basis for analysis. It is unavoidable. The reader who knows the language reads and comprehends. The competent reader can apply experience to discern patterns that are revealing, and that provide guides to the discovery and correction of problems. In short, the ability to give advice, to consult, is inherent in the very process of auditing. It is obvious in the relationship of the accountant and the small businessman. It may be obscured in large organizations, and get separated, but it is nonetheless inherent.

There is a critical difference between the relationship of the accountant and management in a private corporation and that in a public corporation. It is the separation of ownership and management control in the latter from what it is in the former. It is where the auditing-consulting conflict is born. In the private corporation, the auditor can, and usually does, both audit and consult, and does so without a conflict of interest in his/her relationship with either owners or managers, because they are not differentiated. In the public corporation, they are separated, and consulting that aids management may harm owners (shareholders) when the accounting-consultants cover up management misbehavior in the audit that they also do. The Enron–Arthur Andersen case is the perfect illustration. The carrot which is the lure that the auditing horse seeks to eat is the consulting fee. The issue has a vitally important regulatory dimension, because the conflict in the case of the public corporation has called forth major provisions in the Sarbanes-Oxley Act to separate the functions in those companies, which, if applied to private corporations, could destroy the useful advising role of the accountant in their case. Precisely this issue is a matter of deep concern to the accounting profession, small businesses, and regulators (especially in the states). Regulation run rampant can be very destructive; a danger that needs to be kept in mind.

Another aspect of the auditing-consulting conflict involves the question of whether or not the separation of the two functions under Sarbanes-Oxley, which has led three of the Big Four accounting firms to adopt separation in their organizational structure, somehow harms the quality of the auditing process done by those firms. Deloitte & Touche has held out against the separation, maintaining that such is the case. Price Waterhouse Coopers, Ernst & Young, and KPMG have opted for separation, to insure avoidance of the conflict in their audits. Deloitte & Touche argues that the auditing process, by itself, lacks the glamour and intellectual stimulation generated in consulting, so that the best and most able entrants to the profession avoid the auditing segment of the profession, with consequent harm to the quality of recruiting for auditing. Deloitte & Touche argues also that the ability to move accountants between consulting and auditing improves the quality of auditing, because the sometime consultants become experienced in the devices that may be used by misbehaving managements. Of course, the validity of this argument is not easily susceptible to proof, although useful but not available evidence on the actual flow of accountants between the two functions would be instructive. Possibly, time will reveal the truth.

Consulting activity is not the only relationship that can compromise the independence of an auditor. Almost any business relationship with an audited firm apart from the auditing itself may be questioned. A partnership arrangement between Ernst & Young and PeopleSoft, a company that sold software programs for managing human resources, payrolls, and accounting procedures, caused the SEC to challenge Ernst & Young's independence as PeopleSoft's auditor, even though the audit itself was not challenged. Ernst & Young helped promote PeopleSoft's software to other firms, making some $500 million over a 5 year period. It was that activity that compromised its auditing of PeopleSoft, and that the SEC found unacceptable. To stop Ernst & Young, and prevent others from following suit, the SEC prosecuted Ernst & Young. On April 16, 2004, SEC's chief administrative law judge, Brenda P. Murray, levied a fine of $1,686,500, plus interest of $729,302, against Ernst & Young. The judge ruled also that Ernst & Young be barred from accepting any new auditing clients for a period of 6 months. Finally, Ernst & Young was required to retain an outside monitor to insure its future compliance with the SEC prohibition of non-auditing business relationships with an audited client. Note should be taken of the fact that throughout Ernst & Young had in its employ an internal partner in charge of independence issues. It was no doubt embarrassing that he was the SEC's chief accountant prior to his joining Ernst & Young in 1991.[4]

Would Disclosure Ease the Problem?

The SEC has long required that prospectuses and financial audits issued by public corporations disclose material, i.e., significant data bearing on the condition of the corporation, so that investors will be informed when they make their investment decisions. Unfortunately, disclosure has too often been buried in footnotes and fine print, as well as distorting the truth through obscure and excessively complex language.

Selective disclosure is another aspect of the disclosure issue. It occurs when some people receive significant information before others, e.g., financial analysts and investment bankers before shareholders. The SEC attempted to solve the latter matter by issuing Regulation Fair Disclosure in Fall 2000. Its goal was to achieve the distribution of important corporate information to all market participants at the same time. It caused considerable concern among analysts and investment firms at the time, although vocal opposition appears to have gone away since Enron and the passage of Sarbanes-Oxley. Also, the strictures of that law have probably had an impact on the language, completeness, and transparency of footnotes to financial statements and prospectuses.

Perhaps the most notable action of the SEC under Regulation Fair Disclosure came against the Schering-Plough pharmaceutical company and its former CEO, Richard J. Kogan. The company paid a penalty of $1 million, and Mr. Kogan paid $50,000. They neither denied nor admitted guilt of selectively giving information to several institutional investors; namely, Wellington Management, Sun Life Financial, FMR, and Marsh & McLennan. The news that was given involved adverse earnings developments at Schering-Plough. Receiving the news earlier than the public at large enabled the favored investors to sell stock early and save money as the stock declined. Paul R. Berger, associate director of enforcement at the SEC commented that Mr. Kogan had conveyed the earnings information by "providing guidance to a select few through a combination of spoken language, tone, emphasis, and demeanor," giving an unfair advantage to the favored few.[5] Interestingly, the SEC did not impose any penalties on the institutional investors who benefited from the early disclosure.

Disclosure is undoubtedly helpful, and it is right to require that it be full and fair. But it is not a final and definitive answer to the problem of greed and the fraud it engenders. We will still require regulation, appropriate punishment (severe, if not draconian), and measures designed to remove the incentives to misbehavior.

The Impact of Sarbanes-Oxley

When we deal with the impact of Sarbanes-Oxley on the accounting profession, we must return to the distinction between public and private corporations (including partnerships and individual proprietorships). The reason is simple: Sarbanes-Oxley deals essentially with public corporations, because it is concerned with the danger of public harm when ownership and management control are separated. Public corporations sell their securities through national and international markets, and so are subject to federal law as well as the law of the state where they are chartered. But private business entities are essentially governed by state securities laws, and there are possible problems involving the spill-over, or cascading, effect of Sarbanes-Oxley on them and their relationships with the accounting profession. A brief look at the regulatory structure affecting the accounting profession may be instructive, as we explore the impact of Sarbanes-Oxley.

The Regulatory Structure

Accounting firms performing auditing services for public companies are subject to federal regulatory agencies, and those agencies have important powers to regulate and to punish violators of their regulations. The newly created Public Company Accounting Oversight Board (PCAOB), which is subject to the SEC, has the power to oversee auditing standards, which are prepared by the non-governmental Financial Accounting Standards Board, and to discipline auditors who are in violation. The Sarbanes-Oxley Act covers this terrain. Its central thrust is to stiffen the spines of public corporation auditors, to insure their independence and willingness to speak to the power of executives who might be infected by greed.

Accounting firms that do not perform auditing services for public corporations are subject to regulation by state boards of accountancy, and to the organizational rules of the AICPA and the state boards. The precedent set by New York State in 1896, when it created a formal structure for licensing CPAs, was eventually followed by the other states, although there were differences from state to state. All 50 states, Puerto Rico, the District of Columbia, the U.S. Virgin Islands, and Guam now have such laws. Each jurisdiction has a state board of accountancy to carry out the provisions of its law. But the state differences create problems for businesses and accountants working interstate, where one state's requirements may conflict with those of another. To meet this difficulty, the AICPA and the National Association of State Boards of Accountancy produced a model bill in 1984, known as the Uniform Accountancy Act. Most state accountancy laws eventually followed the model's main provisions.

A point needs to be made with respect to the mixture of auditing and advising that the accountant may do for privately held businesses. I have argued that the two roles are inherent in such cases, and I hold to that view. But there is a limitation. If the advising becomes significant consultation that directly impacts upon management's operational decisions, then it could impair the objectivity of the audit. For example, if the accountant is doing the actual bookkeeping for the client, then a real conflict with him/her doing the audit arises. In effect, the accountant, in the auditing function, would be exercising judgment on decisions made pursuant to his/her advice, and, therefore, having to judge himself/herself. The rules of professional conduct prohibit that mix of activities.

There is one advisory activity that warrants a special note. It involves tax advice, and it is likely to be a significant service in the case of the private corporation. The inherent problem is the temptation of the owner-manager to seek tax avoidance, and to look to the accountant for help toward achieving that goal. The matter is subtle, because there is a distinction between tax minimization within the law, and tax avoidance that involves activity and decisions calculated to avoid taxes that are beyond the law and illegal.

Perhaps the best example is provided by the once popular real estate tax shelters, which were made illegal in the mid eighties. Those shelters involved real estate transactions where a relatively small investment could yield "losses" that were deductible on tax returns, and thereby shielded income produced by another business from taxation. The critical point in assessing the integrity of a business decision is whether it is for a valid business purpose. If its sole purpose is tax avoidance, then it should be viewed with suspicion. These comments apply to both private and public corporations. However, in the case of the public company the owner-management relationship is severed, so that tax advice to management may be at the cost of the corporation's shareholders. Interestingly, the Internal Revenue Service now requires accounting and law firms to indicate and register tax shelters that they sell to clients. KPMG, the smallest of the Big Four accounting firms, has been in considerable trouble because of aggressive tax shelter schemes that it had been selling to clients. Having run afoul of the IRS, it fired several partners who had been active in that promotion, and gave up that service to its clients. The case is discussed at length in Chapter VII, in the section on plea bargaining.

Finally, apart from governmental regulation, the AICPA has machinery for monitoring and disciplining member auditors. The organizational units involved are the Professional Ethics Division, the Joint Trial Board, and the Peer Review Board. Of course, these bodies do not have the muscle possessed by the governmental bodies, but their censure is not a cause for merriment by those subject to it.

The Federal Impact: Sarbanes-Oxley

We have already noted the regulatory role of the SEC and its newly created subsidiary, the Public Company Accounting Oversight Board. The board is appointed and overseen by the SEC. The PCAOB has five full-time members, who investigate and oversee the audits and auditors of public corporations. Public companies support the board through mandatory fees. Also, accounting firms that audit public companies must register with the board, and must pay registration and annual fees. Two of the 5 board members must be or have been CPAs. The other 3 must not have been CPAs. One of the CPA members can serve as board chairman, but must not have practiced accounting during the 5 years before appointment. Standards can be issued by the board or adopted from those set by other groups or organizations. The standards cover auditing and related attestation, quality control, ethics, independence, and other matters necessary to protect the public interest. The board has investigative and disciplinary powers. These powers include revocation or suspension of the license to audit public companies, and civil penalties. The board's authority also covers foreign accounting firms that perform audit services for U.S. public companies.

The Sarbanes-Oxley Act impacts directly upon the relationship between the auditor and the audit committee of the public corporation's board. Most important, the auditor will now report to the audit committee, not to management. Audit committees are charged with pre-approval of all audit and non-audit services performed for the public company. But a number of non-audit services are prohibited; i.e., bookkeeping, information systems design and implementation, appraisal or valuation services, actuarial services, internal audit management and human resources services, broker/dealer and investment banking services, legal and expert services unrelated to audits, plus other services ruled out by the board. Services not banned are allowed subject to prior approval of the audit committee. Lead audit partners and audit review partners must be rotated every 5 years on public company audits. If top management, e.g., CEO, CFO, Controller, or Chief Accounting Officer, worked for the auditing firm during the prior year, then the auditing firm is barred from doing the audit.

The law provides criminal penalties for violators who destroy records, commit securities fraud, and fail to report fraud, but whistleblowers are protected. Prison terms running up to 25 years can be imposed, and the statute of limitations was extended to 2 years from date of discovery, and 5 years after the violation. Second partner review and approval of audit reports are now mandatory, as is management assessment of internal controls.

Consideration of penalties brings up the issue of punishment for the accounting firms, in addition to the individual accountants found guilty of violations of the law. The point is especially significant when one realizes the size of the Big Four accounting firms, and considers the devastation visited upon thousands of employees and innocent partners when such a firm collapses. Arthur Andersen, which was destroyed by the Enron case, is the prime example. Also, any reduction in the number of firms, large enough to provide audit services for public corporations, would severely reduce competition in the profession. Paula Dwyer pointed out in *Business Week* that "businesses audited by the Big Four now account for an astounding 99% of all public-company sales." She added: "The Big Four dwarf the rest of the profession: Annual revenues of the 20 next-largest firms combined don't equal the $3.2 billion in U.S. sales of KPMG, the smallest of the Big Four."6

The Cascade Effect on the States

The accounting profession is deeply concerned that the state boards of accountancy may adopt many of the provisions of the Sarbanes-Oxley Act, and apply them to private business enterprises and the accounting firms that perform auditing services for those businesses. One hazard is that the existing variation in state codes could be multiplied as the state bodies choose different regulations and standards to emulate. The long-continuing effort by the profession to achieve uniform standards might be set back severely. No less important is the burden on the operational efficiency of small businesses that do not have large boards, or no boards (partnerships and proprietorships) to navigate the requirements spelled out for audit, compensation, and nominating committees. In short, many provisions of Sarbanes-Oxley simply do not apply to private business enterprises.

International Accounting Standards

The problem of uniform standards across state lines in the United States has a parallel across national boundaries. The huge advances toward globalization of economic activities, with giant public corporations doing business internationally, creates great pressure to achieve substantial uniformity of auditing and accounting standards that are applied to those activities. Essentially uniform standards would improve comparability of corporate financial statements across national lines, and would yield better informed investment decisions and improved capital markets.

In October 2002, the Financial Accounting Standards Board (FASB) of the AICPA and the International Accounting Standards Board (IASB), located in London, issued a memorandum of understanding (the Norwalk Agreement). It made formal the commitment of the two bodies to develop compatible standards of high quality that could be applied internationally; and that, once established, would be maintained. The nature of the FASB was described earlier. The IASB was founded on April 1, 2001, as successor to the International Accounting Standards Committee, and is based in London, but its parent body, the International Accounting Standards Committee Foundation, was incorporated in Delaware, US in March 2001. The IASB consists of 14 members, of whom 12 are full-time, i.e., employed only by IASB. Five must be former auditors, 3 former preparers of accounts, 3 former users of accounts, and one an academic. The other 2 can be any of those categories, or with other backgrounds.

The IASB planned to release its standards by March 31, 2004. Those standards would apply in some 90 countries world wide. Europe's 7,000 listed public corporations would be covered. Unfortunately, a rift between IASB and the European Commission upset IASB and FASB efforts to arrive at mutually agreed standards. Specifically, IASB's standards 32 and 39 were at issue. They involved the accounting treatment of certain financial instruments, i.e., derivatives and stock options. The FASB, the SEC, and the IASB wanted such instruments valued by marking them to the current market. That meant periodic re-evaluation and some volatility. Alternatively, valuation at "cost," i.e., value at time of issue, yielded stability. The latter treatment makes it easier to smooth corporate earnings over time. Banks and insurers, in particular, favored that practice. The issue came to a head due to heavy lobbying of the European Commission by those institutions, especially those in France.[7]

Hopefully, this issue will be settled, and international accounting standards given a boost. Unfortunately, the issue remains open, with the European Commission still opposed to the standard approved by the IASB and the FASB, i.e., to expense options and mark derivatives to market. At their meetings in April and October 2005, the IASB and the FASB reaffirmed their commitment to the convergence objective. While the European Commission can block the IASB standard in Europe, it cannot do so in the United States. And, as Volcker and Levitt have observed (Appendix I), the end result would be to confirm American accounting standards, despite their shortcomings, as the gold standard for protecting investors and the public interest. But, the tendency of foreign firms to avoid American standards (section 404 of Sarbanes-Oxley), by not seeking to raise capital on the American stock exchanges, could inhibit wider application of those standards.

Notes

1. Paul M. Healy and Krishna G. Palepu, "The Fall of Enron," *Journal of Economic Perspectives*, Vol. 17, No. 2, Spring 2003, 3, 15-16.

2. Floyd Norris, "When Politicians Write Accounting Rules, Reality Can Be Forgotten," *New York Times*, July 23, 2004, C1.

3. Baruch Lev, "Corporate Earnings: Fact and Fiction," *Journal of Economic Perspectives*, Vol. 17, No. 2, Spring 2003, 48.

4. Floyd Norris, "Big Auditing Firm Gets 6-Month Ban on New Business," *New York Times*, April 17, 2004, A1, B2.

5. Floyd Norris, "S.E.C. Penalizes Schering-Plough Over a Fair Disclosure Violation," *New York Times*, Sept. 10, 2003, C1, C5.

6. Paula Dwyer, "The Big Four: Too Few To Fail?" *Business Week*, Sept. 1, 2003, 34.

7. *The Economist*, March 6, 2004, 65.

Chapter V

The Lawyers

Chapter IV showed how the accounting profession became complicit in the abuses committed by powerful CEOs. What about the legal profession? If any profession is charged with the responsibility to confront and speak to power, it is surely the legal profession. After all, public corporations and their CEOs operate in a framework of laws and regulations. What happened in the case of the lawyers?

The Concept of Law

Over the millennia, philosophers and theologians have thought and written about the concept of law. The subject is vast, and far beyond the modest needs of our present purpose. For our needs, we can divide law into two broad categories: natural law; and civil or positive law. The former concerns the rules of nature, and is immutable, i.e., beyond man's capacity to change or to disobey. The latter is man-made, i.e., posited by a civil agency and imposed upon society by a human authority; king, dictator, or legislature. Being man-made, it is susceptible to being violated, i.e., man has the option to disobey, as well as to obey. We are concerned with the civil law.

Operationally, there are three important characteristics of civil law. First, civil law can only be promulgated by a person or agency that possesses the power to enact it and to enforce it. Second, civil law is mutable; it can be changed by that same person or agency. Finally, courts, judges, and lawyers are indispensable to the operation of the system, because the issue of violation needs to be determined when the facts are often in contention. Fairness and notions of justice mandate that accused and plaintiffs have their day in court, and the judicial system is supposed to provide that opportunity.

In our own time and here in America, there is an unhappy prejudice against lawyers and the judicial system, because its operation is so often cumbersome and imperfect, and subject to abuse. A common joke illustrates the matter. An engineer, a man of surpassing skill in his profession who is also a good man morally, dies and goes before the Bar Eternal. The heavenly clerk checks his behavioral record on earth and finds it possesses nothing of merit. To the contrary, it reveals an immoral and misspent life. The poor engineer is thereupon cast down to the proverbial Hell, despite his pleas that there must be an error in the record. Upon arrival in the lower regions, he discovers the heat and general discomfort that characterizes the place. But, being an engineer, he goes to Satan, and explains that he could greatly improve the situation by air conditioning Hell. Satan is impressed with the suggestion, and tells the engineer to go ahead. He does so, and succeeds in his task. Satan, and all the residents of Hell are delighted, and Satan asks the engineer if he has any additional suggestions. The engineer does, and in due course, Hell comes to have lush golf courses and very pleasant residential areas. Eventually, news gets up to Heaven about the transformation of Hell. The Almighty is deeply disturbed at this reversal of the role ascribed to Hell, as the place for punishment of miscreants. Whereupon, the Almighty calls Satan, and demands the return of the engineer, who it turns out upon re-examination of his record on earth was really a moral and splendid person. Satan rejects the Almighty's demand, and the latter threatens to sue Satan. Satan laughs at the threat, and the Almighty asks why he is laughing. To which, Satan replies: "You can't sue me!" The Almighty says: "Why not?" And Satan replies: "Because all the lawyers are down here."

The Code of Conduct

No matter how criticized or satirized the legal profession may be, it is vital to the effective functioning of an organized society. It is the key element in the society's judicial system, and that system is the instrument through which society enforces its rules of conduct. Without rules of conduct, society disintegrates into anarchy. Order disappears, and we become predators, with the strong devouring the weak. Some idealists, with a vision of primitive man as pure and uncorrupted by civilization's evils, have argued that anarchy would not be like I have described it, but beautiful in its behavior. No evidence has ever been forthcoming to sustain this lovely dream, and so we must face the reality that society needs laws, i.e., rules of conduct, and a system for its enforcement. It is the courts, the judges, and the lawyers who make up that system.

Through most of the history of organized societies, the judicial system has been an instrument of the state. It is characteristic in such states that the individual is subordinate and subject to the state, and whatever figure or agency holds the power of the state. But in democratic societies, the model created in America and the one to which we proclaim our allegiance, the reverse is true, and the judicial system is *independent*, with each citizen subject to the rule of law rather than the rule of man.

In such a system, the role and conduct of the lawyer has profound purpose and importance. Being human, some lawyers become corrupt, but I have no doubt that most enter the profession imbued with a sense of high and noble purpose, seeking to strike down unbridled and corrupt power, and to protect the weak from those who would seek to exploit them. To that end, they may enter the world of politics, or seek to serve pro bono, or engage the many fields of specialization in the law which afford the opportunity to help those who appear weak, i.e., unorganized labor, often ignorant and helpless immigrants, abused children and women, and so on. There are also many specializations that relate to business, either generally (corporate law, tax law) or specific to an industry (real estate law, copyright law). We are concerned most with those last areas of the law, i.e., the relationship of lawyers to business.

Whatever the area of practice, lawyers are governed by rules of conduct set forth by the American Bar Association. They are, therefore, essentially self-governing. But, one of the consequences of the corporate accounting scandals is the intrusion of government into that self-governance arrangement, especially into the lawyer-client relationship, and the confidentiality that has heretofore been central in the relationship. Since the terrorist attacks of September 11, 2001, that relationship has also been questioned where the client may be suspected of a connection to or participation in a terrorist organization.

The rules of conduct may best be grasped by a look at *The Model Rules of Professional Conduct* published by the American Bar Association in 2003. The Preface of the publication reviews briefly the development of the rules, originally referred to as the ethics of the profession.

The Preamble of the work contains the essence of the rules of professional conduct. Excerpts follow:

> As a representative of clients, a lawyer performs various functions. As advisor, a lawyer provides a client with an informed understanding of the client's legal rights and obligations and explains their practical implications. As advocate, a lawyer zealously asserts the client's position under the rules of the adversary system. As negotiator, a lawyer seeks a result advantageous to the client but consistent with requirements of honest dealings with others. As an evaluator, a lawyer acts by examining a client's legal affairs and reporting about them to the client or to others.

> . . . a lawyer who commits fraud in the conduct of a business is subject to discipline for engaging in conduct involving dishonesty, fraud, deceit or misrepresentation. . . .

> . . . A lawyer should keep in confidence information relating to representation of a client except so far as disclosure is required or permitted by the Rules of Professional Conduct or other law.

> In the nature of law practice, . . . conflicting responsibilities are encountered. Virtually all difficult ethical problems arise from conflict between a lawyer's responsibilities to clients, to the legal system and to the lawyer's own interest in remaining an ethical person while earning a satisfactory living. . . . Many difficult issues of professional discretion can arise. Such issues must be resolved through the exercise of sensitive professional and moral judgment guided by the basic principles underlying the Rules. These principles include the lawyer's obligation zealously to protect and pursue a client's legitimate interests, within the bounds of the law, while maintaining a professional, courteous and civil attitude toward all persons involved in the legal system.[1]

To the layman, the language of the Rules is somehow dimmed by what seems an excess of verbiage. Yet, it is understandable, when one realizes that the lawyer tries to encompass in his language the multiple contingencies and possibilities that life's reality confronts humanity with. The accountant's Standards and the physician's Hippocratic Oath seem blunter in their strictures. Nonetheless, those professions are not more ethical in the behavior of their practitioners than is the legal profession. Perhaps what is most important is that the three professions profess adherence to the highest ethical standards, so that the ideal is always present as a needed reminder of what is right in practitioner behavior. And all three hold out the "stick" of professional opprobrium and punishment before the miscreant.

Whatever the language, a number of major concerns are imbedded in the foregoing language of the Rules, and they require more than passing comment. They are: (1) confidentiality, fraud, and disclosure; (2) conflicts of interest; (3) independence from external power; and (4) zeal and the adversarial nature of the legal system.

Confidentiality, Fraud, Disclosure, and Sarbanes-Oxley

The lawyer is bound by the Rules to be an effective advocate for the client, and to be zealous in that advocacy. But effective advocacy presupposes that the client fully informs the lawyer of *all* the facts and evidence relevant to the case, even if those facts and evidence are damaging to the client's case. Otherwise, during the proceedings involved in the case, the lawyer may be unpleasantly surprised by the unexpected disclosure of adverse material, and be compromised in the effectiveness with which he pursues the client's side of the matter.

Of course the client does not like the idea of divulging damaging information to the lawyer, fearing that doing so may somehow doom him to lose in the prospective adjudication and disposition of the case. The guarantee of confidentiality in the client-lawyer relationship is the needed protection to elicit *all* information available from the client. Even an occasional viewer of TV shows dealing with the law knows about this guarantee of confidentiality, just as the viewer knows of the same guarantee in the fields of medicine and religion. So, it would appear that confidentiality is sacrosanct.

Confidentiality would seem to preclude disclosure by the lawyer to any third party of any information given by the client. Yet the Rules of Professional Conduct allow for some exceptions: mainly, to prevent death or substantial bodily harm (presumably "moderate" bodily harm would be acceptable); to defend the lawyer, if he/she somehow gets implicated in the client's activities or is embroiled in a controversy with the client; to obtain legal advice about the lawyer's compliance with the Rules; or, to comply with a court order or other law. But, suppose the client appears to be using the lawyer to further a criminal or fraudulent course of conduct. In that case, the lawyer must withdraw from the case, but, having done so, the rule of confidentiality continues to be in force.

The foregoing provides context for a look at the Sarbanes-Oxley Act, as it applies to lawyers. Sections 307 and 602 are relevant.

Section 307 mandates that the SEC "shall issue rules, in the public interest and for the protection of investors, setting forth minimum standards of professional conduct for attorneys appearing and practicing before the Commission in any way in the representation of issuers, . . ." The section goes on to specify that the lawyer is required "to report evidence of a material violation of securities law or breach of fiduciary duty or similar violation by the company or any agent thereof to the chief legal counsel or the chief executive officer. . . ." If those corporate officers do not respond with appropriate action, the lawyer is required to report the violation to the audit committee of the board of directors, or to another committee, or to the entire board (but only the independent directors).

Section 602 states the power of the SEC to censure, temporarily suspend, or permanently disqualify anyone who: (1) lacks the requisite qualifications to represent others; (2) lacks character or integrity, or has engaged in unethical or improper professional conduct; or (3) has willfully violated, or aided and abetted the violation, of any provision of the securities laws or the rules and regulations issued pursuant to them.

Sections 307 and 602 seem plain enough. Being confronted with wrongful behavior by the corporate client, the lawyer is charged with the responsibility to *disclose* that behavior to responsible top management, or, failing appropriate action at that level, to the independent directors of the board, who are then charged with the responsibility to act. Failure to disclose under those circumstances exposes the lawyer to significant punishment.

How does this square with the confidentiality requirement of the Rules? Unhappily, the answer is not clear and unequivocal, because the Washington attorneys bar association issued a 7 page Interim Formal Ethics Opinion which states among much other language that "To the extent that the SEC Regulations authorize but do not require revelation of client confidences and secrets under certain circumstances, a Washington lawyer should not reveal such confidences and secrets unless authorized to do so under the RPCs" (Rules of Professional Conduct). The Opinion adds "As a general matter and with the current lack of case law on the pre-emption issue, a Washington attorney could not fairly claim to be complying in "good faith" with the SEC Regulations, as that term is used in section 205.6(c) of the Regulations, if (s)he took an action that was contrary to this Formal Opinion."

It is that sort of language that causes the layman's eyes to glaze over, while the person seeking clear guidance gnaws the lip or hits the table in frustration. It would seem that the lawyer's advocacy role is primary, at least until case law develops. That may mean until a lawyer is actually punished, either by disqualification from practicing before the SEC, or by a court.

What about the case where the lawyer has disclosed misbehavior to the CEO and/or the independent directors, and neither one has taken action. Could the lawyer then disclose the misbehavior to the SEC or other regulatory body? The answer appears to be negative, given the language of the Rules and the Interim Opinion. Can society then count on the lawyer to speak to power?

A relevant case arose, which promised to produce case law applicable in the future. But, that outcome appears to have been stillborn. The case involved a Mexican owned company, TV Azteca, which planned to issue bonds for sale in the United States. Also, TV Azteca had depository shares that were traded on the New York Stock Exchange. TV Azteca retained the New York law firm of Akin Gump Strauss Hauer and Feld to represent it in connection with the bond offering.

A dispute arose between the law firm and TV Azteca, its client, with respect to disclosure of certain financial transactions that would yield a personal gain of some $100 million to TV Azteca's CEO and principal shareholder, Ricardo Salinas Pliego. The law firm demanded that TV Azteca disclose those transactions, and TV Azteca's executives refused. In response and citing section 307 of Sarbanes-Oxley, Akin Gump et al notified the independent directors of TV Azteca that it was withdrawing as counsel to the bond offering. This action became public. The law firm indicated also that it *might* notify the SEC, although Akin Gump et al did not take that action formally.

What did follow is most instructive. Two of Azteca's most prominent independent directors resigned, thereby delivering a stinging rebuke to its chairman, Mr. Salinas Pliego. Probable stimuli to the directors' action were an investigation into Mr. Salinas's actions that had been initiated by the SEC, as well as the impact of Sarbanes-Oxley and the actions taken by the Akin Gump law firm. The two directors are James R. Jones, who had been chairman of the American Stock Exchange and an ambassador to Mexico, and George F. Jankowski, who had been chairman of the CBS broadcast group. It is important to note that the publicity created by these events significantly harms Azteca's and Mr. Salinas's credibility in the financial markets, and their ability to finance future ventures. In fact, it was precisely this consideration that had led Mr. Salinas to earlier bring significant independent directors onto Azteca's board. What was an effort to establish credibility has now been undone, and the significance of truly independent directors clearly revealed.[2] However, that was not the end of the matter. On January 4, 2005, the SEC filed a lawsuit against Mr. Salinas Pliego in a federal court in Washington. The suit charged him with fraud, called for his being barred from serving as an officer or director of any company whose shares were traded on an American exchange, and demanded that he pay over $110 million gained from trading in TV Azteca's securities. Finally, Mr. Salinas Pliego came under investigation by the Mexican regulatory agency (the Comision Nacional Bancaria y de Valores), which found him to have broken that country's securities laws.[3] Two aspects of this case are especially remarkable: (1) for the first time, a law firm used the disclosure provision of Sarbanes-Oxley against a recalcitrant client, and dropped the client; and (2) the SEC exerted its authority against a foreign firm that traded on an American exchange. Although these seemed important precedents at the time, the final outcome was less remarkable. On September 14, 2006, Mr. Salinas Pliego and the SEC announced a settlement of the case, with Salinas Pliego neither asserting innocence nor admitting guilt. Under the terms of the agreement, Salinas Pliego agreed to pay $7.5 million in penalties and compensation to settle the fraud charges. He was also forbidden to serve as an executive or director of any publicly listed American company. Earlier, in 2005, Salinas Pliego had delisted his companies from the New York Stock Exchange, citing the burden of "excessive regulation." Also in 2005, he paid $3.3 million in fines to Mexican regulators. But, there was no prosecution against him in Mexico.[4]

Conflicts of Interest and Disclosure

The Rules set forth explicitly the likelihood that lawyers will encounter conflicts of interest in the course of practice. There is one such conflict I have come across in the business world that should be a clear violation.

It involves a lawyer serving as a director on the board of a client corporation. In today's climate, the likelihood of this occurring is probably negligible. But it should be non-existent, and disclosure of the dual role does not clear away the inherent problem.

Another case that would seem to be equally clear involves a situation where the lawyer winds up simultaneously on both sides of the table. This situation can arise when a lawyer represents a client, or clients, on one side of an issue, but is asked by the other side to act concurrently in the capacity of a negotiator of a settlement.

Fortunately for our discussion of this issue, a perfect case can be reported. It was revealed in the *New York Times* in March 2003.[5] The case involved Joseph F. Rice, a well-known class action lawyer who was reported as accepting "a $20 million fee from the parent of a company that he is suing, in addition to the fees that he will collect from his clients for settling their claims against that very company."

The suit involved a company called Combustion Engineering that manufactured boilers, with liners made of asbestos. Thousands of present and former employees of the company filed a class action lawsuit alleging that they had been injured by the asbestos and seeking compensatory payments. Among the lawyers retained by the plaintiffs to represent them was Joseph F. Rice, who was a leader among the plaintiff's lawyers. Combustion Engineering was bankrupt, so it was a shallow pocket from which to extract any compensatory payments. But, it happened to be a fully owned subsidiary of a Swiss company that was financially stable.

The parent company became the real target of the class action lawsuit. That company, known as ABB, realizing the complexity of the case and the prospect of lengthy, expensive litigation, asked Joseph Rice to settle the matter, and offered him the noted $20 million fee to do so. He agreed, and obtained the assent of the other plaintiffs' lawyers to the arrangement and the proposed settlement. Everything was disclosed and public.

Legal ethicists, when asked, said "the payment raised ethical concerns because he (Rice) was in effect being paid by both sides in the dispute, . . ." Obviously, Rice did not agree. He was reported as saying that he saw no conflict because he was paid by ABB, not by Combustion Engineering, which was the direct target of the lawsuit. He maintained that he was not suing ABB, so it was okay. Also, Rice pointed out that neither he nor his firm advised any clients on whether to vote in favor of the agreement, which was approved by presumably impartial experts including lawyers representing future claimants against Combustion Engineering.

The conflict issue was put also to George Kuhlman, ethics counsel for the American Bar Association. Kuhlman was unable to give a clear response. He observed that the ABA did not have absolute rules that prohibit lawyers from being paid by both sides in a case. He said that "There are things that you are supposed to avoid, but it does not boil down to that you are supposed to avoid a fee from someone you are otherwise suing."

Rule 1.7 of the Rules of Professional Conduct deals specifically with conflicts of interest. While the rule prohibits concurrent representation where there is a conflict of interest, it provides some exceptions. One exception involves representation that does not involve the assertion of a claim by one client against another client represented by the lawyer in the same litigation or other proceeding before a tribunal. Since Mr. Rice did not view ABB as a party to the basic lawsuit, he could construe this exception as justifying his actions. But to the layman, like me, it does seem to be splitting hairs. The language of the lawyers seems disappointing, especially if one is focused on their playing a leading role in speaking to power in behalf of the public welfare.

Independence from External Power

The Rules consider independence from two aspects: first, freedom from governmental influence or pressure; and, second, freedom from involvement with third parties that might compromise the completeness of the relationship between the lawyer and the client. Both aspects are important. The first one goes to the heart of the American judicial system, and protects the nation from falling under the rule of men, rather than the rule of law. The second one seeks to prevent obligations, implied or explicit, to third parties that might conflict with the lawyer's responsibilities to the client. The Rice case provided an illustration of the difficulty that can attend the effort to preserve the second aspect of freedom.

There is a third aspect from which the independence of the lawyer can be viewed. Although it is not directly noted and discussed in the Rules, it is there in the form of statements that require the lawyer to be honest and truthful in explaining carefully to the client the legal implications of any action that the client may wish to pursue, even if the client does not want to hear those contrary to his/her desires. It involves the idea held in the heads of some clients that the lawyer's acceptance of a fee requires the lawyer to justify and enable the client to do whatever he/she wants, i.e., get around the law, rather than comply with the law. The problem arises when the fee is very large, so large that it tests and strains the lawyer's obligations under both the Rules and the law.

That problem goes to the lawyer's character and moral fiber, as it would in the case of the physician or clergyman (where a large donation to the church might be the lure, rather than a personal payment). Here the independence of the lawyer involves speaking to the power of the client's purse, and the too common notion that everyone has a price. I view this aspect of independence as possessing critical importance, because it is basic to the effort to provide a bulwark against the exercise of unbridled executive power. Laws and rules of conduct are useful, as are punishments for misbehavior, in stiffening the spine of the potential miscreant to withstand the lures and enticements of power backed by wealth. But the real bedrock is the society's moral standards, and their influence on the citizenry.

Zeal and the Adversarial Nature of the Judicial System

America has an adversarial judicial system. There is a plaintiff, or group of plaintiffs. There is a defendant, or group of defendants. Each side retains lawyers to represent them. They go before a jury, or before a judge. And each side argues its respective case.

What is the role of the lawyer or lawyers on each side? The Rules are very clear on this matter. The lawyer must be zealous in behalf of the client. The dictionary defines zealous as ardently active, devoted, diligent. Those are very strong words, implying passion. They are words filled with emotion and feeling. But emotion can easily conflict, indeed is likely to conflict, with objectivity, and objectivity is necessary to rational and logical legal advice and representation. Of course the Rules have language intended to qualify zealousness, where it may lead to dishonest, fraudulent, or even criminal actions in the lawyer's efforts to win the case. But, in any adversarial contest the aim is to win. And America is a competitive society, with a profound urge toward winning, whether in sports or the larger contests of life. More subtle and dangerous still is the situation where the urge to win is whetted by the size of the retainer.

The Class Action Suit

Class action lawsuits are a hot topic, inflaming political passions as large sums are spent in lobbying efforts by business, on one side, and tort lawyers, on the other side. The Rice case was such a suit, because it brought together a large class of individual plaintiffs who alleged that they had been injured by asbestos in the workplace. And the Rice case was only a small part of asbestos related litigation that had been going on for years, and involved many billions of dollars in legal fees and in settlement payments. Many firms were driven into bankruptcy by that litigation. The tobacco industry is another case in point. Again, the legal fees and the settlements amounted to hundreds of billions of dollars. More recently, medical malpractice suits have raised physician insurance costs so high that doctors are, here and there, quitting practice, or sporadically withholding their services from patients in protest.

The foregoing illustrations seem to have a negative aspect. The case of WorldCom (now MCI), a giant telecommunications company that went through bankruptcy following disclosure of large accounting irregularities, presents a more positive face for the class action suit. WorldCom's bondholders and shareholders suffered huge losses when the corporate collapse occurred. The injured victims of the debacle instituted class action suits against the executives and directors of WorldCom. They also sued the investment banks whose financial analysts had touted the company's securities, alleging misleading and dishonest behavior. A leader among them was Citigroup, parent of Smith Barney; a firm that led in promoting WorldCom. The lead plaintiff in the class litigating the case was New York State's Common Retirement Fund. Rather than carry its defense forward through the expense and danger of a possibly unfavorable verdict, Citigroup (i.e., Citibank) negotiated a settlement of $2.65 billion (with no admission of guilt). The class action suit continued against other defendants.[6] As of mid-2004, they were balking at accepting the terms that applied to Citibank. But, their resoluteness collapsed, and, on January 5, 2005, ten former directors of World Com agreed to a settlement which is both rare and remarkable. Under its terms, they agreed to pay personally a penalty of 20 percent of their net worth (apart from the value of their residences and pensions). Normally, directorial liability would be covered by insurance, but this time the penalty went beyond that and came out of the directors' personal pockets. In addition, the ten directors agreed to cooperate with the prosecution against other defendants. All this was agreed to, despite the proviso by the ten directors that they neither admitted nor denied any wrongdoing. While the directors may have settled due to fear of the huge liabilities possible in a jury trial, it is also possible that their decision reflects their own sense that they had failed to be sufficiently alert and vigorous in meeting their fiduciary obligations to shareholders. I have no doubt that this case got the attention of other directors, although it may have been so egregious an example of directorial shortcomings that its spill over may have been limited somewhat by that fact.[7]

It soon became clear, however, that the personal exposure and liability of individual directors had become more likely. On January 8, 2005, there was an announcement that ten former directors of the defunct Enron Corporation had agreed, in a confidential settlement arrived at in October 2004, to pay collectively $13 million of their own money to Enron's former shareholders. The directors agreed to do this despite the fact that a federal court in Houston had earlier dismissed claims of fraud against them; claims of negligence remained outstanding before the settlement. The message to directors should be loud and clear; pay attention and be active because passivity is dangerous.[8]

What are the positives and negatives of class action lawsuits? The major positive point is that they make it possible for a multitude of individually weak people, who have been injured by powerful entities (businesses, hospitals, etc.), to join together and jointly sue the party who has caused them injury. Here the tort lawyer becomes the instrument that provides otherwise unavailable recourse, acting as a sort of private attorney general. Typically, the tort lawyer takes the class of clients, indeed, organizes the class, on a contingency fee basis under which he/she collects only if a settlement or favorable court award is achieved. The lawyer can see him/herself as acting in behalf of the public weal, and doing so in consonance with the spirit as well as the letter of the profession's rules.

Unfortunately, the class action lawsuit can be abused, and it is. When the lawsuit exposes the defendant business or other entity to huge legal costs and distracting litigation over a lengthy time period, the cost of a quick settlement makes practical sense, even if the class action is without merit or is "frivolous." It is even possible that the lawyer, looking to a contingency fee of 30-40 percent of a settlement, may go for a quick settlement and a "fast buck" as against the cost in time, effort, and money required for a larger settlement or court award that may be more favorable to the plaintiffs.

It must be pointed out that, if the lawyer honors the spirit of the Rules, then this unhappy outcome will not occur. At least it seems to me that such an interpretation is implicit in rule 1.7 (Conflict of Interest). Although the rule deals with conflicts where the lawyer has two or more clients with conflicting interests, its spirit would appear to apply where the conflict is between the client's interest and the personal material interest of the lawyer. In any case, rule 1.7 requires that the client give the lawyer "informed consent, confirmed in writing," to indicate that the client has been told of the conflict, knows and understands it, and approves of the lawyer's conduct. Presumably, as in the Rice case, clients represented by other lawyers who are also party to the lawsuit may be considered to have given informed consent if their lawyers agree to the settlement. The assumption, in that instance, is that the other lawyers obtained informed consent from their clients.

Is the tort lawyer a public defender, or the proud possessor of a savory honey pot? Oddly, the answer can be both. In which case, the real question is: Should we tolerate the possible abuse in order to have the benefit? I'm inclined to answer affirmatively, although I think that some legislation that would cap settlements and awards at reasonable levels is appropriate.

The Opinion Letter

Management and/or boards of directors may turn to a reputable legal firm, one of substantial professional reputation, for advice on the legal status of a proposed course of corporate action. The proposed action may involve a host of matters, e.g., taxes, mergers, acquisitions, IPOs (Initial Public Offerings of stock), disclosure, and so on. Acting as an advisor, the lawyer "provides a client with an informed understanding of the client's legal rights and obligations and explains their practical implications."[9]

That is the language used in the Preamble to the Rules. Rule 2.3 may also apply to opinion letters (Evaluation for Use by Third Persons). The lawyer's opinion may be used by management and/or the board as providing a legal basis for going forward with a proposed course of action. The lawyer's fee for providing the opinion letter can be substantial, amounting to millions of dollars in some instances. The intriguing and troubling question is: Does the size of the fee incline even a lawyer of high reputation to color or slant his opinion in favor of the action that he knows management and/or the board favors? We know of cases in medical research funded by pharmaceutical firms where researchers have been charged with "adjusting" research results in favor of the drug company's product. Why would lawyers not be tempted by the same enticements, at least some of them?

The temptation to provide questionable legal opinions for a fat fee may now be tempered by a significant court ruling. It involved the now defunct Long-Term Capital Management hedge fund, which collapsed in 1998 and almost caused an international financial crisis. Long-Term Capital was a partnership that entered into a series of complex transactions allegedly designed to avoid income taxes otherwise payable by the partners. The IRS held the transactions to be illegal tax avoidance schemes, because they lacked a valid business purpose. The IRS sued the partners, in a civil action. It seems appropriate to note that two of the partners were Nobel Prize winners in Economics, and one of them was the author of a textbook on "Taxes and Business Strategy." They had also been professors at two of America's leading business schools (one still is). Yet, the partners, in their defense, claimed that they relied on legal opinion letters from two law firms (Shearman & Sterling and King & Spaulding), and that those letters opined that the transactions were legal. Judge Janet Bond Arterton, of the Federal District Court in New Haven, who presided in the case, ruled that the transactions were tax evasion schemes and illegal, thereby upholding the IRS. Eileen O'Connor, an assistant attorney general in the tax division of the Justice Department, commented that ". . . unreasonable legal opinions will not protect investors from monetary penalties."[10]

Although the Rules of Professional Conduct prohibit dishonesty, society's defense lies in the threat of punishment and the opprobrium attached to discovery of the dishonesty. The possibility of enticement is an ever present danger, because a misbehaving management and board can use the opinion letter as a legal defense against prosecution and punishment for actions taken pursuant to the cover provided by the opinion letter. In short, we must remain alert to the possibility of abuse, but not take foolishly drastic action, such as prohibiting legal firms from issuing opinion letters. They do provide a useful service, and are a legitimate advisory function of the legal profession.

Notes

1. American Bar Association, *The Model Rules of Professional Conduct*, 2003, Chicago, Ill., 1-3.

2. Elisabeth Malkin, "As Inquiries Press Ahead, 2 Directors Quit Azteca," *New York Times*, May 10, 2004, C2. Patrick McGeehan, "Get the Wrong Answer, Ask Another Lawyer," *New York Times*, November 21, 2004, BU4.

3. Patrick McGeehan and Jenny Anderson, "Chairman of TV Azteca Is Charged With Fraud," *New York Times*, January 5, 2005, C3.

4. *New York Times*, September 15, 2006, p. C3.

5. Alex Berenson, "A Cauldron of Ethics and Asbestos," *New York Times*, March 12, 2003, C1, C22.

6. Gretchen Morgensen, "Citigroup Agrees to a Settlement Over WorldCom," *New York Times*, May 11, 2004, A1, C4.

7. Gretchen Morgensen, "10 Ex-Directors From WorldCom To Pay Millions," *New York Times*, January 6, 2005, A1, C8.

8. Kurt Eichenwald, "Ex-Directors At Enron To Chip In On Serttlement," *New York Times*, January 8, 2005, B1, B2.

9. Preamble to the Rules, 1.

10. Lynnley Browning, "Tax Ruling Casts a Long Shadow," *New York Times*, August 30, 2004, C1, C2.

Chapter VI

Investment Bankers, Financial Analysts, and Institutional Investors

Imperial executives could do nothing without the capital markets of the nation. Those markets are the source of the funds which are the life-blood of their corporate dreams and ambitions. Their corporate stocks and bonds are sold through those markets. And the values commanded by those securities in the markets are the symbols of success or failure. But the markets are in the hands of intermediaries, human beings who handle the sale of corporate securities, who analyze them and seek to provide guidance as to their fair worth, and who invest in them in behalf of millions of individual savers. Why didn't these intermediaries check executive malfeasance, by exposing it to public view?

Investment Bankers

Investment bankers are at the nexus of the nation's financial markets. They are the key middlemen who bring together the savers and inves-tors, who provide the capital that stimulates the nation's economic growth and future well-being, and the businesses that apply and activate that capital. In performing this critically important economic role, they expe-rience an inherent and inescapable conflict of interest.

On the one hand, they represent the interests of the savers and inves-tors, who want to buy the securities (stocks and bonds) available at the most favorable price possible, i.e., the lowest reasonable price. On the other hand, they represent also the issuers of the securities, who want to sell them at the price most favorable to them, i.e., the highest reasonable price. Morally and in the interest of their own good name and reputation, the investment bankers should analyze the true and fair value of the prospective business investment, and set that price as the one at which the securities in question change hands.

The fair value analysis is done by experts with detailed knowledge and experience in the firms and industries issuing the securities. Suppose the financial analysts are employees of the investment banking firm that is acting as the middleman in the transaction. Suppose further that the investment banker gets paid by the issuer of the security in the form of a fee that is a percent of the value of the security. Obviously, the higher the fair value placed on the security, the larger the investment banker's fee will be. If the financial analyst, an employee of the investment banker, can be prevailed upon to "tout" the desirability of the security as a buy then the sustainability of a high value-price is greatly enhanced.

The incentive to mischief should be plain. It resides in the opportunity to gain materially by favoring the issuer of the security as against the saver-investor. Of course, this game works best when the buyers are either ignorant or stupid, a possibility that is enlarged as ever greater numbers of people buy corporate securities for their 401(k) and other retirement plans.

I do not argue that the kind of behavior described is usual or characteristic of the investment banking industry, but that it exists and, especially during periods characterized by an economic bubble driven by "irrational exuberance," can seize the investment banker's psyche and unduly affect his behavior. At any rate, that is what seems to have happened during the nineties, and it is the reality that underlies Sarbanes-Oxley and the other corrective actions that have been taken, and will continue to be taken.

The investment banker's role as a financial middleman is more varied than the foregoing description indicates, because he does not always represent both sides of the financial market. He/she may be arranging financing in a leveraged buy-out offer by the top management of a public corporation, who seek to take the company private. In such a case, the investment banker is really representing the interest of the management, not the public shareholders. And the independent directors, in that instance, have to be especially alert that the "fair value" placed on the company's stock is not low-balled in behalf of the management. A truly alert and independent board would, in that case, insist on retaining its own investment banker to do a separate financial analysis and fair value evaluation. Note! The estimation of fair value is still central to the investment banker's function.

Mergers and acquisitions are also transactions in which investment bankers perform an important function. An acquisition may be entirely for cash, in which case the estimation of fair value involves only the amount of money to be paid for the stock of the company being acquired. Of course, even that presumably simple valuation process, where one has the current market value of the stock as a guide to its value, is complicated when the prospective shareholder-sellers think that their stock is undervalued by the market, a not infrequent attitude and one sure to invite a class action shareholder lawsuit if the price accepted by the board of the selling firm is considered too low. The situation is greatly complicated, and the likelihood of a class action shareholder lawsuit enhanced, if the deal involves part cash and part stock of the acquiring company (whose stock must also then be valued). Or, to go a step further, if the deal is entirely in the form of stock in the acquiring company.

The investment banker can also function as a venture capitalist, becoming itself the investor. The intention is then probably not to remain as the owner in the long-term, but to get the business up and running, so that it looks promising as a viable long-term investment by others. At which time, the investment banker would probably do an Initial Public Offering (IPO), take the company public, and cash out.

There is another role that is played by investment bankers, and it is very important. It involves the activities of investment banking firms as operators of multiple mutual funds, with each fund specialized by type of security (stock or bond), investors' financial goals (growth or income), type of industry (high tech or more conventional), degree of risk, nature of fee structure (front-end or back-end, commission rate, etc.), and so on. These mutual funds require especially careful scrutiny, because they cater to the public at large, and because they represent an additional layer of removal of the ownership from the underlying enterprises, i.e., there are two layers of management between the basic enterprises and the mutual fund owners. Does the management of the mutual fund in this case have as its true goal achieving the maximum financial results for the fund investors, or the maximum income generated for the investment banking firm that employs its managers? The temptation to look to the interests of the investment banking firm is strong.

Investment bankers act also as investment managers for very wealthy clients. This function is private banking, and has a long history of dealing with the estates and heirs of family fortunes. Here, as much as anywhere, the integrity and moral fiber of the banker is vital.

Across this panorama of activity, the investment banker faces conflicts of interest that will test his/her integrity. In performing the functions presented above, not only his/her moral fiber will be tested. His/her financial acumen and skill will be tested as well, daily and even hourly. The working life style can easily become frenetic and all-absorbing, to the point of short-changing the banker's family and social life. Particularly in periods of great market activity, with all sorts of deals underway and usually conducted in an atmosphere of urgency, the pressure and the time demands stretch human strength. A sense of severe competition will probably be present, with other bankers and rival bidders in the picture. One thinks of Tom Wolfe's *Bonfire of the Vanities*, and the investment banker anti-hero who is a "Master of the Universe." It is very heady stuff, and one's judgment can easily stray away from the financial fundamentals that are supposed to provide the bedrock for fair value analysis. After all, if the market, responding to exuberant investors who are focused only on the fact of rapidly rising stock prices, grossly overvalues a company's stock, is the banker or the analyst wrong to use that value as the basis of a fair value judgment? It's a nice question, but the ethical judgment is not likely to earn the one who broadcasts it much praise or any encomiums.

A further thought is appropriate. The shift in the form of business organization characteristic of investment banking, from the partnership to the public stock company, may have had a largely unrecognized and unhappy impact on the motivation and behavior of investment bankers. When the former type of organization prevailed, investment banking was essentially a relationship type of business. The partners in the firm depended on each other's honor and integrity to do the right thing in their business dealings with clients. After all, each partner was personally liable for the financial consequences of another partner's misdeeds. And clients felt a personal bond to the banker, and vice versa.

The intellectual and moral climate is different when the public stock company is the form of business organization, as it is now. The emphasis on maximizing the company's earnings and market value, in behalf of the shareholder as well as the management, takes hold. Corporate competitiveness rises. The focus easily shifts from maximum benefit for the client to maximum benefit, and probably in the short-term, for the firm.

The problem is maximized during an economic bubble. For example, at such a time, stocks in an IPO tend to surge upon being issued, perhaps doubling or more in the first day. People are carried away and think that every IPO will jump in value. They don't bother to look at, let alone study, the prospectus. They simply want to get their order in to buy. In that fevered climate, the investment banker who gives favored customers the stock at the issue price is, in effect, giving them a gift. It is so easy for the banker to give favored customers, i.e., corporate chiefs whose future company security issues are sought, large amounts of the current IPO. The corporate chiefs make a substantial personal gain, and have an implied obligation to give their own company's future business to the investment banker. It smells like a bribe for the future business, and is certainly unethical, if not illegal.

The situation may change somewhat, due to the procedure Google (the internet search company) chose to use in its IPO. At the end of April 2004, Google announced that it would do an IPO in the near future, but it would use an auction procedure instead of the usual offering through a group of investment banking firms. Consequently, bids by prospective buyers of Google stock would set the initial value of the equity, instead of the usual fair value set by the investment banks handling the offering. Google chose Morgan Stanley and Credit Suisse First Boston as the intermediaries who would gather the bids and announce the price that would clear the market (the price at which all the shares offered would be sold). Bidders who bid at or above the clearing price would get the stock at the clearing price. They might not get as many shares as they collectively bid for, because that amount might exceed the amount of stock offered. But they would get a portion of what was offered. The attractiveness of the procedure is that it treats small investors as well as larger ones. And, it presumably avoids the practice where the investment banking firms treat their prime customers preferentially. Of course, the clearing price may be more than the fair value estimate of a skilled financial analyst, due to the exuberance of the bidders. But, subsequent economic reality and market trading would eventually bring it down to an appropriate value.[1]

At year end 2006, there was no evidence that the auction method had taken hold in doing IPOs.

The Financial Analysts

Financial analysts have already been referred to, since they play a central role in the evaluation of securities. And we have noted that they can get caught up in conflicts of interest when they perform that role while in the employ of investment banking firms. It happens whenever they are pressured to slant their analysis in favor of a present or prospective client of the investment banking firm. And the pressure becomes very difficult to resist when it is accompanied by the lure of a handsome bonus, especially if the "slant" leads to additional business from the client to the investment banking firm.

Ideally, financial analysts should be, indeed must be, free of such untoward influence. Their analysis of the value of corporate securities should be dispassionate and objective, based upon company financial statements and a careful analysis of the balance sheet and the profit and loss statement. They should view that data over time, and compare it against similar data of other firms in the same industry. Where a firm faces competition from abroad in a global industry, that factor needs to be weighed in evaluating future trends and projecting future earnings prospects. Technological developments have to be considered, as do legal and tax factors relevant to the industry; tobacco, asbestos, steel, and automobiles are a few examples. In short, financial analysis is a highly complex and sophisticated exercise, requiring extensive technical knowledge and experience. Out of such analysis come recommendations from the analyst, advising prospective investors to buy, sell, or hold a security. The integrity of those recommendations is profoundly important to the efficient performance of the nation's capital markets. We must not tolerate or smile benevolently when we discover efforts to tamper with their honesty. Mistakes are understandable, but chicanery is intolerable.

The U.S. Bureau of Labor Statistics *Occupational Outlook Handbook, 2002-2003*, indicates that some 143,000 people work as financial analysts, with about 36,000 of them employed by security and commodity brokers, exchanges, and investment services firms. About 29,000 worked for banks, credit institutions, and mortgage bankers and brokers. The rest worked for insurance carriers, computer and data processing services, and management and public relations firms. We are concerned mainly with the first two groups.

Typically, the nature of the work and life style of the investment banker and the financial analyst are very different. We have already spoken of the former, and the pressure, competition, and risk taking characteristics of the banker's life. But the financial rewards of success are large, sometimes huge, and a great material lure to those who are quick-witted, venturesome, and driven by ambition. The average analyst's life is very different, usually consumed by careful study of data that is done largely in private, although there will be important personal contacts and visits to executives and operations sites of companies being analyzed. Demands of the job are not as intrusive into the analyst's family and social life as is the case with the investment banker. And the compensation is usually significantly less. But, in the case of the analyst who is willing to slant his/her analysis, bonuses and cuts of investment banking fees can become very substantial. Of course, that is wrong and every effort must be made to stop it.

How can we combat wrongful behavior by the financial analyst? One way that has been suggested, and is reflected in section 501 of the Sarbanes-Oxley Act, is to build a so-called Chinese wall between the analyst and the investment banker. The term Chinese wall is probably drawn from the famous wall constructed millennia ago by the Chinese to protect that nation's inhabitants from the incursions of hostile invaders. In the financial world, the purpose is to insulate the analysts from any pressure by the investment bankers, perhaps by removing them from the employ of the latter and placing them under a different and separate employing agency. Or, alternatively, by placing them in a special research department of the investment banking firm and keeping that department completely free of any influence from the bankers, not an easy thing to accomplish. Another possibility, mentioned by a knowledgeable banker but not widely discussed, would be to limit the analyst to simply describing the financial and other relevant facts applicable to a corporation, without any recommendation to buy, sell, or hold its securities. In that case, the analyst's report would bear the statement: "This report is only factual, and expresses no opinion as to the desirability of owning the stock." Finally, whenever an analyst changed jobs, and moved from one investment banking firm to another, he/she would be precluded from doing so if the new employer held out the prospect of rewarding the analyst for drawing clients from the old employer to the new one. Negative covenants, or similar "no compete" agreements might serve that purpose.

Section 501 of Sarbanes-Oxley (discussed in detail in Appendix III) requires full disclosure of any conflicts of interest by financial analysts.

The SEC is the enforcement agency, with the authority to designate a registered securities association or national securities exchange as the regulatory and enforcement body for adopting and overseeing implementation of the rules requiring such disclosure. Of course, these bodies remain under the supervision of the SEC. Section 501 provides an overview of the conflicts to be avoided, the measures needed to improve research objectivity, and the steps required to achieve full disclosure. Unfortunately, detailed rules and strong enforcement do not guarantee the total elimination of conflicts of interest and inadequate disclosure. Two cases seem relevant; one demonstrating compliance; the other seeming non-compliance. Both cases involve the requirement of Sarbanes-Oxley that there be a Chinese wall between financial analysts and investment bankers.

The first case involved an IPO by Warner Music Group in mid 2005. The IPO was handled by an impressive group of investment banking firms, including Goldman Sachs, Morgan Stanley, Lehman Brothers, Citigroup, Bank of America, and Deutsche Bank. Merrill Lynch was originally part of the group, but it withdrew after Ms. Jessica Reif Cohen, its expert financial analyst on the music industry, objected to the original offering price as being too high. That price was in the $22-$24 range. Although the offering price was lowered to $17, Ms. Cohen felt it was still too high, and, at that point Merrill withdrew from the sponsoring group. Despite that loss of business and fees, there is no indication of any adverse actions against Ms. Cohen by Merrill, her employer. I believe that such an outcome would have been most unlikely before Sarbanes-Oxley was enacted.

The second case was reported in April 2006. It involved an experienced financial analyst, Matthew N. Murray, who was employed as a portfolio manager by Rodman Renshaw, a small, privately held investment banking firm. Murray downgraded his evaluation of the stock of Halozyme Therapeutics, a small biotechnology firm that was a client of Rodman Renshaw. The market price of the stock had hit the value that he believed it was worth, and so he downgraded it from "outperform" to "market perform," a reasonable and appropriate action consistent with the thrust of section 501. But, he was discharged by Rodman Renshaw, which disclaimed any connection between the downgrading and the discharge. Subsequently, in July 2006, while discussing the matter with investigators for the Senate Finance Committee, former General Wesley K. Clark, now chairman of Rodman Renshaw, repeated the denial of any connection between the downgrade and the discharge. The SEC also entered the picture, and is pursuing its own investigation of Mr. Murray's discharge. All the while, Rodman Renshaw stoutly maintained that it discharged Murray for just cause, disclaiming any connection between its action and his downgrade of Halozyme stock. And, Murray and his attorney just as vigorously maintained the two actions are connected. The disclaimer of any connection does test my credulity, causing me to wonder about the knowledge and understanding of Sarbanes-Oxley by Rodman Renshaw's top executives. Although I have no relevant evidence, I wonder further if smaller and possibly less scrutinized firms suspect that inappropriate actions by them might get by under the supervisory radar. In any case, we see the bite of Sarbanes-Oxley, as well as its possible limits.[2] In light of this episode, it is interesting to read Rodman Renshaw's promotional blurb on its web site. Rodman Renshaw describes itself as "a privately held, full service investment bank committed to fostering the long term success of emerging growth companies through capital raising, strategic advice, insightful research, and the development of institutional support. Rodman employs dedicated, experienced, and talented professionals within its equity research, corporate finance, and sales & trading divisions." Is it possible that its insightful research is too strongly dedicated to its capital raising objective?

Institutional Investors

We have usually assumed, to this point, that corporate shareholders are individuals, and that there is consequently just one layer of management that separates ownership and control. It is necessary now to recognize explicitly that that assumption is some distance from reality. Apart from the substantial segment of the American economy that is actually owner operated, i.e., family businesses, individual proprietorships, partnerships, professional practices, and S-type corporations, individual saver-investors invest through institutions that group their savings into pools of funds that are then invested by the institution into corporate and government securities of great variety. The financial experts who actually manage the investment portfolios of those institutions constitute a second layer of separation between the individual investor-owners and the managers in control of the actual enterprises that constitute the foundation of the economic edifice. The additional layer of separation offers room for further conflicts of interest to intrude themselves between the individual owners and the management in control of the underlying enterprises. In an effort to counter the conflicts, the SEC, in late June 2004, issued a rule requiring that the chairman of each mutual fund be an independent individual, i.e., not a part of the company that manages the fund. James K. Glassman, a fellow of the American Enterprise Fund, opposed the rule, arguing that the rule was unnecessary, because dissatisfied individual investors could always withdraw their savings from a fund and go to another one that put the investor's interests ahead of any other interest. The issue was finally resolved when the U.S. Court of Appeals overturned the rule, as well as the companion SEC rule requiring the board of a mutual fund to be at least 75 percent independent.

On August 18, 2004, the SEC significantly extended its regulatory rules over mutual funds, by adding ten new provisions. While the industry did not agree readily with the SEC's earlier rule that independent directors chair fund boards, it quickly expressed its approval and support of the additional rules. Specifically, the Investment Company Institute, a trade group, and the Securities Industry Association, a lobbying group for brokerage firms, publicly announced their approval. The new rules ordered mutual funds to no longer pay higher commissions to brokers who promoted their funds than to those who did not do so. Further, portfolio managers were ordered to reveal personal investments in funds under their supervision. Also, mutual funds must now inform investors how their mutual fund managers are compensated, e.g., incentive arrangements, as well as any manager involvement in other investments sold by the mutual fund. Clearly, disclosure is the critical operative requirement, so that possible manager conflicts of interest become visible to investors.[3]

To understand the nature of the situation, we must look more closely at the several types of institutions that gather together individual savings, and pool them into investment funds. They are: (1) pension funds that are for the benefit of employees, both government and private, and are usually part of collective bargaining agreements; (2) mutual funds, usually managed by investment banking firms, and already referred to above; and (3) endowment funds of charitable foundations, educational institutions, and medical entities, e.g., hospitals and research centers. While the pooling of savings for investment by pension funds and mutual funds reduces individual risk by providing diversification of investments, and presumably enhances returns by providing expert financial analysis to investors, the managers of the funds may have goals that conflict with those in the minds of the prospective pensioners and mutual fund owners, as just noted above. And, in the investment of foundation type funds, the managers of the funds may be subject to pressure from politically motivated groups that seek ends that conflict with maximizing returns to meet the purposes of the foundations.

Let's get more specific, and take a look at some sample cases. Beginning with pension funds, it seems logical that the prospective pensioners want, more then anything else, to maximize the future income that they will receive, with the minimum possible risk. That goal presumes consistent investment decisions. But, unions may have influence over the funds that are created under their collective bargaining agreements. Suppose the union leaders want to enlarge membership in unorganized firms whose securities are held by the very pension funds they have created. Suppose further that that goal will have bad financial consequences for the target firms. Which goal will triumph? Which goal should triumph? Should the choice be carefully explained to the union members who are beneficiaries, and left to a referendum decision by them? Will it ever be? We know from experience that senior union members frequently choose their interests over those of less senior members; think of seniority provisions in contracts when layoff or promotion decisions are to be made.

A relevant illustration involves Calpers (California Public Employees Retirement System); the largest public employee pension fund in the nation, and a leader also in its activism in behalf of good corporate governance. In 2000, Sean Harrigan, a leading official of the United Food and Commercial Workers union and a member of the Calpers board, was elected to be president of the board. He had earlier been appointed to the Calpers board as a representative of the five person California State Personnel Board, a body that settles disputes involving civil servants. In 2004, the food workers union became embroiled in a bitter, lengthy strike against the Safeway food chain. Mr. Harrigan appeared to use his position with Calpers to pressure the board and management of Safeway to settle the strike on terms sought by the union. That effort was vigorously opposed by people who argued that it involved a conflict between the fiduciary obligation of a board member to present and future retirees, and Mr. Harrigan's interest as a union leader; being somewhat comparable to a corporate director, who was also involved in another company that was doing business with the first one. It is the potential conflict of loyalties that clouds the picture. On December 1, 2004, Mr.

Harrigan was replaced as the representative of the State Personnel Board to the Calpers board, thereby losing his position as president of Calpers.[4] The change was attributed to the controversy surrounding Mr. Harrigan's efforts to use the power of Calpers in behalf of the food workers union in its dispute with Safeway, as well as his activist position in other areas where Calpers influence was exerted on corporate governance.

Another relevant case, involving a mutual fund, comes to mind. It involves the Bank of America, and was reported in the *New York Times*.[5] Kenneth D. Lewis, the bank's CEO, determined to enlarge the bank's profits by quickly increasing its business in managing investments. That goal stimulated special arrangements with wealthy persons and the financial entities they controlled, e.g., special trading privileges that harmed the interests of long-term mutual fund shareholders managed by the bank. The specific case that broke open the situation involved *Canary Capital Partners*, a hedge fund controlled by Edward Stern. That case also involved Bank One, Strong Capital, and Janus Capital. Bank One agreed, on June 29, 2000, to a joint settlement with the SEC and Eliot Spitzer's office. The settlement required a $90 million payment by Bank One, of which $40 million was penalties, $10 million was restitution and disgorgement, and $40 million was a reduction of its mutual fund fees. Mark A. Beeson, who had been CEO of One Group Mutual Funds, a division of Bank One, paid a personal penalty of $100,000 and agreed to a ban of 3 years against service as an officer or director of an investment manager, as well as a 2 year ban from the mutual fund industry. Strong Capital and Janus Capital had also agreed to settlements.[6] In aggregate terms, as of August, 2004, the SEC, with Attorney General Spitzer and some other State Attorney Generals, had imposed about $3 billion in penalties on mutual fund firms.[7]

In the case of university endowments, we know well of pressure from faculty, students, and other groups seeking to compel boards of trustees (and fund managers) to withdraw investments from countries and companies that are political targets. Think of the campaigns aimed at companies with manufacturing operations in third world countries. People with an understanding of the long-term economic benefits of free trade and comparative advantage see such efforts as aimed to protect high cost domestic producers, at the expense of profoundly impoverished third world people. Whatever the merits of the conflicting pressures, the goal of the universities' endowments is presumably to maximize returns on the endowments, so that they can be applied to student financial aid, research activities, and faculty compensation. Having spent my life in academe, I come down on the side of furthering the educational and research goals of the university, and keeping the institution itself from becoming a party to partisan preferences.

A relevant illustration is provided by a group of students and alumni. On April 22, 2004, they announced that they were organizing The Responsible Endowments Coalition, "to promote socially responsible investment policies for American college's endowments." The group included students and alumni from 35 leading universities and colleges, e.g., Yale, Columbia, Brown, University of Pennsylvania, Amherst, Swarthmore, etc. By the end of 2004, the institutions presently or formerly attended by the students and alumni had combined endowments of some $102 billion, according to the coalition. The activist group said that they would seek to influence endowment investment policy toward companies they labeled progressive, and against companies they claimed undermined economic and social democracy. They would also seek to influence voting on shareholder resolutions as a method of changing corporate policies.[8] The financial results achieved by the endowments was nowhere to be found among the group's concerns or objectives, although the fiduciary obligations of the trustees of the endowments made that a primary concern for them. Significantly, a survey of 741 colleges, done by the National Association of College and Business Officers showed that in 2004 seventy-three percent of the institutions did not consider social responsibility in their investment decisions, up from 61.4 percent in 2001.

Note should be taken of the magnitude of the funds in the hands of institutional investors. I provide only a partial indication. Pension funds, including large public labor funds and corporate pension funds, are organized in a Council of Institutional Investors. In 2003, the Council had 130 pension fund members whose assets exceeded $2 trillion; certainly not small change. The Council states its aims as protecting plan assets and obtaining the best return on their investment, taking cognizance of the fiduciary obligations of the funds' managers. The Council points out that it was organized in 1985 "in response to controversial takeover activities that threatened the interests of pension fund beneficiaries."

I read into that statement the implication that the purpose was to prevent takeovers, and maintain employment of unionized workers in the target firms. It is possible that the job protection goal, while clearly in the interest of the workers in the target companies, may have had a cost in terms of protecting assets and getting the best return for workers covered by the pension plan but not employed in the target firms. The clash of interests is intriguing, but one could certainly argue that job protection in unionized firms was a legitimate concern and goal for the pension fund managers. However, if the long-term consequence is the gradual death of a highly unionized, high cost industry, perhaps from global competition and the movement of production overseas, then the contrary argument would also make sense. Precisely this internal conflict between a narrow focus on investing to maximize pension benefits, and a broad focus that includes social and political goals, may have led to the resignation of Sarah Ball Teslik, the Council's long-time executive director.[9]

A quick look at college and university endowments in America also indicates very substantial amounts.[10] The *Chronicle of Higher Education* reported that in 2005 there were 236 such institutions with endowments in excess of $175 million each. I scanned the list to get an approximate idea of the aggregate magnitude of the endowments. The top 40 colleges and universities had a total endowment of some $177 billion, with about $103 billion concentrated in the top ten. Harvard and Yale alone had about $41 billion. While the amounts are not nearly as great as those in the pension plans, they are still considerable, and very important to the operations of the colleges and universities involved. That they are a target of political pressures is therefore a matter of concern, especially if one is a trustee bound by fiduciary obligations.

A few words about hedge funds are in order. They are funds which typically gather together the funds of wealthy investors (individuals and institutions) and pool them for investment in promising enterprises; which may be riskier than ones that attract individual investors. Because hedge fund investors have been seen as wealthy, and presumably financially sophisticated, they have not been as closely regulated as mutual funds. But, in recent years, that assumption has been questioned. Consequently, the SEC announced on December 13, 2006, that it would tighten its rule on who might invest in a hedge fund. Instead of the former rule limiting such investors to those with a net worth of at least $1 million or an annual income of $200,000, the new rule limits them to those with a minimum of $2.5 million in investment assets (excluding primary residences).[11]

Perhaps this final point should be made. Peter Drucker, the famed management guru, observed a number of years ago, that the growth of institutional investment funds in the United States would eventually socialize its capitalistic system. He thought that this would happen as a consequence of the wide dispersion that would come about in the owner-ship of corporate securities. Presumably, the profit motive would be modified as a consequence, and that would have an impact on the functioning of the market system. It does not appear to have happened yet, and the idea has not had much attention in recent times. Yet, we saw something of the point in connection with our brief review of possible conflicts of interest in the management of institutional investment funds.

The Impact of Sarbanes-Oxley

Title V of the Sarbanes-Oxley Act, in entirety, deals with "Analyst Conflicts of Interest." In its two main parts, it deals with: (1) analyst protections; and (2) disclosure. The analyst protection segment seeks to erect Chinese walls that will separate and insulate the analysts from any influence or pressure by investment bankers. The disclosure segment calls for disclosure of any conflicts of interest by both analysts and investment bankers. Title V requires registered securities exchanges and national securities exchanges to be the regulatory instruments through which its aims are achieved, and to accomplish the charge within one year of the passage of the Act. The exchanges operate under the overall supervisory authority of the SEC.

With the stated purposes of enhancing public confidence in the research done by analysts, and protecting their objectivity and independence, the Act: (1) restricts prepublication clearance or approval of research reports by anyone employed in investment banking, including anyone not directly responsible for investment research, except legal or compliance staff; (2) limits the supervision and compensation decisions involving analysts to officials who are not involved in investment banking; and (3) requires that anyone involved with investment banking may not, directly or indirectly, retaliate against or threaten any analyst, where the threat is a result of an adverse, negative, or otherwise unfavorable research report. Disciplinary actions against an analyst that are based on other causes are not prohibited, so long as they are within the policies and procedures of the employing firm.

Also intended to protect analysts is the requirement that blackout periods shall be defined during which brokers and dealers involved with public offerings of securities should not publish or distribute reports relating to the affected securities or the issuing firms. Finally, to further strengthen the separation between bankers and analysts, the protection segment of Title V requires the establishment of "structural and institutional safeguards within registered brokers or dealers to assure that securities analysts are separated by appropriate informational partitions within the firm from the review, pressure, or oversight of those whose involvement in investment banking activities might potentially bias their judgment or supervision; . . ."

The disclosure segment of Title V seeks to inform the public of any conflicts of interest involving both analysts and investment bankers. Specific references are made to: (1) any personal investment in or debt to an issuer firm by an analyst who is involved with a research report on the firm; (2) any compensation by an issuer firm to either analysts or bankers involved with research about the issuing firm, other than exemptions determined by the SEC to be appropriate in the public interest and consistent with the protection of investors; (3) client relationships between issuers and brokers or dealers in the year preceding the appearance of a research report, in which case the types of service provided to the issuer are disclosed; (4) whether an analyst received compensation related to a research report that was based upon the investment banking fees paid by the issuer to the investment banking firm; and (5) an omnibus provision mandating "such other disclosures of conflicts of interest that are material to investors, research analysts, or the broker or dealer as the Commission, or such other association or exchange, determines appropriate."

Time will tell how effective these efforts at analyst protection and disclosure of conflicts of interest will be. Time will also tell if these efforts at regulation overreach, and have a stifling impact on the efficiency of the capital markets. For the moment, the impulse is to regulate, in an understandable effort to immunize us from repetitions of the corporate scandals that marked the turn of the millennium.

Notes

1. "Investors Eagerly Anticipate Google's IPO," *Wall Street Journal*, April 30, 2004, C1, C4.

2. *New York Times*, June 19, 2005, section 3, pp.1, 10; *New York Times*, April 9, 2006, section 3, pp. 1, 12.

3. *New York Times*, August 19, 2004, C3.

4. *Wall Street Journal*, December 2, 2004, C3.

5. Patrick McGeehan and Riva D. Atlas, "How Bank of America Stumbled," *New York Times*, September 28, 2003, Section 3, 1, 9.

6. Riva D. Atlas, "Bank One Settles Trading Case for $90 Million," *New York Times*, June 30, 2004, C1-C2.

7. *New York Times*, August 19, 2004, C3; and *Wall Street Journal*, September 8, 2004, C1.

8. John L. Pulley, "Students and Alumni of 22 Colleges Push for Socially Responsible Investing of Endowments," *The Chronicle of Higher Education*, April 23, 2004. (http://chronicle.com/daily/2004/04/2004042301n.htm).

9. Mary Williams Walsh, "Leader Quits Corporate Governance Group Amid Clashes," *New York Times*, September 22, 2004, C8.

10. *The Chronicle of Higher Education*, Vol. LIII, No. 1, August 25, 2006, 32.

11. *Wall Street Journal*, December 14, 2006, pp. C1, C6.

Chapter VII

The Regulators

The Regulatory Objective

The focus of this book is the protection of shareholders who buy the securities issued by public corporations. To that end, public companies are regulated, to contain conflicts of interest between their executives and those who interact with them and have influence on their decisions and the earnings and values of their securities. Laws are enacted, both federal and state, which establish regulatory agencies, and empower them to oversee corporate governance and the behavior of executives, directors, and their professional advisors (accountants, lawyers, investment bankers, and financial analysts). Prior chapters have shown that, in addition to the governmental agencies, there are non-governmental agencies that are part of the regulatory structure, i.e., the securities exchanges and professional associations that set forth rules of professional conduct. To the degree that the regulatory structure is successful, investor confidence will be strong and the nation's capital markets will operate effectively. What kept the regulators from blocking executive abuses of power?

The Regulatory Structure

The regulatory structure is not a single, coherent, or neatly articulated system. It is multi-faceted, and grew to its present state over a lengthy period of time. We saw in chapter I that it began in the 1890s and early 20th century with the anti-trust laws that marked that period, Then, in efforts to restore public confidence in our capital markets following the collapse of 1929 and the Great Depression that ensued, the Securities Act of 1933 and the Securities Exchange Act of 1934 were enacted. The latter law created the Securities and Exchange Commission, a federal agency dedicated to: (1) enforcing the obligation of public corporations to tell the truth about securities that they were selling to the public, and the risks involved in investing in those securities; and (2) enforcing the obligation of people who sell and trade securities, i.e., brokers, dealers, and exchanges, to treat investors fairly and honestly.

With the memory of the economic bubble of the nineties and the collapse that followed the dawn of the new millennium, it is obvious that the protections created by the New Deal in the 1930s failed. As collective memories of the Great Depression dimmed and boundless enthusiasm took their place, "irrational exuberance," to borrow Alan Greenspan's memorable term, joined seemingly insatiable greed and executive power, and overrode the behavioral checks and balances created in the gloom of that earlier time.

Congress returned to the legislative corrective and enacted the Sarbanes-Oxley Act. That law extended the power and reach of the SEC, in ways that we have already examined, and will examine further. The individual states have also enacted laws relevant to public corporations, the securities markets, and the brokers and dealers involved in the sale and trading of securities. A review of those laws is beyond the scope of this work. Relevant, however, is the enforcement activities of the States' Attorney Generals, as they impact on and occasionally collide with the enforcement activities of the SEC. We will deal only with the activities of Eliot Spitzer, the Attorney General of New York State, because the most important securities exchanges are located in New York, and because he took the lead in enforcement action.

In addition to the governmental agencies noted above, there are two main types of non-governmental organizations (NGOs) that are important parts of the regulatory structure: (1) the securities exchanges; and (2) the professional associations that set the rules of professional conduct for the accounting and legal professions. Both are known also as self-regulating organizations (SROs).

The major exchanges that we will examine are the New York Stock Exchange (NYSE), the American Stock Exchange (AMEX), and the NASDAQ. The last two were owned by the National Association of Securities Dealers. Now, the AMEX is owned by its member firms, while NASD owns the NASDAQ. All are headquartered in New York

City. The professional associations are the American Institute of Certified Public Accountants (AICPA) and the American Bar Association (ABA). We have already taken a close look at the two professional associations in chapters IV and V.

The interactions of the several types of organizations noted above can become an issue when they collide during enforcement efforts. Perhaps the most serious potentially is a collision between a State Attorney General and the SEC. A danger in that type of collision may well be the ambitions of an Attorney General with an eye on the Governor's mansion or on a Senate seat. Such an ambition could color the nature and conduct of a prosecution, with the possibility of compromising the effectiveness of SEC enforcement activity. To this point, the danger does not appear to have been an impediment to enforcement activity. In any case, the regulatory structure is a work in progress.

The SEC and the PCAOB
(Also Fannie Mae and Freddie Mac)

The SEC. Prior chapters have examined the oversight role of the SEC, as it carries out its responsibilities under the Securities Acts of 1933 and 1934, as added to and strengthened by the Sarbanes-Oxley Act. Here, we take a look at the make-up and structure of the agency itself, and finally, confront the question: Why did the Agency fail when confronted with the actions that culminated in the collapse of 2000-2002?

At the apex of the SEC are five commissioners, who are appointed by the president with the advice and consent of the Senate. The president also designates one of the five to serve as Chairman of the Commission and CEO of the Agency. The terms of the commissioners are five years, and they are staggered, so that one commissioner's term expires per year (on June 5th). In an effort to guarantee that the Commission is a nonpartisan body, no more than three commissioners can belong to the same political party. The meetings of the Commission are open to the public and the media, unless confidential matters are to be discussed, e.g., the initiation of an investigation that involves possible enforcement action.

The effort to encourage non-partisan outcomes by the Commission, while constructive, does not eliminate party-line cleavages among the members. As of mid-2006, three Republicans were members (Christopher Cox, chairman, Cynthia A. Glassman, and Paul S. Atkins), plus two Democrats (Annette Nazareth and Roel C. Campus). Two years earlier, when William Donaldson was chairman and Harvey Goldschmid, a Democrat, were still members, the Commission often split along party lines. Donaldson sided with the two Democrats on a number of major regulatory issues. An important illustration, as of June 24, 2004, involved new regulations for the mutual fund industry. Donaldson joined Goldschmid and Campus in pressing for adoption of these two rules: (1) a requirement that board chairmen of mutual funds be independent directors (rather than management executives); and (2) a further requirement that at least 75 percent of mutual fund boards be comprised of people who are independent. Glassman and Atkins expressed substantial reservations about the two rules, and when the final vote was taken later they voted against adoption.[1] Two years later the situation appeared fluid. In early April 2006, the U.S. Circuit Court of Appeals overturned and sent back to the SEC, for the second time, the rule requiring that 75 percent of a mutual fund's board of directors be independent, as well as the requirement that the chairman of the board be independent. The first time the Court simply stayed the rules. But, the second time the Court vacated the provisions of the rule, while the first time it merely ordered a restudy of the rules, plus an analysis of the cost impact of the rules and a consideration of alternative rules.[2] It should be noted that in the interim period the membership of the SEC board has changed. Former Congressman Christopher Cox is now chairman, and Goldschmid has been replaced by Annette Nazareth.[3] It could be significant that Chairman Cox, in a *Wall Street Journal* interview, emphasized that his major aim as chairman was not to pile up regulations, but to achieve greater transparency and clarity in corporate accounts, thereby enabling investors to make intelligent decisions based on accurate information.[4] Note should also be taken of Chairman Cox's success in obtaining unanimous votes in the commission; a healthy and welcome sign.

Probably reflecting Chairman Cox's objective of greater transparency, the SEC is working on amending the rules relating to corporate reporting of executive compensation, seeking greater transparency in reports to shareholders on: (1) pay for performance criteria, e.g., based on corporate earnings, market value of stock, and/or revenue growth; (2) specific arrangements with compensation consultants, if one is employed, e.g., did management or the board hire the consultant?, does the consultant do other work for the corporation that might influence its recommendations?; (3) any future compensation arrangements for executives, e.g., deferred compensation, interest payments in behalf of executives; (4) retirement benefits; and (5) any hidden benefits, e.g., dividends on restricted stock issued to executives, perquisites provided for executives, etc. These prospective requirements were made public in January 2006. Concurrently, the SEC adopted the requirement that subject corporations report total compensation of the CEO, CFO, the next three senior management executives, and all directors. On July 26, 2006, the SEC finally adopted, by unanimous vote, the executive pay rules, with minor changes, to be effective in December, in time for the following year's corporate proxy season. Clearly reflecting the objectives of transparency and full disclosure, the new rules require the "creation of a section in a company's proxy statement that would broadly discuss the compensation committee's objectives, policies, and decisions. This so-called Compensation Discussion and Analysis would be filed with the commission and certified by the chief executive and chief financial officer." Also, ". . . In a new chart, companies will be required to disclose the lump-sum value of an executive's pension based on a series of standard assumptions, not the estimated annual pension benefit that was previously proposed. They also must report the cost of severance, change-of-control and deferred compensation plans.[5] As noted on page 30, these rules were eased in December 2006, especially the matter of reporting the value of stock options. Despite the easing, the reporting of executive compensation is now substantially more informative than was previously the case.

It should be noted that the SEC interest in executive compensation, although strongly denied, may reflect widespread public concern that such payments have gotten greatly disproportionate to average worker pay in recent decades. *Fortune* magazine reported a long-term study that showed that the median compensation of executives at large corporations was 33 times average worker pay in 1980, 55 times in 1990, 110 times in 2000, and slightly less, at 104, in 2004. If we take only the peak executives, i.e., the top 10 percent, the numbers become astronomical. In 2000, probably fed by stock options, that group of executives received compensation that was 785 times the average received by workers, dropping from that breath-taking multiple to a still awesome 350 times in 2004.[6]

We should note here another instance in which the federal courts have rejected an extension of SEC rule making authority. In this case, hedge funds were involved. In December 2005, the SEC extended its regulatory power over hedge funds, which had been growing explosively, by redefining the meaning of the word "client." The issue was whether the fund itself was the client, or the funds investors were the clients (15 or more had been the boundary). If the former was the case, then the fund was exempt from SEC rule, while in the latter case the opposite would be true and the fund would be covered. In June 2006, the U.S. Court of Appeals rejected the SEC's changed interpretation of "client," and thereby forced the Commission to reconsider its decision. The growing importance of the hedge fund segment of the country's financial system makes it unlikely that the SEC will simply abandon its concern. And, we noted in the last chapter that the SEC tightened the rule regarding the minimum wealth required of an investor in a hedge fund.[7]

Some other noteworthy SEC rules involve: (1) actions on fining companies guilty of fraud; and (2) delisting of foreign owned firms leaving U.S. exchanges. In the first case, the SEC faced significant complaints that fining companies hurt innocent shareholders, while the guilty parties were the executives. They were presumably the proper targets for investigation and prosecution. The SEC will now decide whether to proceed against a tainted company on the basis of: (1) whether the company itself benefited from the fraud, as against the executives; (2) the degree to which the penalty will recompense or further harm injured shareholders; and (3) the pervasiveness of the fraud within the offending company.[8] In connection with the delisting of foreign firms, the SEC initially delayed the effective date of Sarbanes-Oxley section 404 requirements for such firms. Beyond that, such firms can leave the U.S. exchange market if less than 5 percent of the trading volume of the stock occurs in U.S. markets, and less than 10 percent of the firm's shares are owned by U.S. residents. If less than 5 percent of the firm's shares are owned by U.S. residents, then the firm can delist despite the trading volume.[9] In December 2006, the SEC changed the rule; by basing it only on trading volume.[10]

The structure of the Agency consists of four Divisions and eighteen Offices, with about 3,100 people. It is located in Washington, D.C., and has eleven regional and district offices around the nation. The four Divisions are: (1) Corporation Finance; (2) Market Regulation; (3) Investment Management; and (4) Enforcement.

Corporation Finance reviews the documents that public corporations file with the Commission. These are the documents intended to insure complete and accurate disclosure of financial data and risks to investors, and are: (1) registration statements for newly-issued securities; (2) annual and quarterly filings; (3) proxy materials distributed to shareholders before annual meetings; (4) annual reports to shareholders; (5) documents related to tender offers; and (6) filings related to mergers and acquisitions. This division also issues administrative interpretations of relevant laws, and works closely with the Office of the Chief Accountant in overseeing the accounting profession (especially in connection with setting accounting standards).

Market Regulation sets and maintains standards for the securities markets, and for all those who are participants in the operation of those markets, i.e., the stock exchanges, the broker-dealers, the analysts, etc. More specifically, this Division's work embraces: (1) implementing the SEC's financial integrity program for broker-dealers; (2) reviewing and approving new and changed rules filed by self-regulating organizations, e.g., the stock exchanges; (3) setting rules and issuing interpretations related to the operation of the securities markets; and (4) overseeing the markets.

Investment Management, aiming to enhance disclosure and reduce risks for investors, oversees and regulates the investment management industry, administers the securities laws relating to investment firms (such as mutual funds) and investment advisers. In carrying out these responsibilities, the division also performs an interpretation function with respect to laws relevant to investment companies and advisors. It reviews relevant enforcement matters and filings, and develops new rules and amendments to existing rules as circumstances change and require adjustments in the regulatory structure. This division also has oversight responsibility for registered and exempt utility holding companies; an important matter as the utility industry moves from a regulated monopoly to a competitive, market driven industry.

The Enforcement division investigates alleged violations of the securities laws, recommends action by the Commission when deemed appropriate, and negotiates settlements. It can bring actions before either a federal court or an administrative law judge. Although the SEC is limited to civil enforcement authority, it does work closely with criminal law enforcement agencies across the nation when the violation warrants severe measures.

Of the eighteen Offices of the SEC, I will emphasize the Office of the Chief Accountant. The reason is simple: that is the Office that is intimately involved with the accounting profession. It works closely with national and international bodies that are concerned with accounting and auditing standards, i.e., the Public Company Accounting Oversight Board, the Financial Accounting Standards Board, the International Accounting Standards Board, and the American Institute of Certified Public Accountants. Its work is not limited to the development of accounting and auditing standards. It is involved also with the application of those standards, and in dealing with problems that may lead to enforcement actions. Two other SEC Offices warrant special note: (1) the enforcement office; and (2) the Office of Compliance, Inspection, and Examination. They have become the subject of Congressional attention, apparently because of questions raised in connection with an inquiry into Pequot Capital Management, a $7 billion hedge fund involved in an insider trading investigation. There appeared to be suspicion that the inquiry was, at some point, hindered by the discharge of Gary J. Aguirre, an SEC staff lawyer seeking testimony from John J. Mack, a prominent Wall Street executive. Senator Charles E. Grassley, chairman of the Senate Finance Committee, in September 2006, asked the Government Accountability Office, Congress's investigative body, to undertake a broad examination of the SEC's activities in the foregoing two offices. Perhaps seeking an extra "bang for the buck," the GAO will also look into the SEC's monitoring of self-regulatory agencies; most notably the NYSE Group and the NASDAQ. Whether such investigations enhance SEC effectiveness or hinder it, because of the inhibiting effect of Congressional second-guessing, is an important and interesting question?[11]

And so we come to the question: Why did this elaborate "gate keeping" structure fail to prevent the corporate scandals that befell us as the new millennium arrived? To start with, I suspect that the magnitude and extensiveness of the misbehavior was beyond anything anyone expected. The scale of the debacle became apparent only after the collapse of Enron and Arthur Andersen took the lid off this financial Pandora's Box. The triumph of executive power, coupled with greed and the silence of directors, accountants, lawyers, investment bankers, and financial analysts as they became complicit in the wrongdoing, was more important. In a real sense, everyone got into the act. Still, what about the SEC, the regulatory body of the government that had been set up to prevent this very situation?

Arthur Levitt, the longest serving chairman of the SEC, who held office during the high-flying nineties, provides an answer. He lays the blame at the doorstep of Congress, across party lines, as well as the influence of special interests. He notes the undue influence of special interests, gained through contributions to Congressional campaign coffers, over regulatory agencies like the SEC. Whenever unpalatable regulatory action was in prospect, lobbyists would go to work, and members of Congress would make inquiries of the involved agency, sometimes subtle, sometimes not. If that failed to influence the agency, as was probably true on many occasions, the pressure could escalate to budgetary action that limited the funds and enforcement staff of the agency.

Mr. Levitt referred to specific Congressional members in his book *Take on the Street: What Wall Street and Corporate America Don't Want You to Know; What You Can Do To Fight Back.*[12] He described how pressure was brought to bear on the SEC. Lobbyists for special interest groups would contact relevant Congressmen and Senators. Their aides would contact Commission staff. If desired results were not forthcoming, the contacts would go to higher levels of officialdom, and eventually could involve threats or reprisals against Commission budgets. In the end, the enforcement ability of the Commission could be hindered.

Members of Congress did not always succumb to special interests and pressure from lobbyists. Mr. Levitt tells of an incident, when the SEC was working on a rule that would require Fair Disclosure of information by public corporations to all shareholders simultaneously. The securities industry strongly opposed the rule, arguing that it would have a stifling effect on the efforts of analysts to get complete and reliable information directly from corporate officials. In the course of their opposition, the Security Industry Association, speaking for the industry, approached members of Congress. Mr. Levitt wrote:

> . . . I pre-empted them by going to Senator Phil Gramm, the Texas Republican who chaired the Senate Banking Committee. . . . Gramm believes in fair and efficient markets, which to him means that all players should have access to the same information. He never interfered.[13]

A current example, which may be less happy in its outcome, involves Pequot Capital Management, a leading hedge fund. Senator Arlen Spector, chairman of the Senate Judiciary Committee, and Senator Charles E. Grassley, chairmen of the Senate Finance Committee, in mid-August 2006, were inquiring into allegations that political pressure was exerted to interfere with an SEC investigation that sought testimony from John J. Mack, now CEO of Morgan Stanley. No charges have been filed against

Pequot, Morgan Stanley, or Mack, and there may be no evidence of wrongdoing, other than the allegation of exertion of political pressure. But, the bogeyman of political pressure persists in rearing its head.[14]

It was public outrage over the market collapse of 2000-2002, and the severe losses suffered by investors, pensioners, and employees of the companies that were caught up in the misbehavior of their managements, that blew things up, and resulted in the enactment of Sarbanes-Oxley, and a sudden, public, and verbal conversion to rectitude. Will it hold? Time will tell.

Some now fear that we are in danger of over-regulation. The danger should not be overstated. While the SEC was chaired by a pro-active chairman following enactment of Sarbanes-Oxley, he knew the capital markets well as a former investment executive and chairman of the New York Stock Exchange. William H. Donaldson did not aspire to be chairman of the SEC, and did not seek any larger political office. He had made his fortune, and appeared beyond temptation. He had a reputation as a moderate person, able to bring people together; yet, he did not fear to speak to power. In 2005, he was succeeded as chairman by former Representative Christopher Cox. So far, his leadership appears to be successful in winning moderate, consensual judgments from his fellow commissioners.

The persistence and pervasiveness of the problem posed by special interest lobbying of Congress is illustrated most recently by the controversy over the expensing of options granted by public corporations to executives. Stock options have become a major element in many corporate compensation plans, and are especially significant in start up technology firms. The SEC, under the leadership of Mr. Donaldson, adopted a rule in 2004 that required options to be expensed. The rule was to become effective in January 2005. In mid-October 2004, intense lobbying by opponents of the rule led over 50 senators, including such leading Democrats as Edward Kennedy and Hillary Rodham Clinton, to press the SEC to delay the implementation of the rule. While most of the senators requesting delay were Republicans, some 15 were Democrats; an interesting example of at least a degree of bipartisanship in the Senate. In any case, Mr. Donaldson held fast to the implementation of the rule.[15]

I do not want to leave the reader with the impression that any and all oversight of regulatory agencies by the Congress is somehow to be seen only as a reflection of special interest lobbying that is contrary to the public interest. The public must have access to its representatives, and they, in turn, must be able to exercise some checks and balances over regulatory agencies. Otherwise, an all powerful bureaucracy could develop, and bury normal business activity under mountains of stifling regulations and the attendant record keeping activities. History, both contemporary and old, is rich with illustrations.

PCAOB. Section 103 of the Sarbanes-Oxley Act established the Public Company Accounting Oversight Board, and required the SEC, in consultation with the Secretary of the Treasury and the Chairman of the Federal Reserve Board, to appoint a five member Governing Board. On October 25, 2002, Harvey L. Pitt, then chairman of the SEC, announced the five people selected to be founding members of the PCAOB. As with the SEC, their terms of office are staggered, with one board member retiring each year. Of course, this arrangement required that, beginning in 2003, one of the five would retire per year until 2007, when the then members would be serving five year terms. They were all highly regarded, with extensive relevant experience. The chairman and chief executive officer of the board was William H. Webster, a former federal judge, who had also served as director of the FBI and the CIA. Daniel L. Goelzer had served as General Counsel of the SEC. Kayla J. Gillan had served as chief legal adviser to the California Public Employees' Retirement System. Willis D. Gradison, Jr. was a former Congressman, who had served nine terms in the House. Charles D. Niemeier was Chief Accountant in the SEC's Division of Enforcement.

Unfortunately, a public fuss arose over the appointment of Judge Webster, partly over some disclosure item and partly over what seemed to some to be high-handed behavior by Mr. Pitt in connection with the appointment process. In the end, Judge Webster withdrew, and Mr. Pitt was forced out of the chairmanship of the SEC, where he was replaced by Mr. Donaldson.

Judge Webster was replaced by William J. McDonough, who was appointed on June 11, 2003. Mr. McDonough had been president and CEO of the Federal Reserve Bank of New York for ten years, and had a distinguished career with the First Chicago Corporation and its bank, the First National Bank of Chicago before that. He has begun his term effectively, and the Board's staff is actively into its work of standard setting for registered accounting firms that do audits and such consulting as remains permissible for public companies. In general, the Board oversees the audits of the financial statements of public companies through registration, standard setting, inspection, and disciplinary programs. It will set standards through an open process, with participation by the accounting profession, preparers of financial statements, and others. Also, the Board has established a standing advisory group, from which it will seek expert input. Rules established by the Board will not take effect until approved by the SEC.

One thing seems sure: a major focus of the Board's attention will probably be the continuing issue of the conflict between the auditing and the consulting functions of the accounting profession. Arthur Levitt devoted a lengthy chapter V to the issue in his book, telling there of the intense fight between the SEC and the profession when the Commission tried to issue a rule preventing firms from auditing clients for whom they were doing consulting work. In the end, the Commission was forced to back down at that time and settle for a compromise.[16] The issue continues to be live. A strong indication of that was clear from the PCAOB's action in mid-December 2004, when the Board proposed a rule that would prohibit an auditor of a public company from also: (1) selling an IRS listed "abusive" tax shelter, or one with a similar strategy, to that public company; (2) selling the company's executives, but not its directors (an odd exception), any tax services; and (3) making contingent fee arrangements with the company, where the fee would be related to any tax savings resulting from the tax services. The proposal, subject to a 60 day comment period; became effective in October 2005.[17]

Another problem facing the PCAOB may involve its relationship with the Financial Accounting Standards Board, which, until the creation of the PCAOB, was the body that established accounting standards. That problem was alluded to in chapter IV. What is made explicit now is the possible diminution in the power of the FASB. Remember that the FASB has been particularly sensitive to the influence of its constituent groups, as a consequence of which it had difficulty arriving at a consensus on important and controversial accounting issues. The PCAOB may well be less constrained, and readier to take strong actions. Interestingly, the relationship appears to have strengthened the FASB. A significant illustration is the rule, promulgated by the FASB, compelling public corporations to expense stock options. That rule, which was to become effective on January 1, 2005, was subsequently postponed to July 1, 2005, but thereafter became effective. Its enforcement has disclosed major misbehavior by too many corporate executives (through backdating and other illegal practices, which were discussed in chapter II).

By late 2006, the effectiveness of the PCAOB was being revealed through its impact on the audits done by smaller accounting firms, i.e., those auditing smaller public corporations listed on NASDAQ or trading over the counter. Of course, this is another reflection of the impact of the Sarbanes-Oxley Act, which created the PCAOB, and which brought the smaller accounting firms and their clients under closer scrutiny than they had ever experienced before. Floyd Norris reported the evidence in the *New York Times*, writing:

> AuditAnalytics, a company that is trying to secure a niche in analyzing audit problems, reports that in 2005, the number of companies filing restatements was 1,395, up 72 percent from the previous year. And in the first half of this year, 928 companies filed restatements, a 14 percent increase from early 2005. But an interesting trend emerges when you study the numbers. Clients of auditing firms you have heard of are filing fewer restatements. AuditAnalytics reports that the eight largest firms—the Big Four plus the next four—had 424 restatements in the first half of 2006, down 31 percent from a year earlier. But restatements more than doubled in the same period for smaller firms, which deal largely with small Nasdaq companies and with those that trade over the counter. . . . For the first time, these firms accounted for more than half the restatements. What's going on? Thanks to Sarbanes-Oxley, which established the Public Company Accounting Oversight Board, someone is looking at those firms for the first time.[18]

The matter has particular importance, because the impact of that law's section 404 on small firms has become a heated issue, with much heated complaining that it reflects overregulation that is unduly onerous and costly. It has led to SEC consideration of possible changes in section 404 that would ease its impact on the small firms and their clients. Clearly, the matter requires careful study and consideration of ways to ease the burden without losing the benefits to the invesating public of greater transparency in the accounts of small companies.

Fannie Mae and Freddie Mac. Both organizations were created by the Congress to advance homeownership in America, through making low cost mortgage funds more available to prospective homeowners. Originally created in 1938, Fannie Mae aimed to expand available mortgage money beyond the then existing capacity of local banks. It did that, and also pioneered the idea of long-term, fixed rate mortgages, that could be refinanced. For thirty years, Fannie Mae operated well, but limited by the funds available to it. In 1968, Congress expanded its capacity and nature by privatizing it, creating a private, shareholder-owned corporation with a federal charter and a public mission of expanding homeownership by raising private capital. By September 2003, Fannie Mae had accumulated over $30 billion of equity capital and was financing $2 trillion of mortgages.[19] The organization had helped over 50 million American families become homeowners. But, the leverage was great, and became a source of controversy and concern.

Freddie Mac was created by Congress in 1970, also as a private corporation under federal charter, to stabilize mortgage markets in America and expand affordable rental housing, in addition to expanding opportunities for home ownership. However, Freddie Mac does not make mortgage loans to individual prospective homeowners. Rather, it creates a secondary market for mortgage loans. It buys mortgages from lenders nation-wide, and packages them into securities that are sold to investors, i.e., mortgage derivatives. The organization also invests directly in mortgages, by selling bonds, based on those mortgages as assets, to investors world-wide. As of July 2003, Freddie Mac had over $600 billion in assets, and was the fourth largest financial institution in America.[20] Freddie Mac and Fannie Mae are under the oversight of the Office of Housing Enterprise Oversight, although there has been some consideration of strengthening the regulatory situation by placing the supervisory authority in the Treasury Department.

The regulatory issue arose because Freddie Mac disclosed, as a consequence of a board directed investigation, that the company had obscured its true earnings picture. Following a FASB mandated change in accounting rules in late 2000, Freddie Mac had a large, one-time financial gain. Rather than report the gain in that time period, Freddie Mac's top management sought to manage the earnings picture by spreading the gain over time. This objective was achieved through sham transactions that created offsetting losses that could be reversed as time passed. The situation was discovered as a result of two anonymous letters to the board that alleged that management had misstated 1999 results. While those allegations did not hold up on examination, the investigation uncovered the earnings manipulations of late 2000. The disclosures led to the separation, by discharge or resignation, of the CEO at the time, his successor as CEO within several months, the chief operating officer, and the chief financial officer. Subsequently, it turned out that Fannie Mae was not immune to similar financial manipulations. On September 22, 2004, the

Office of Federal Housing Enterprise Oversight released a 200 page report, based on an eight month long investigation that alleged accounting manipulations at Fannie Mae. The allegations involved efforts to manage earnings, to smooth them over time, presumably with an eye on executive bonuses.[21] An especially interesting and relevant aspect of the Fannie Mae situation is the shift in its former influence with the Congress and other governmental agencies in Washington, along with an apparently seismic shift in the relationship between its board of directors and its top executives. The investigatory muscle now shown by its regulator, OFHEO, is a profound change from that agency's formerly supine role. And, the board of directors is now exerting its power in response to the allegations of accounting, and possibly other, regulatory infractions. In this context, Fannie Mae's powerful CEO, Franklin D. Raines, was placed in a defensive posture.[22] But, he did not surrender meekly. Challenging OFHEO's allegations of accounting abuses, he turned to the SEC to review the allegations. In an odd twist of fate, he was able to do this because Fannie Mae registered its stock with the SEC in 2002, after having fought that step vigorously and ultimately losing under pressure from critics, who were strengthened by the rush to regulate in that year; the year of Sarbanes-Oxley. As a public corporation with its stock registered with the SEC, Fannie's accounting practices are under that agency's authority. Unhappily for Mr. Raines, OFHEO's findings were supported by the SEC in December 2004. As a result, both Mr. Raines and Timothy Howard, Fannie's chief financial officer, were pushed out of their positions. Mr. Raines was replaced, on an interim basis, by Stephen B. Ashley, as acting chairman, and by Daniel H. Mudd, as acting CEO. Mr. Howard was replaced by Robert Levin, as interim chief financial officer.[23] Also, KPMG, Fannie Mae's auditor, will be replaced by another auditing firm. And, Fannie Mae began 2005 with plans to raise new funds to meet OFHEO's minimal capital requirements ($5 billion immediately, but $4 billion more to come later).[24]

The foregoing accounting manipulations, designed to manipulate earnings and maximize management bonuses and compensation, were allegedly aided by: (1) Goldman Sachs, who presumably arranged misleading transactions that shifted income into the future; (2) Lehman Brothers, who presumably designed deals executed by KPMG that improperly deferred taxes; (3) Rodian Insurance, who provided a policy that inappropriately shifted income forward; and (4) KPMG, who approved inaccurate financial statements. All of the parties alleged to have done these things denied the allegations. Unfortunately for them, two separate reports generally supported the allegations.

The first report was authorized by the Fannie Mae board of directors in 2004, after the initial revelation of improprieties came to light. The report reflected an 18 month study of the matter by an independent panel chaired by ex-senator Warren Rudman. Its conclusions were damning, finding that Fannie Mae's accounting practices violated GAAP "in virtually all of the areas that we reviewed." The report also found that Fannie Mae was run with "an attitude of arrogance." It seemed apparent that the main target of this charge was Franklin D. Raines, ex CEO and chairman of Fannie Mae, a former holder of high office in the Clinton administration who was referred to above.

The second report was done by Fannie Mae's regulator; OFHEO. That report was no less damning than the Rudman one was. It too specifically pointed a finger at Franklin D. Raines, who, in the 1998-2003 period, received in salary, bonus, and stock options a total of $90.2 million. Other top Fannie Mae executives also received compensation in the millions of dollars during that time period. They included J. Timothy Howard, Fannie Mae's former CFO, Jamie Gorelick, Daniel H. Mudd, and Robert Levin.

On May 23, 2006, Fannie Mae agreed to pay $400 million to settle federal charges covering the period 1998-2004. On December 6, 2006, Fannie Mae announced that it would reduce its reported earnings by $6.3 billion for the period from 2001 through the first two quarters of 2004. Of course, the overstatement of earnings was related to the large bonuses that Raines and other executives had received during that period. During the longer period from 1998 to 2003, Raines's bonuses, presumably tied to overstated earnings, were estimated to amount to $52 million; which Fannie Mae is now trying to recoup It is expected that Raines' will vigorously oppose that effort, especially since Fannie Mae is paying his legal bills.[25] On December 18, 2006, OFHEO sued Raines and the former two top financial executives, seeking $215 million. Of that sum, $100 million represented allegedly improper bonus payments, and $115 million represented penalties. The SEC and other agencies are proceeding against the major figures involved, possibly on criminal as well as civil grounds, while civil actions against the outside firms that allegedly aided Fannie Mae's activities are underway. But, the Justice Department announced on August 24, 2006 that it would not proceed with criminal charges against the firm itself, presumably reflecting recognition of the consequences following the prosecution of Arthur Andersen.[26]

Concern about Freddie Mac's and Fannie Mae's operations rose in the context of those developments. Both organizations have small equity bases backing their large-scale mortgage operations. Should they fail, there would be enormous pressure on the federal government to bail them out, although they are private and their securities are not government guaranteed. But, because they are federally chartered, there is a general impression that the federal government stands behind them. Also, the housing market is a major segment girding current economic activity, and a failure of Fannie Mae and/or Freddie Mac could be a severe blow to that economic sector. Powerful lobbying activity had formerly frustrated efforts to tighten regulation of Fannie Mae and Freddie Mac through congressional action. Now, as noted above, the existing regulatory agencies are tightening oversight through regulatory orders and other punitive measures. The long-term effectiveness of such action remains to be seen, but at this time it is having a real impact.[27]

The States' Attorney Generals and Regulatory Agencies

In addition to federal laws and regulatory bodies, there are securities laws and agencies at the state level. The state agencies have a national organization, the North American Securities Administrators Association, headquartered in Washington. It maintains an updated list of state regulators and phone numbers. They license brokers and investment advisers in their respective states, investigate complaints, frequently cooperate to advance industry-wide reforms, and offer investor educational programs. But effective enforcement activity at the state level, with a significant impact also at the national level, has been most prominently achieved by the New York State Attorney General, Eliot Spitzer. One reason for his prominence is the importance of the New York securities markets, and the investment firms that are centered in New York City. Another reason is undoubtedly the vigor and effectiveness with which Spitzer has pursued malefactors.

Three principal phases have marked Attorney General Spitzer's efforts. The first phase, in 2002-2003, involved major investment banks and financial analysts, and disclosed unconscionable activities, in which the bankers pressured the analysts to hype certain client stocks, even though the analysts thought the stocks were not as good as the claims made. The bankers were after the fat fees gained when the clients issued new securities. The second phase began in late summer of 2003, and involved mutual funds. In that case, investigation disclosed that a number of mutual funds were engaged in after hours and "timing" trades that were contrary to accepted rules, and that favored some investors over others. Questions were raised also about the fee charging practices of some mutual funds. The third phase became public in mid-October 2004, when Spitzer went after Marsh & McLennon, the largest insurance brokerage firm in the country. Insurance brokers, presumably acting in behalf of client firms seeking coverage against various business risks, find such coverage with insurers, again presumably at terms most favorable for their clients. For this service, the clients pay the brokers a fee. Spitzer alleged that the process was rigged, with the broker also receiving payments from the insurers for giving them the business. He charged also that in some cases a fixed competitive bidding process was arranged by the brokerage firm, to make it appear that the client had gotten favorable premium rates. By late October 2004, Spitzer expanded his probe to include Aon, the second largest insurance brokerage firm. In any case, Eliot Spitzer was once again leading the prosecuting pack.

The upshot of Spitzer's efforts was a $1.4 billion dollar settlement with ten investment banking firms, most prominent among them being the Smith Barney subsidiary of Citigroup and Morgan Stanley. The settlement amount, a tidy sum indeed, remained in state hands. Some people didn't like the fact that the states didn't distribute the money to investors who had been harmed, but used it for other purposes. Also, the arrival at a settlement, rather than continued prosecution that would include federal involvement, seems to have precipitated some controversy between the two levels of government, and might betoken future difficulty. All in all, Spitzer's investigations and prosecutions got some $4.4 billion from his target firms.

Of all Spitzer's investigations into the insurance industry, his examination of AIG, a giant in the industry, and its leader, Maurice "Hank" Greenberg, have probably attracted the most media attention. A non-substantive but large reason may be the degree to which apparent personal confrontation is involved; Greenberg is not in the mood to submit meekly to any plea bargain or settlement. Consequently, a real donnybrook has developed with suits and countersuits being fought. The opening shot appears to have been fired by Spitzer, when he opened a probe into a questionable transaction between AIG and General Re, an insurance subsidiary of Warren Buffet's Berkshire Hathaway company. Spitzer questioned whether the transaction was truly a valid insurance deal, or an accounting arrangement designed to boost AIG reserves and improve its financial statements. Spitzer, as well as other regulators, was also interested in AIG's relationships with other Greenberg controlled companies, principally CV Starr (Starr is a Greenberg controlled private company, with a major ownership position in AIG, a public company). The issue was whether there were conflicts of interest that were detrimental to AIG shareholders. Greenberg, facing a Spitzer led deposition hearing in March 2005 and under intense pressure from his heretofore docile AIG board, resigned as CEO of AIG. He remained as a director of AIG briefly, but appears to have been pushed out of that position as well by a nervous board. Martin Sullivan, a protégé and long time colleague of Greenberg's succeeded him as CEO. But, he was no proxy for Greenberg, moving, with other directors, to come to a settlement with Spitzer and other regulators in other proceedings. The settlement with Spitzer (and the New York State Insurance Department) involved a payment by AIG of $1.6 billion. In addition, AIG agreed to some governance changes, i.e., the chairman of the board would be an independent director, the board would create a regulatory and compliance committee, and a mandatory retirement age policy would be set for directors. Concurrently, AIG retained Arthur Levitt, former SEC chairman, as a special advisor to the board. It seems clear that this agreement represented a complete capitulation by the board, possibly worried by personal exposure to prosecution and shareholder lawsuits. But, Greenberg is in fighting mode. He has begun a vigorous campaign against AIG and its board. His major weapon was the relationship between CV Starr and Starr International Company (SICO), private companies under his control that have a major ownership position in AIG (estimated to be worth some $21 billion). AIG claims that the stock actually belongs to it, probably believing that AIG's claim reflects some past manipulations by Greenberg. AIG is also suing CV Starr, in an attempt to block it from competing for business with other insurance firms.

One might think that the picture presented above would represent a sufficiently complex web of suits and countersuits. But, that thought would be wrong. There is more. Perhaps to intensify the pressure on Greenberg, Spitzer charged that Greenberg had defrauded the CV Starr Foundation, which was created upon Starr's death some 38 years ago. CV Starr was the founder of AIG. He had hired Greenberg, after the latter's discharge from the military at the end of World War II, been his mentor, and put him in the position to apply his large business talents to making AIG the giant insurance company that it became. When Starr died in 1968, his estate went into the Starr Foundation, and having no heirs, his will designated Greenberg and several colleagues (Houghton Freeman, John J. Roberts, and Ernest Stempel) as executors. Spitzer alleged that, under Greenberg's leadership, the Foundation had sold off its assets, at less than true value, to corporate entities controlled by Greenberg and his colleagues. The defendants argue that all these transactions occurred almost 40 years ago, and were approved by the Attorney General's Office, as well as the IRS and the Surrogate's Court. To which Spitzer maintains that those approvals were not based on full, true, and complete information. Perhaps of some relevance, Spitzer announced, concurrent with the fraud charge, that he would not seek a criminal indictment of Greenberg. Of course, the burden of proof requirement in a criminal proceeding is greater than it is in a civil one. A final note: entirely apart from the foregoing proceedings, the SEC, in 2003, investigated AIG about questionable accounting practices, The investigation involved Brightpoint, a cell phone distributing company that was allegedly helped to hide losses through certain insurance transactions. This action was a civil suit and was settled by AIG for $10 million. In 2004, AIG settled with all federal and state agencies having criminal claims involving the Brightpoint transactions. The settlement amount was $126 million.[28] Later, in September 2006, Spitzer dropped several civil charges from his suit against Greenberg, noting that his action was motivated by a desire to "streamline" the case. Greenberg's attorney, David Boies, had a very different interpretation of the action, maintaining that the remaining issues were not significant, i. e. material (important) in legal language. The ultimate outcome of the clash of these two large egos will be of considerable interest.[29] But, that outcome may be avoided by the settlement, announced on December 5, 2006, of 18 cases in dispute between AIG and CV Starr (controlled by Greenberg). The details of the settlement were kept private, including any disclosure of possible money payments. But, it was disclosed that, in the future, AIG will not use CV Starr's name, nor will Starr use AIG's name.[30]

All of which brings us to the mutual funds mess. The realization that mutual funds were also tainted by serious improprieties came late in the evolving scandals that infected the securities' markets, and the companies and organizations that are an integral part of those markets. The realization was especially shocking because mutual funds had become so popular, and were so widely regarded as clean. Even Harvey J. Goldschmid, a member of the Securities and Exchange Commission had remarked publicly that "The mutual fund industry has been blessed—and blessed is the only word—by being relatively free of scandal."[31]

The popularity of the mutual fund industry was reflected in the huge sums that American savers invested in them. In early October 2003, mutual funds had some $7 trillion invested in them by 95 million customers. At their peak in August 2000, they had held $7.47 trillion, and the intervening three years had witnessed a very large market collapse.[32] Remember that the mutual fund industry's importance rested on the wide diversity of investment options it afforded investors, along with its capacity to achieve diversification in an investment portfolio. These characteristics are vital to millions of small investors, seeking to prepare for their retirement.

Eliot Spitzer began his investigations by looking into the operations of Canary Capital Partners, a hedge mentioned in chapter VI that had been involved in after-hours trading. Canary settled for some $40 million. Spitzer followed up immediately, launching an investigation into the operations of Bank of America's Nations Funds, Bank One's One Group, Janus Capital Group, and Strong Financial Corporation. All of these firms announced that, if any malpractices were uncovered, they would provide restitution to their shareholders. They also discharged employees alleged to have been involved in misbehavior. Investigation of other firms was also launched, and is proceeding. It is important to note here the case of Thomas Sihpol III, an important investment broker with Bank of America. Sihpol was involved in the Canary Capital Partners case, and was charged by both the SEC and Spitzer in separate proceedings. In the SEC case, Sihpol was charged with grand larceny and fraud. The case went to trial, the jury acquitted him of 29 counts, and deadlocked on 4 others. The judge thereupon declared a mistrial on the 4 outstanding counts. The SEC then settled with Sihpol. Under the terms of the settlement, Sihpol agreed to pay $200,000, neither admitting nor denying guilt. In October 2005, Spitzer dropped his charges against Sihpol, demonstrating, again, the difficulty of obtaining a court conviction after trial, as against a plea bargain.[33]

Returning to the insurance brokerage investigations, Spitzer's attack on Marsh & McLennon had major effects, before any actual punitive actions were taken, i.e., court actions. Alleging lack of cooperation, even actual hindrance of the investigation, by Jeffrey Greenberg, CEO of Marsh, Spitzer announced that he would not negotiate any settlement with the company and its directors, so long as Greenberg remained CEO. This was a major power play, because Greenberg had been CEO for a long time, and was the undisputed "boss" of the firm. The upshot was stunning. The directors forced Greenberg's resignation, and replaced him with Michael Cherkasky, a former CEO of Kroll, Inc. Cherkasky, an attorney by training, had years before been Spitzer's chief in the New York district attorney's office. With that, settlement negotiations will occur, presumably without the threat of criminal charges against the directors. Also, Marsh announced that it would no longer accept any commissions from the insurers with whom it placed policy coverage for clients.

Once again, Eliot Spitzer led the field in opening up a large and highly important area of scandal in the securities markets. The SEC had entered the picture earlier, but was following his lead. A continuing problem with overlapping jurisdictions is likely to be a collision between those who seek to settle, as against the inclination of others to pursue prosecution. The inherent tension became clear in the mutual fund situation.

While feelings have undoubtedly been bruised and feathers ruffled, that is not necessarily bad. SEC's commissioner Harvey J. Goldschmid's praise of the mutual fund industry, cited earlier, indicated a degree of complacency that was clearly in error. Although the wakening has been rough, it was necessary and will hopefully have beneficial results. But internal conflict between regulators must be contained within bounds, so that the results are beneficial. In any case, in April 2004 the SEC took its first step to control the market timing trades that Spitzer's investigative activities had disclosed. The SEC imposed a rule requiring mutual funds to disclose, in their prospectuses, their actions to forestall such trades.[34] In prospect are further rules to reveal fees paid to investors, to mandate that mutual fund boards be chaired by independent directors, and to enforce the 4 PM market closing time for buy-and-sell orders. Progress, however slowly, is being made.

Spitzer's activity produced a shake-up in the management personnel of many of the affected mutual funds. Another impact is likely to be on the boards of directors of the funds, as they review what went wrong and what it implies for them as individuals and as directors. For one thing, being a fund director will appear less attractive to many of them.

The denouement of Spitzer's prosecutorial zeal was reported by the *New York Times* to have been reached on December 24, 2004, when it announced that he was turning over his investigations and prosecutions to federal regulatory bodies, i.e., the SEC and other agencies. In so doing, the Times reported specifically that: (1) the increased vigilance and zealousness of the federal agencies since the enactment of Sarbanes-Oxley reduced the need for states' attorney generals to be so active; and (2) the inherent danger of tension and conflict in overlapping investigations and prosecutions could pose a serious problem to regulatory enforcement. On the political front, Spitzer's announcement was greeted with some skepticism by New York State Republican leaders, who saw it as a move related directly to his announcement, some two weeks earlier, that he was a candidate for the State governorship. Spitzer denied any such connection, attributing his decision entirely to the reasons he had given. It is worth noting that Arthur Levitt, Jr., SEC chairman during the Clinton administration, did not agree that matters could now be left to the federal agencies. He is reported to have said: "If Spitzer is saying that now he's turning the whole thing over to the S.E.C., I think that's wrong. I think that we need a diligent New York State protector of investor rights working with the S.E.C."[35] However, the Times report was wrong, according to Spitzer himself, who told me so in a personal phone call. He stated bluntly that he intended to continue his investigative and prosecutorial activities unabated so long as he continued as Attorney General.

There is a substantial regulatory issue of overlapping jurisdiction between state and federal levels of government, and it is highlighted by Spitzer's zeal as contrasted with the past history of federal agencies like the OFHEO (Office of Federal Housing and Employment Opportunity) and the SEC, and the Office of the Comptroller of the Currency. The last named agency challenged Spitzer's jurisdiction when he moved to investigate whether a group of national banks was discriminating in residential lending practices. The Office of the Comptroller of the Currency argued that it had exclusive authority over national banks, and Spitzer's initiative was therefore unlawful. In this case, Judge Sidney N. Stein, of the Southern District of New York, upheld the position of the federal agency.[36] While some other States' Attorney Generals have followed Spitzer's lead, none have equaled the breadth and aggressiveness of his efforts. It seems likely, once he has moved on to the governorship of New York State, that the federal level will more completely reassert its primacy in regulating the financial records and activities of public corporations.

Plea Bargaining

Attention has been directed in our analysis to plea bargains as a significant method of settling regulatory and other investigations of corporate and personal wrongdoing, but the nature of the plea bargaining process itself has not been carefully scrutinized. To start, it must be understood that the plea bargain is arrived at in the context of a threatened prosecution, possibly criminal rather than civil and therefore more dangerous in terms of possible prison sentences. That is the danger in the case of an individual defendant. It is interesting and significant that in Enron's case Andrew Fastow, who cooperated with prosecutors, wound up with a six year prison sentence, while Jeffrey Skilling, who fought, received more than 20 years. And, in the WorldCom Case, Scott Sullivan, former CFO, who made a deal and cooperated in the prosecution of his boss, Bernard Ebbers, former CEO, received a five year sentence, while Ebbers got 25 years. In the case of a corporate defendant, however, the danger is the possible, if not probable, death of the firm, as happened in the prosecution of Arthur Andersen. I believe the fate of Arthur Andersen hangs heavy in the consciousness of corporate boards, when confronted with an investigation of alleged wrongdoing, especially the realization that, despite Supreme Court reversal of that famous accounting firm's conviction, its corporate body remained dead and inert, and its thousands of innocent employees had to seek alternative employment. The famous claim of American jurisprudence that a defendant is "innocent until proven guilty" pales against the harsh possibility that a jury of average Americans may have small sympathy for multi-billion dollar corporate defendants charged with allegedly wrongful acts. There is also the real impact of an investigation and possible prosecution on stock values and the market for the firm's product. It is no wonder that a plea deal, with no admission of guilt or lack thereof, makes sense, and appears very attractive. But, there are important negative aspects to the plea bargain, only one of which is the fact that the alleged wrongdoing is never subjected to the acid test of proof in a court of law. There is also the fact that the defendant may accept terms that are excessively onerous and damaging to his/her legal rights. Perhaps the best illustration of these points is the case of KPMG, the smallest of the Big Four accounting firms.

KPMG was especially aggressive in promoting complex tax shelters to its clients, and prospective clients. Its efforts were allegedly aided and abetted by Deutsche Bank, attorneys who provided opinion letters supporting the legality of the shelters, and investment firms (Presidio and the Quellor Group). Eventually, KPMG's tax shelters were challenged by the Justice Department and the IRS as being abusive, with the latter ruling them invalid and proceeding against the clients who had purchased them, and paid substantial fees to KPMG. An abusive tax shelter is one which lacks any economic justification apart from the avoidance of taxes. A hotly contested concept, the issue appeared to have been resolved by the U.S. Court of Appeals, which upheld the interpretation of the IRS in the Coltech case in its decision on July 12, 2006.[37] But, back in 2005, Justice and the IRS initiated criminal proceedings against KPMG and a number of the individuals involved in promoting the tax shelters. KPMG entered into a plea agreement with Justice and the IRS. The firm's clients, who had so gullibly and perhaps greedily accepted the promise of tax savings, turned around and sued KPMG and its legal advisors for the monetary damages they had sustained.

On August 29, 2005, KPMG entered into its plea agreement with the IRS and the Justice Department.[38] The deal involved severe penalties, to match the extent of the fraud that was perpetrated, because, in this case, KPMG "admitted criminal wrongdoing." There was no face saving statement here that the defendant neither admitted nor denied guilt, for an outright admission of criminal guilt was part of the agreement. The magnitude of the case is clear when one realizes that the fraud was estimated to have generated $11 billion of phony tax losses that cost the U.S. Government at least $2.5 billion in evaded taxes. It is the largest criminal tax case filed in this country until now. The fraud covered the period 1996-2003, and involved 9 former KPMG partners. Indeed, it was egregious, for it was perpetrated against forceful warnings from KPMG tax experts and others that the tax shelters were almost "frivolous" and would not stand up under IRS scrutiny.

The plea agreement involved a corporate fine of $456 million, plus a list of severe conditions. The conditions were: (1) permanent restrictions on KPMG's tax practice; (2) prohibition of KPMG involvement with pre-packaged tax products; (3) restriction of KPMG acceptance of any fees not based on hourly rates (rather than fees based on a percentage of the alleged savings of fancy tax shelters or other tax avoiding arrangements); (4) implementation and maintenance of an effective compliance program; (5) installation of an independent government appointed monitor to oversee KPMG's compliance for a three year period (Richard Breeden, former chairman of the SEC); and (6) full and truthful KPMG cooperation with the pending criminal investigation of the individuals involved in the fraudulent tax shelters, including voluntary provision of documents and information (presumably to overcome the problem of documents withheld on the grounds of attorney-client privilege). Criminal prosecution of 16 KPMG involved defendants, plus two involved outsiders, was scheduled to go to trial in September 2006, but was delayed pending the outcome of a prosecutorial proposal to presiding Judge Lewis A. Kaplan that the trial be divided in two, with the defendants separated into two groups; one consisting of former KPMG senior partners and executives and the other of junior employees. A number of these defendants had been discharged when the prosecution was begun. Normally, the firm would have advanced funds to them for their legal defense, but, in this instance, and likely intended to impress the prosecutors with the firm's commitment to cooperate, KPMG refused such financial support. Significantly, on June 27, 2006, this action by KPMG was overruled by Judge Lewis A. Kaplan of the U.S. District Court in Manhattan, as a violation of the constitutional rights of the former employees (partners). In November 2006, Judge Kaplan further postponed the trial date for the KPMG defendants because he thought the issue of financial support for them by KPMG would not have been settled in time to meet the trial date of January 15, 2007.[39] The issue of financial support for employees charged with corporate misconduct was a significant element in a Justice Department memo known as the Thompson Memorandum. That memo apparently suggested the withdrawal of such corporate support as an important indicator of corporate cooperation for prosecutors. Judge Kaplan's action probably awakened wider concerns over the matter of constitutional rights, because Paul J. McNulty, U.S. Deputy Attorney General, while defending Justice Department tactics used in investigations of corporate misconduct, announced that the Department would review its policy.[40] On December 12, 2006, he announced the results of that review. Specifically and most notably, the revision modified the Thompson Memo's thrust regarding waiver of attorney-client privilege, and its pressure against target firms paying the legal expenses of employees facing prosecution for actions taken in the course of their employment. But, the modifications were not absolute and clear-cut. Rather, instead of routinely asking for a waiver of attorney-client privilege, the Justice Department prosecutor must now obtain written approval to do so from the Deputy Attorney General (which is assumed to be rare). But, in considering whether to indict a firm, the prosecutor may no longer consider whether the firm is paying the legal expenses of employee defendants.[41] In any case, and this is the point, KPMG has been saved as a going concern. The client suit against KPMG by some 200 investors was settled for $153 million, and the settlement was approved by Judge Dennis M. Cavenaugh. But, in an interesting twist, Fannie Mae sued KPMG for $2 billion (including $1 billion for costs), alleging that its problems were due to KPMG's negligence, which led it to violate accounting standards and thereby run afoul of the law. KPMG responded by announcing that it would pursue its own claims against Fannie Mae. The spectacle of a round-robin of everybody suing everybody would be like a circus, if it was not so difficult, even tragic, for the people involved.[42]

KPMG's plea agreement, which originally seemed to confirm the power of the Thompson Memo, was upended by Judge Kaplan's decision relating to corporate financial support for defendant employees, charged with wrongdoing in their corporate related activities. It was upended also by his other decision, in which Judge Kaplan decided, on July 26, 2006, "that statements made in 2004 by two of the defendants . . . had been coerced by the firm (KPMG) under pressure by prosecutors and thus could not be used as evidence."[43] I have no doubt that plea bargaining will continue to be used widely, because it is far les expensive than extended litigation, and avoids the uncertainty and anxiety attendant on a court trial. At the same time, it can impose undue burdens on the defendants facing alleged infractions that, if tried, would not be upheld by a judicial decision. Hopefully, balance will be achieved in the long run.

The Securities Exchanges

The SEC is deeply concerned with corporate board structure and governance. The concern has taken on special significance as the agency reviews the governance of the securities exchanges, especially the New York Stock Exchange, the American Exchange, and the NASDAQ. The issue erupted with particular passion when the compensation arrangement between NYSE and its former CEO, Richard Grasso, was made public.

On March 26, 2003, William H. Donaldson, Chairman of the SEC, sent a letter to the three exchanges. In it, he reminded them of the critical role of the exchanges, as self-regulatory organizations, in setting governance standards for the companies whose securities they listed. He emphasized that their role in this connection had become even more vital, in light of the corporate scandals that had accompanied the market crash of 2000-2003. He wrote:

> It is now more important than ever that self-regulatory organizations be examples of good governance. Therefore, I ask you to engage in a review of your own corporate governance practices, including board structure and representation, and oversight of management policies and practices to ensure that they serve the public well. Bottom line, how do your governance practices reflect those expected of corporations traded on your market?

> When you have completed a review of your governance structure, we would appreciate receiving a report of your principal findings and any proposed changes to your governance arising from the review. Please provide this report by May 15, 2003.[44]

The responses of the three exchanges varied sharply, especially those of the NASDAQ and the NYSE. At least, that is my reaction to them. The NASDAQ response was one of whole-hearted agreement and willingness to comply with both the letter and spirit of the Donaldson letter. The NYSE response was to agree with SEC's governance goals and to express its desire for "the highest standards of ethics and transparency in its own governance."[45] But, the Devil was in the details.

NYSE informed Donaldson that, in furtherance of the SEC goals, the NYSE board had established a special Governance Committee, which would then engage in an elaborate process of consultation with its constituent groups (the very organizations that it regulated), followed by public hearings, the formulation of reforms, and final action by the board. After all that, the recommendations would be forthcoming and submitted to the SEC.

With no personal knowledge as to the feelings and the reactions of the parties, my guess is that Donaldson and his SEC colleagues perceived significant stalling. It was in this context that Grasso later called Donaldson and told him about his compensation arrangement with the NYSE board, under which Grasso stood to receive $139.5 million, with a subsequently revealed further amount of $48 million. Whether correct or not, it is easy to conclude that the public outrage over the magnitude of the sums involved created the pressure that finally ousted Grasso from his position as NYSE's CEO, led to the subsequent resignation of H. Carl McCall as a director, and created further pressure that will likely lead to the eventual replacement of all or almost all of the current directors. More important, it blasted open the governance issue at the NYSE, and resulted eventually in its conforming closely to the governance standards required of its listed public companies.

No less important, the issue of separating the regulatory authority from the other activities of the NYSE had to be settled. In this connection, radical surgery was not likely. Donaldson, in an appearance before the Senate Banking Committee, signaled that outcome. Reported in the *Wall Street Journal*, Donaldson was quoted as saying that, "The stock exchange is going to have to come up with a governance structure that guarantees the independence of the regulatory aspect of what they're doing but somehow keeps its proximity" to those it regulates, . . . The NYSE can't become "Just a bureaucracy out here somewhere who doesn't really understand how difficult it is to conform to, let's say, trading regulations."[46] There was speculation that Donaldson might support a half-way solution that would require the exchange to form two separate boards: one for regulation; and the other for the marketplace. That outcome came to fruition, but was subsequently changed by the November 28, 2006 announcement of the NYSE Group and the NASDAQ to merge their regulatory bodies and functions.

The AMEX's response was positive, and indicated a readiness to meet SEC goals. But that case was more complicated than the other two, because the AMEX was jointly owned by two interests: the National Association of Securities Dealers (NASD), whose interest was controlling; and the Amex Membership Corporation, which was owned and controlled by the Amex seat owners. That problem was finally settled at the beginning of 2005, when NASD sold its interest in Amex to the members of the exchange, making them its sole owners. Apart from the ownership issue, the AMEX response to Donaldson's letter clearly showed that its existing governance arrangements were already in substantial compliance, and indicated readiness to go further when it could be done.

Despite those pious promises, by November 2004 the SEC notified the top three executives of the AMEX that it might file civil charges against them, for not properly enforcing the AMEX rules. The so-called Wells Notice provides an opportunity for those charged to provide a defense, and is not necessarily followed by a formal complaint and court action. But, it is another manifestation of the SEC's regulatory energy.[47] It should be noted, of the three exchanges, that the Amex is the most lenient in its listing standards, serving generally smaller companies than the NYSE or the NASDAQ. Also, the composition of the securities it trades has shifted from stocks to options, and to other types of securities such as hybrid/structured ones. Finally, the AMEX, which was second to the NYSE in the early 90s, had slipped badly by 2005 in relative importance. But, under the leadership of its new CEO, Neal Wolkoff, it is making a determined effort to regain market share.

The NASDAQ response indicated the likely future direction of the exchanges. Its response detailed its actions; namely, (1) NASDAQ's board and its major committees are balanced, with an independent majority that meet a stringent definition of independence; (2) the market and regulatory functions are divided, with separate boards; (3) the positions of Board chairmen and CEO are being separated; (4) disclosure obligations will insure transparency and broader public knowledge of NASDAQ policies, financial practices, and operations; (5) NASDAQ's CEO and CFO are required to certify the accuracy and completeness of its financial statements; (6) the NASDAQ Code of Conduct precludes any officer from serving on the board of a NASDAQ listed company, without prior written approval of its Audit Committee, and no NASDAQ employee serves as a director of a company listed on the NASDAQ or any other exchange; (7) although not technically subject to its own listing standards, NASDAQ has acted as though it was; (8) independent directors meet regularly in executive session; and (9) the Nominating Committee is composed entirely of independent members.[48]

Historically, skepticism has characterized the views of many who examined the rigorousness of the NYSE's regulatory function. There was a feeling that the member firms that owned the exchange influenced its regulatory activities in their favor. The situation today is quite changed, as the organization and nature of the NYSE itself has changed. Following a merger of NYSE and Archipelago, a for-profit trading firm, in December 2005, the NYSE became a for-profit corporate entity, with its stock owned by former member firms and the public (after an IPO in

2006). The new entity is known as NYSE Group. It continues to have a regulatory function, but it is performed by a separate unit known as NYSE Regulation. NYSE Regulation is structured so as to minimize any possible influence by NYSE Group. NYSE Regulation has its own board of directors; ten in number. That board is composed of three directors from NYSE Group, but they are nominated by the entire board of NYSE Regulation. Six directors of the NYSE Regulation board must be unaffiliated with NYSE Group, and the tenth member of the NYSE Regulation board is its CEO (Richard G. Ketchum). Mr. Ketchum reports solely to the NYSE Regulation Board, and he has primary responsibility for the regulatory oversight of the NYSE Group exchange subsidiaries. Moreover, the NYSE Regulation board oversees all compensation decisions for its employees. With regard to disciplinary actions, the decisions of NYSE Regulation and its board are final, except for appeals to the SEC itself. It is worth noting that a stiffening of the NYSE's regulatory posture was already evident prior to the merger with Archipelago, and the restructuring into NYSE Group and NYSE Regulation. In September 2005, NYSE's then regulatory enforcement body put more than 20 exchange firms on notice (so-called "blue sheets") that they were filing incomplete or inadequate trading data. That action was taken despite a negative reaction by the charged firms that it was heavy handed and abrupt.[49]

In any case, the NYSE Group is probably the leading stock exchange in the world, in terms of assets and trading volume. According to it,

Nearly 400 of the largest securities firms in America are members. . . . These firms service 92 million customer accounts, or 90 percent of the total public customer accounts handled by broker dealers, wit assets of $3,28 trillion. They operate from 19,000 branch offices around the world and employ 146,000 registered personnel.

Further, according to NYSE Group,

In 2005, . . . (it) was the leading market for non-U.S. companies. As of December 31, 2005, . . . (it) listed more than 450 non-U.S. companies representing a total global market capitalization of $7.9 trillion. The market capitalization of the 17 mainland Chinese companies on the NYSE increased to $329 billion, and the NYSE added its ninth listed company from India in 2005.

NYSE Group's pride in its international listings must be viewed against considerable worry expressed by others that the reporting burden and cost of section 404 of Sarbanes-Oxley are driving foreign firms away from listing with U.S. exchanges.

There has been discussion of whether the NYSE Group and NASDAQ should retain any involvement at all with regulatory oversight of the exchanges, especially since the NYSE Group was created as a for-profit corporate entity. The matter came up at the meeting of the Securities Industry Association meeting at Boca Raton, Florida in November 2005. The discussion reflects the feeling among some that the current arrangement involves an element of self-regulation and possible conflict of interest. But, Robert Ketchum, CEO of NYSE Regulation, opposed the idea, probably feeling that the current arrangement offers strong protection against conflicts, while allowing for some input from those governed.[50] And the Chicago Mercantile Exchange, a for-profit entity, is already apparently carrying out a regulatory function in a satisfactory manner. The *Wall Street Journal*, however, favored separation of the regulatory function from any connection with for-profit NYSE Group. It favored also uniting regulatory functions of both NYSE Regulation and NASDAQ into a single agency completely independent of the exchanges.[51] This position appears to have triumphed, since the joint announcement by NYSE and the NASDAQ that they would merge their regulatory bodies, subject to approval by the 5,100 members of the NASDAQ. Significantly, the announcement was made with the participation of Christopher Cox, chairman of the SEC; indicating that agency's support. It is hoped that this action will simplify the regulatory system, and reduce its cost. Preliminary indications are that the new regulatory body will have a 3 year interim organization managed by senior executives of the merged bodies, with an oversight board of 23 members. Eleven seats will be occupied by public governors. Large broker firms (500 or more brokers) will be guaranteed 3 seats, as will small broker firms (150 or fewer brokers), and medium size firms will be assured 1 seat. The new organization will be responsible for broker examination, enforcement, arbitration, and mediation activities. It will regulate, by contract, the NASDAQ, the Amex, ISE, the Chicago Climate Exchange, and the OTC Bulletin Board. The NYSE Regulation body will continue to oversee its own trading activity. Mary L .Schapiro, the NASDAQ CEO, will serve as CEO of the new regulatory body, and Richard G. Ketchum, CEO of NYSE Regulation, will be the non-executive chairman of the board during the interim organizational period. The ultimate shape of the new regulatory body will be created during that period.[52]

International and National Exchange Consolidations

Enormous advances in communications technology and the globalization of economic activity, as well as a great increase in the variety of types of securities traded on exchanges, have created pressure for international, as well as national, consolidation of exchanges. In Europe, we have seen it in the creation of Euronext, which merged the exchanges of Paris, Brussels, Amsterdam, Lisbon, and the London Derivative Exchange. We have seen it also in NASDAQ's purchase of a 28.75 percent stake in the London Stock Exchange, and its further effort late in 2006 to buy the LSE entirely. To further that effort, NASDAQ announced its intention, in an SEC filing in November 2006, to raise $5.9 billion.[53] As of mid 2006, there was a contest between Deutsche Borse and NYSE Group to merge with Euronext, with NYSE Group having reached an agreement, on June 1, 2006, to buy Euronext for $10.2 billion. But, the agreement was being resisted by leading European political figures (Jacques Chirac, President of France, Romano Prodi, Prime Minister of Italy, Jean Claude Trichet, Chairman of the European Central Bank, and Angela Merkel, Germany's Chancellor). They are supporting the efforts of Deutsch Borse, despite the fait accompli of the NYSE Group-Euronext merger. But, there are internal stresses among them, because, while it may seem juvenile, Deutsche Borse wants the headquarters to be in Frankfurt, while the Euronext exchanges want to keep their existing headquarters location. NYSE-Euronext, the merged U.S. holding company, is subject to approval by regulators and shareholders. But, if approved, it would keep the present headquarters locations. Rumors circulated that Deutshe Borse, in the event its efforts failed, might seek a cross ocean tie with the Chicago Mercantile Exchange. In mid-November 2006, further rumors circulated that Deutsche Borse would withdraw its offer to buy Euronext; rumors that turned out to be true.[54] Along with these developments, in October 2006, the Chicago Mercantile Exchange announced plans to buy the Chicago Board of Trade, making the combination the world's largest financial market; to be known as the CME Group, Inc. The two exchanges, each over a century old, trade in options and futures contracts in commodities (cattle, lean hogs, corn, soybeans, and wheat), as well as stocks, Treasury bonds, and derivatives. At the time of the announcement, the market capitalization of the Chicago Mercantile Exchange was $17.75 billion; and that of the Chicago Board of Trade was $8.03 billion; and their respective average daily trading volume was 5.4 million contracts and 3.2 million contracts, amounting to a "notional" value of $4.2 trillion. The comparative market value of these exchanges, as of October 17, 2006 was: ICE (Intercontinental Exchange)—$4.62 billion; NASDAQ—$3.90 billion; London Stock Exchange—$4.92 billion; NYSE Group—$11.43 billion; Euronext—$11.26 billion; Deutsche Borse—$16.11 billion; and the new CME Group—$25.78 billion.[55]

In addition to the $10.2 billion purchase price, these organizational details of the proposed NYSE Group–Euronext merger need to be noted: (1) John Thain, NYSE Group CEO, will be the CEO of the new firm, but he has announced that he will retire after 2-3 years. Jean Francois Theodore, CEO of Euronext, will be Deputy CEO, Jan Michiel Hessels, Chairman of Euronext, will be Chairman of the new entity. Presumably, Theodore will succeed Thain as CEO after the latter retires, a rather neat movement around the executive suite; and (2) The NYSE-Euronext board will consist of 11 NYSE executives and 9 Euronext executives (in October 2006, Thain, in Paris and seeking European support for the deal, indicated that he was open to adding additional European directors) Although the preponderance of power appears to favor the NYSE side of the organization, time will tell how things sort themselves out. Presumably, the structural arrangements reflected the relative economic facts marking both organizations. As of the end of 2005, NYSE was valued (market cap) at $10.1 billion, while Euronext was valued at $10.73 billion ($8.4 billion Euros). NYSE had had a 2005 revenue of $1.1 billion, with a profit of $41 million, while Euronext's revenue was $1.14 billion with a profit of $287 million. Those figures would inspire wonder at the relative power arrangement in the new merged firm. But, the answer lies in the relative size and global importance of the two operations. The value of the equities traded on NYSE in 2005, amounted to $14.125 trillion, while Euronext's volume amounted to $2.901 trillion. And, NYSE's volume amounted to 27.7 percent of the global market, while that of Euronext amounted to 5.7 percent. Together, they will be a global giant. And, Euronext's all electronic trading system might be applied to the NYSE floor based exchange, with potentially great efficiencies. In an interview with the *Wall Street Journal* in November 2006, Thain indicated that he envisaged eventual long-term international consolidation arrangements that would tie together the burgeoning markets of China and India with those of America and Europe.[56]

The foregoing consolidation efforts raise a major issue: to what regulatory agency, in what country, are the firms listed on the several exchanges subject? We know that non U.S. firms are resistant to being subject to SEC authority, mainly because of distaste for the section 404 internal controls provision of the Sarbanes-Oxley Act, which they see as inordinately costly and onerous. Recognizing that concern, a number of American leaders have sought to reassure the Europeans, e.g. Annette L. Nazareth, an SEC commissioner, U.S. Senator Charles Schumer, and John Thain, prospective CEO of NYSE-Euronext. The message being transmitted is that the country in which each exchange is located will be the one to possess regulatory authority. If that is the case, then a further question arises: will listed firms shop around to find the exchange location with the least regulatory oversight, setting in motion a movement to the location with the least protection for investors? Of course, there is the large counterweight that attracts firms to the NYSE market; its huge ability to raise large amounts of capital. In any case, the forces impelling the exchanges to consolidate appear to be irresistible.[57] And, in fact they were irresistible; the NYSE and Euronext merger was approved by their respective shareholders in December 2006. Concurrently, European political resistance to the merger collapsed, and the new, giant international exchange became a reality. The next step is already underway; NYSE announced in January 2007 that it, along with three other investors (Goldman Sachs, General Atlantic LLC, and Soft Bank Asian Infrastructure Fund) were buying an aggregate 20 percent stake in India's National Stock Exchange. Meanwhile, NASDAQ's efforts to buy the London Stock Exchange continued, despite LSE's efforts to thwart the buyout.

Professional Associations

Two self-regulatory organizations are most important; namely, the American Institute of Certified Public Accountants (AICPA), and the American Bar Association (ABA). We examined them at length in chapters IV and V, where we discussed their respective rules of professional conduct. It is important to note here that their regulatory authority covers all practitioners in their respective fields, where the regulatory authority of the SEC and the PCAOB covers only those accountants and lawyers who audit and advise public corporations subject to Sarbanes-Oxley and predecessor laws.

With respect to lawyers, Sarbanes-Oxley calls upon them to report client behavior that violates the law. Of course, this requirement runs into conduct rule 1.6, which requires lawyer confidentiality in the client relationship. The *New York Times* reported that:

> The American Bar Association approved a change today to its model code of conduct to allow a lawyer advising a company to disclose client confidences to protect the company from harm caused by an employee's crime.

> For example, under the provision, if a lawyer learns of an employee's or officer's illegal act that may injure the company, the lawyer should report the concerns to top executives. If the executives do not address the problem appropriately, the lawyer may—but is not compelled to— then disclose the client's confidences to protect the company.

> . . . In the fall, the agency may consider requiring lawyers to report such concerns to regulators.[58]

I do not read as much into the ABA's actions as the *Times'* does. First, although rule 1.6 on confidentiality was broadened as indicated above, the SEC rules, under Sarbanes-Oxley, *require* disclosure, while the ABA's new rule uses the word *may* instead. The former term is mandatory. The latter term is permissive. Time will reveal whether that is a distinction that makes a difference, or not. Second, Sarbanes-Oxley directs not only disclosure to top management. It indicates, in the event of a failure of management to take appropriate action, disclosure to the independent directors of the board of directors. If there is failure to act at that level, then disclosure to the regulatory authority may follow, but is not yet mandatory.

Recall the TV Azteca case discussed in chapter VI. Another relevant case has been in the news. It involves a former investment banker, Frank Quattrone, who worked for Credit Suisse First Boston, and David Brodsky, who was general counsel for that firm. The case centers on an alleged destruction of papers in an investigation of Credit Suisse. David Brodsky was called as a witness, to testify as to whether the destruction of those papers came subsequent to discussion and the passage of e-mails between Brodsky and Quattrone. Brodsky came forth as a witness, and testified.

An especially interesting aspect of the case is that Brodsky's relationship with the company makes the company, rather than Quattrone, the client. From that angle, action by the company releasing its lawyer from any confidentiality stricture can be seen as freeing the lawyer to testify against another employee. It is significant, and must be noted, that the prosecution of Quattrone ended in a mistrial, because of a deadlocked jury. In mid-April 2004, a retrial was instituted, and it ended on May 3rd with Quattrone's conviction. Subsequently, in 2005, an Appeals Court overturned the conviction on the ground the judge gave erroneous instructions to the jury. Remember, the issue involved the destruction of documents, and, more directly, whether Quattrone was aware (knew) at the time that their destruction was illegal. Foreknowledge of illegality would evidence intent to do wrong, and hence warrant conviction. But, the judge's instructions to the jury allowed a conviction even if the defendant (Quattrone) was unaware that his actions would be illegal. Almost concurrent with the overturn of his conviction, the SEC reversed its earlier decision to ban Quattrone from the securities industry for life.[59]

The mistrial in the Tyco case (Kozlowski and Swartz) resulted in a retrial in 2005, and the outcome was the conviction of both Kozlowski and Swartz of grand larceny, conspiracy, securities fraud, and falsification of business records. They received jail sentences of 8½-25 years, plus combined fines of $240 million. Kozlowski was to pay $97 million to Tyco in restitution, plus $70 million in fines. Swartz was to pay $38 million to Tyco in restitution, plus $35 million in fines.[60] Subsequently, Tyco itself settled with the SEC on April 17, 2006, and agreed to pay a fine of $50 million, to go to shareholders.[61]

The situation with accountants seems simpler. The AICPA rules do not seem to collide with the requirements of the SEC and the PCAOB to the degree found in the case of the ABA and rule 1.6. After all, the very nature of the certification process is to report true financial facts to shareholders and the investment community. To the degree auditors stray from that ideal, they violate the spirit of their professional code of conduct.

Hopefully, the outcome of recent events will be a large shift in professional attitudes, resulting in a cultural shift that will encourage professionals to speak to the power of wrongdoing executives and directors.

Warning! Regulation is not a Final Solution: The Refco Case

Despite the pious hope just expressed, reality dictates recognition that strong regulation, plus vigorous enforcement, do not and cannot guarantee the total elimination of corporate fraud. The story of the Refco company case illustrates the point most dramatically.

Refco, founded by and named for Ray Earl Friedman, was built into a large brokerage in financial futures by Friedman's stepson, Thomas Dittmer. Dittmer took control of the firm in the 1970s, and brought in a Texas businessman, Edwin Cox, Jr. In August 1999, Dittmer retired and was succeeded as CEO and chairman by Phillip R. Bennett. The late 90s were marked by a financial collapse among leading Asian economies, and Refco, which was heavily involved in those markets, suffered serious losses from customer bad debts. Bennett, presumably to hide those losses, allegedly secretly transferred the debts to a separate company that he controlled. The amount involved has been estimated to approximate $430 million. It appears that Bennett was aided in the deception by an Austrian bank, Rawag PSK Bank of Austria, because the bank later entered into a plea deal with the U.S. In that plea deal, the bank admitted that it had helped Bennett hide hundreds of millions of dollars in losses from investors and creditors, by "manipulating certain inter-company accounts." The deal, in addition to the admission of guilt, required Rawag to pay $675 million, of which half was to go to the Refco bankruptcy estate (Refco filed for chapter 11 bankruptcy on October 17, 2005) and the victims of the fraud.

The amazing aspect of the Refco case is that the company, despite the foregoing fraudulent activities, carried out a much publicized IPO of its stock in August 2005. The IPO was handled by Goldman Sachs, Credit Suisse First Boston, and Bank of America. The Refco prospectus accompanying the IPO revealed: (1) that Refco's internal auditors reported two significant deficiencies in its internal financial controls; (2) that Refco was deficient in its ability to prepare financial statements "that are fully compliant with all SEC reporting guidelines on a timely basis"; and (3) that Refco's brokerage subsidiary and the subsidiary's CEO, Santo C. Maggio, were under investigation by the U,S. Attorney in New York and the SEC, with the SEC suspending him from supervisory duties at the brokerage for 1 year (although he continued to be employed by the firm). How did all this get by the investment banks that handled the IPO, let alone the regulatory agencies that were presumably awake while this much publicized IPO was taking place? As noted, the IPO took place in August 2005. Bennett's actions became public shortly after, and, on October 10, 2005, he was suspended by the Refco board, apparently suddenly awakened from its lethargy. Concurrently, federal prosecutors in New York charged him with criminal securities fraud. On October 17, 2005, Refco filed for chapter 11 bankruptcy, and the NYSE suspended trading in its stock on the next day, after which the firm's liquidation was pursued. On October 24, 2006, Robert C. Trosten, former CFO of Refco, was indicted and charged with having conspired with Bennett in arranging and implementing the fraudulent activities described above. Concurrently, additional charges were filed against Bennett (a count of securities fraud and two additional counts of wire fraud).

Incredible! But those are the facts as reported in the *New York Times*, the *Wall Street Journal*, and *Business Week*. There is a moral in this story, and it is this simple truth: Fraud remains an ever present danger, even in a climate of Sarbanes-Oxley and vigorous legal and regulatory action. And! Caveat emptor remains the rule for investors.[62]

Notes

1. Stephen Labaton, "S.E.C. to Order That Funds Have Outsiders As Chairmen," *New York Times*, June 22, 2004, C1, C2.

2. *Wall Street Journal*, April 11, 2006, p. A16.

3. *New York Times*, July 22, 2005, p. C4.

4. *Wall Street Journal*, May 20, 2006, p. A8.

5. *Wall Street Journal*, January 17, 2006, pp. C1, C7; *New York Times*, January 18, 2006, pp. A1, C2; *New York Times*, July 27, 2006, pp. C1, C10.

6. *Fortune*, July 10, 2006, p. 81.

7. *Wall Street Journal*, June 24, 2006, pp. A1, A9.

8. *New York Times*, January 5, 2006, pp. C1, C5.

9. *New York Times*, December 15, 2005, p. C14.

10. *New York Times*, December 7, 2006, p. C6.

11. *New York Times*, October 27, 2006, pp. C1, C8.

12. Arthur Levitt, with Paula Dwyer, *Take on the Street*, Pantheon Books, N.Y., 2002, 12.

13. A. Levitt, *Take on the Street*, 93.

14. *New York Times*, August 15, 2006, p. C3.

15. Gary Rivlin, "Senatos Lobby S.E.C. Chief To Delay New Options Rule," *New York Times*, October 8, 2004, C3.

16. A. Levitt, *Take on the Street*, 113-143.

17. Jonathan Weil, "Accounting Board Seeks To Separate Tax, Audit Services," *Wall Street Journal*, December 15, 2004, C1, C3.

18. *New York Times*, October 13, 2006, pp. C1, C9.

19. Franklin D. Raines, chairman and CEO, "Oral Testimony before House Committee on Financial Services," September 25, 2003.

20. *New York Times*, July 24, 2003, C2.

21. "Regulator Details a Wide Range of Accounting Problems at Fannie," *Wall Street Journal*, September 23, 2004, A1, A6.

22. James R. Hagerty, "Raines Is No Longer In Full Control of Fannie," *Wall Street Journal*, September 24, 2004, C1, C4.

23. John D. McKinnon and James R. Hagerty, "How Accounting Issue Crept Up On Fannie's Pugnacious Chief," *Wall Street Journal*, December 17, 2004, A1, A10. Stephen Labaton, "Chief Is Ousted At Fannie Mae Under Pressure," *New York Times*, December 22, 2004, A1, C4.

24. Eric Dash, "Fannie Mae Agrees to Sell Preferred Stock," *New York Times*, December 30, 2004.

25. *New York Times*, December 7, 2006, pp. C1, C4.

26. *New York Times*, February 24, 2006, pp. C1, C6; *New York Times*, May 24, 2006, pp. C1, C10; *Business Week*, June 12, 2006, pp. 36-38; *New York Times*, August 25, 2006, p. C3.

27. James R. Hagerty and Judy D. McKinnon, "Regulators Hit Fannie, Freddie With New Assault," *Wall Street Journal*, April 28, 2004, A1, A8.

28. *Wall Street Journal*, March 16, 2005, pp. C1, C4; *Wall Street Journal*, March 15, 2005, pp. C1, C4, C11, C13; *New York Times*, March 15, 2005, pp. C1, C8; *New York Times*, October 18, 2005, p. C3; *Business Week*, March 27, 2006, pp. 79, 80; *New York Times*, December 15, 2005, pp. C1, C4; *Wall Street Journal*, January 13, 2006, pp. A1, A10; *Wall Street Journal*, April 15-16, 2006, p. A6; *New York Times*, December 18, 2005, section 3, pp.1, 11.

29. *New York Times*, September 7, 2006, p. C4.

30. *New York Times*, December 6, 2006, p. C2.

31. *New York Times*, October 5, 2003, "Mutual Funds Report," 1, 20.

32. *Wall Street Journal*, "Mutual Funds," October 6, 2003, B1.

33. *Wall Street Journal*, June 10, 2005, pp. A1, A2; *New York Times*, October 13, 2005, p. C3.

34. *New York Times*, April 14, 2004, C2.

35. Patrick O'Gilfoil Healy, "A Top Prosecutor, In a Shift, Will Cede Inquiries to the U.S.," *New York Times*, December 25, 2004, A1, A15.

36. *New York Times*, October 13, 2005, p. C3.

37. *New York Times*, July 13, 2006, p. C2.

38. ArriveNet Press Release, August 20, 2005; *Wall Street Journal*, August 29, 2005, pp. C1, C5; *New York Times*, June 21, 2005, pp. C1, C5; *New*

York Times, February 4, 2006, p. B3; *New York Times*, April 24, 2006, p. C2; *New York Times*, June 3, 2006, p. B2.

39. *New York Times*, June 28, 2006, pp. C1, C2; *Wall Street Journal*, November 15, 2006, p. C4.

40. *New York Times*, September 13, 2006, p. C3.

41. *New York Times*, December 13, 2006, pp. C1, C4; *Wall Street Journal*, December 13, 2006, p. A18.

42. *Wall Street Journal*, December 13, 2006, p. A12.

43. *New York Times*, July 27, 2006, p. C3.

44. Letter, William H. Donaldson to Richard Grasso, March 26, 2003.

45. Letter, Richard Grasso to William H. Donaldson, May 14, 2003.

46. Deborah Solomon, "SEC Won't Push Radical Change on NYSE," *Wall Street Journal*, October 1, 2003, C1, C9.

47. Jenny Anderson, "S.E.C. Warns Amex Leaders It May File Civil Charges," *New York Times*, November 12, 2004, C1, C8.

48. Letter, Hardwick Simmons to William H. Donaldson, May 9, 2003.

49. *Wall Street Journal*, September 9, 2005, pp. C1, C4.

50. *Wall Street Journal*, November 14, 2005, pp. C1, C3.

51. *Wall Street Journal*, December 14, 2005, p. A20.

52. *New York Times*, November 29, 2006, pp. C1, C6; *Wall Street Journal*, November 29, 2006, pp. C1, C4.

53. *New York Times*, November 28, 2006, p. C2; *Wall Street Journal*, November 21, 2006, pp. C1, C4.

54. *Wall Street Journal*, November 15, 2006, pp. C1, C6.

55. *Wall Street Journal*, October 18, 2006, pp. A1, A14, C1, C3.

56. *Wall Street Journal*, November 17, 2006, pp. C1, C2.

57. *Wall Street Journal*, June 5, 2006, pp. A1, A7, A10; *New York Times*, June 15, 2006, pp. C1, C6; *Business Week*, May 22, 2006, pp. 33, 34; *Wall Street Journal*, May 23, 2006, pp. C1, C3; *New York Times*, May 24, 2006, p. C3; *New York Times*, June 2, 2006, p. C3.

58. Jonathan D. Glater, "Bar Association in a Shift on Disclosure," *New York Times*, August 13, 2003, C4.

59. *New York Times*, July 13, 2005, pp. C1, C2; *New York Times*, March 21, 2996, pp. A1, C2; *New York Times*, March 25, 2006, p. B3; *Wall Street Journal*, March 21, 2006, p. C3; *New York Times*, June 2, 2006, pp. C1, C4.

60. *Wall Street Journal*, September 20, 2005, pp. C1, C4.

61. *New York Times*, April 18, 2006, p. C3.

62. *Wall Street Journal*, October 21, 2005, pp. C1, C3; *Wall Street Journal*, October 28, 2005, pp. C1, C3; *Business Week*, November 7, 2005, pp. 114-116; *New York Times*, October 16, 2005, section 3, pp. 1, 4; *New York Times*, June 6, 2006, p. C3; *New York Times*, October 25, 2006, p. C3.

Chapter VIII

Protecting the Public Interest

The preceding chapters have endeavored to reveal how imperial CEOs acquired and then abused enormous power. We turn now to possible correctives. These developments seem most significant in our effort to strengthen the checks and balances that encourage speaking to power: (1) behavior modification, through enhancing countervailing power and/or fear of punishment that balances and counters any fear of executive power; (2) enhancement of shareholder influence over corporate directors; (3) improvement of regulatory consistency and enforcement of the law; (4) reduction and containment of the power of political pressure by special interests; (5) revival of a sense of individual responsibility among the citizenry, so there will be a realization that in a democratic society freedom and checks to unbridled power are everyone's responsibility; and (6) strengthening the ethical component in B-school education. Finally, in seeking to achieve all these goals, we need to be mindful of the danger of over-regulation, and its handmaiden, the law of unintended consequences.

Behavior Modification

A judicious combination of carrots and sticks, perhaps more sticks than carrots, characterizes Sarbanes-Oxley. CEOs and CFOs are now required to personally sign off on the corporate financial statements, making them personally liable and punishable for knowing misstatements. Visualization of being led off to jail in manacles, heretofore unlikely in white-collar crime, gives them pause when greed whispers insidiously in their ears. Separation of the offices of chairman and CEO, or, in the alternative, creation of the position of lead director, checks the CEOs power. The power of directors is greatly enlarged by requirements for independence, and for majorities of boards to be independent. And key board committees must be entirely made up of independent directors. Accountants doing audits for public corporations report to the board's Audit Committee, not to the CEO, and are subject to the standards set by the PCAOB, which now has oversight authority over the FASB. Rules seeking to create Chinese Walls between the auditing and consulting activities of accounting firms have been created. Plainly, an auditor for a public corporation who surrenders to wrongful demands from a greedy CEO, will lose both livelihood and professional reputation on discovery and prosecution. Those consequences are likely to revive any flagging sense of professional propriety, and encourage speaking to power. Attorneys are required to report client behavior that is criminal, a requirement that has led to revisions of rule 1.6 of the ABA's Rules of Professional Conduct. Chinese Walls have been created to separate investment bankers and financial analysts, and significant prosecutions and financial settlements have hopefully frightened those responsible for our securities markets away from future misbehavior.

Enhancement of Shareholder Influence on Corporate Directors

Relevant references to this point have been made in chapters III and VI. In chapter III, we noted that the SEC has moved to expand the ability of shareholders to influence director nominations on the proxies voted at annual meetings of shareholders. In particular, the ability of large institutional investors to influence director nominations has received much discussion. Mention was made earlier of the revolt against Michael Eisner at the Disney annual meeting in 2004. And, in April 2004, Calpers announced that it would withhold votes for Sanford Weill and Charles Prince as directors of Citigroup. Weill and Prince were respectively chairman and CEO of the company.[1] Shortly after, also in April 2004, the New York State Common Retirement Fund joined Calpers in withholding its vote for Weill and Prince as Citigroup directors.[2] While these efforts can be seen as positive in the present climate, we must not forget that the influence of large institutional investors may be applied to goals other than those most important to their investors; namely, goals important to the investment managers who manage the large institutional investors.

There is another potential problem with the idea of expanding shareholder democracy; that it might lead to squabbling and divisiveness among directors that would undermine organizational morale, and endanger corporate efficiency and earnings. No doubt due to recognition of the possible problems, the SEC is showing considerable caution as it moves to empower shareholders. *Business Week* made the point in an article entitled "Board, Interrupted," observing:

> CORPORATE AMERICA is fiercely opposed to opening up the proxy, so the SEC is treading carefully. Under its plan, contested elections are likely to be approved only at the most unresponsive companies. The agency envisions a two-step process, requiring a trigger that shows management is ignoring shareholder wishes before activists can nominate their own candidates. A vote to allow outside nominees or a big vote against a director nominated by management would be enough. The SEC may also allow elections at companies that ignore shareholder proposals backed by majorities, votes that are merely advisory now.[3]

Improvement of Regulatory Consistency and Enforcement of the Law

To achieve these ends, regulatory bodies, both governmental and nongovernmental, ought to conform in their organization and operations to the spirit of the standards they set for the public corporations that they regulate. In both cases, they should not be subject to undue influence from those they regulate. Governmental bodies need to achieve workable consistency between federal and state levels of regulation and enforcement. Fortunately, despite occasional flare-ups, State Attorney Generals have achieved a workable relationship with the SEC. But there is latent tension there, and it may produce real problems in the future. No less serious would be enactments of inconsistent regulatory requirements by the states. And we should not forget the difficulties that can arise from overlapping investigations and prosecutions, where one regulatory agency may favor settlement where another wants to pursue vigorous prosecution.

Non-governmental bodies, being self-regulatory in nature, need to avoid rules and enforcement measures that are weak and pusillanimous, and fail to uphold the spirit of the law. In the case of the stock exchanges, they must achieve an effective separation of their regulatory and market functions, as well as having structural characteristics that are as high as those they require of the public corporations that they list. In the case of the professional organizations, like the ABA and the AICPA, their rules of professional conduct should be consistent with the spirit and letter of the law, and seek to avoid excessively elaborate exceptions that confuse and obfuscate the obligations of their members.

Reduction and Containment of the Power of Political Pressure by Special Interests

This requires an enlightened and active citizenry, which is both just and proper in a democratic society. The problem was clearly, even bluntly, stated by Arthur Levitt in his book, *Take on the Street*. Cited earlier in chapter VII, he explained that special interest groups would seek to subvert the regulatory and enforcement activities of government agencies like the SEC, by exerting influence and pressure through the legislative bodies, e.g., Congress in the case of federal agencies. The source of that influence is campaign contributions made to Congressmen and Senators when they seek election. The expensiveness of political campaigns today, and the ardor with which career politicians seek office, is no secret. Its corrupting effect on the nation's governance is also no secret, as is the fact that it crosses all party lines. So, when corporate America fears enlargement of shareholder influence, it marshals its arguments in opposition, and collects what is due from legislators obligated by prior financial support. The point applies with equal force to all other special interest groups, from every segment of the political spectrum. Once called upon, legislators will at least make "friendly" inquiries of the regulatory bodies involved. If the demands of the special interest groups are blatantly contrary to the legislators' principles, then the matter may be dropped. Otherwise, non-responsiveness by regulatory bodies can lead to successively greater pressure, ending in denial of budgetary requests by the agencies involved. It is clear that regulatory agencies suffering from inadequate support cannot do much regulation or enforcement.

How can we overcome this problem? One effort, much in the news in recent years, is the attempt to achieve campaign reform; principally through the McCain-Feingold law. That law has been upheld by the Supreme Court. In any case, the actual impact of McCain-Feingold will only be known as time passes. What we do know is that earlier efforts at reform have all been overcome by loopholes of one sort or another. In fact, as the 2004 presidential election heated up in July and August of that year, so-called 527 organizations amassed and spent many millions of soft money dollars on attack ads; the very thing that McCain- Feingold was supposed to prevent. Another attempt at reform, put into place a few years ago, was term limitations for political office-holders. The long-term effects of that effort are still unfolding. In the end, an informed citizenry may be the real requirement needed to offset the power of special interest groups. But, that point merely poses this question: If we truly achieved an informed citizenry, then wouldn't special interest groups be an anachronism? I refuse to abandon the ideal, and argue for never-ending striving to achieve it.

Revival of a Sense of Individual Responsibility

Calling for a revival of individual responsibility is a further cry against special interest groups. It is a call for the accountant to hold dearest his/her individual responsibility for the integrity of an audit, uncontaminated by the lure of a fat consulting fee, or the fear of losing a client. It is the lawyer's recognition of the noblest traditions and highest ideals of his profession, and his/her refusal to subvert them to any client's wish for ways, no matter how sleazy, to circumvent the law, either its letter or its spirit. It is the director's loyalty to his/her fiduciary duty, to hold that duty above management pressure to be part of the team, when the team wants to do things that are wrong. It is the obligation of the investment banker, the financial analyst, and the institutional fund manager to put honesty above any greedy pursuit of money. It is for the executive to recognize that the tone and culture of the corporation comes from the signals that he/she sends, not by words alone, but by actions. If the executive is open, approachable, fair of mind, and honest, then that will be the character of his/her corporation. As someone once famously said, "The fish stinks first from the head."

We must, if we are honest with ourselves, stop blaming society for all ills, and recognize that democracy begins with and rests upon acceptance of individual responsibility. In short, our efforts for reform should start with our individual determination to order our own lives in the path of integrity. If we can do that, then we will find the whole healthier and more satisfying. But, given human nature, it is a never-ending struggle. There is no doubt about that, because the struggle is going on for millennia. One need only read the ancient works of religion and philosophy to know that that is the case.

Strengthening the Ethical Component in B-School Education

We saw in chapter II that there are two major ethical aspects to management behavior. One aspect is the fiduciary obligation of management to be honest in its behavior, so that shareholders can trust the corporate accounts and the faithfulness of management and directors in fulfilling their fiduciary responsibilities. The second aspect is the obligation of management to give honest consideration to the well-being of non-shareholder stakeholders in corporate decisions. This is not an easy set of obligations, for they may conflict with each other. For example, competitive pressures may compel outsourcing of some corporate operations, with a loss of employee jobs a consequence. An alternative would be insistence on greater productivity, plus possibly reduced wages, from the present work-force. One of the alternatives, both of which hurt present employees, cannot be avoided, if management's obligation to the shareholders is honored. What is the ethical course of conduct?

How about management's own compensation? Wouldn't ethical values dictate that management cut its own compensation first, before any other alternatives are instituted? What about reducing dividends, or even eliminating them? Under adverse economic conditions, shouldn't the benefits being paid to retirees be reduced, if that action is contractually possible? What are the priorities? And, what are the priorities under prosperous conditions? How does this sound to the ears: "Me first for the benefits, everyone else first for the painful cutbacks!" Finally, how are the ethical concerns to be weighed as against economic and market pressures? Students should wrestle with these questions.

Another interesting possibility comes to mind. It would be a useful exercise for B-schools to have a course titled "CEO Celebrities: Some Ethical Evaluations." Several past and present CEOs, who had achieved celebrity status during their careers, could be evaluated from an ethical point of view, rather than solely on the basis of corporate stock values, or increase in revenues. Names that come readily to mind are Jack Welch, Bill Gates, and Warren Buffet, as well as Donald Trump, Kenneth Lay, and Dennis Kozlowski. History is rich with notable names, like John D. Rockefeller, Henry Ford, Thomas Edison, Andrew Carnegie, and Jay Gould. How about those who made their money with scant regard for ethics, but spent it creating great research foundations, universities, museums, and libraries? Classroom discussion of the careers of these business leaders, evaluated in terms of ethical concerns, might be more exciting and interesting than a purely philosophical and seemingly abstract consideration of ethics.

The Danger of Over-Regulation

A substantial part of this book is taken up by discussion of laws enacted, and regulations issued and enforced. Indeed, that is the principal means through which we are seeking to correct corporate and professional malfeasance. But there is danger there, and we have touched on it in the course of our discussion. We revisit the point now, for a final look.

One danger of overregulation is the so-called law of unintended consequences. The law that is intended to cure one evil may have consequences that are equally evil. When public anger at excessive executive salaries arose in the late eighties, action was taken that limited the salary amount that could be charged as a cost to $1 million. The consequence was the wide adoption of stock options as an alternative means of executive compensation beyond the $1 million amount. Stock options became a major element in the run-away executive compensation packages of the late nineties. They appear to be a larger problem than the use of straight salary compensation packages ever were.

Another example may be the effort to make boards of directors more responsive to shareholders. Taken to an extreme, that effort might make corporations ungovernable. In any case, we noted that the SEC is displaying considerable caution in that connection. Finally, a particularly significant example was provided by Professors Healy and Palepu, who were cited in chapter IV. They described measures taken by the Federal Trade Commission in the 1970s to stimulate competition among the then Big Eight accounting firms, by allowing advertising and other competitive stimulants. Coupled with steps taken by other bodies, the increase in competitive pressures reduced the independence of auditors by making them more sensitive to the desires of the executives who were perceived as having the power to engage or discharge them. And that consequence had very bad further results.

Another danger of overregulation is that it invites ever more complex schemes aimed at evasion. Excessive regulation requires mountains of verbiage, in efforts to consider and control a variety of exceptions that appear appropriate. But language piled on more language increases complexity exponentially, and gives rise to specialists who cleverly build careers on evading the spirit, if not the letter, of the regulation. As an example, Professor Lev of New York University, who was quoted in chapter IV, argued there against excessively detailed rules in accounting. He made the point that "earnings manipulation, . . . actually thrives in a thicket of rules."

Perhaps the greatest danger of overregulation resides in the bureaucratic structures that grow in the regulatory soil. Agencies multiply. They issue rules that often go beyond the bounds envisaged in the original enabling legislation that brought them into being. Their rules and their enforcement activities can create rigidities that stultify and suffocate the entrepreneurial spirit that is the energizing life force of the American economy. Innovation may suffer. We should not lose sight of the profound insight of the late, great Professor Joseph Schumpeter, who observed that the dynamic energy of the capitalistic system was built on "creative destruction."

A few words about excessively enthusiastic prosecution may be in order. When Arthur Andersen, perhaps the most prestigious Accounting firm, was attacked for its involvement in the Enron debacle, the outcome was the destruction of the entire firm. Andersen's collapse brought untold pain and dislocation to its many thousands of innocent employees. Yet, it was the failure of David Duncan in the Houston office, as lead partner on the Enron account, to heed the strictures of the national office that was responsible. Was the destruction of the entire firm a necessary or desirable result? I think that an argument can be made to the contrary. First, focusing punishment on Duncan and those involved with him seems more appropriate, and it would have provided a sufficiently severe example to other possible malefactors. Second, the destruction of the Andersen firm reduced the number of major firms auditing public corporations to only four. Since those four firms audit the overwhelming majority of the nation's public corporations, competition may be harmed. Interestingly, some observers have speculated that future enforcement activity may be inhibited by fear of further reducing the number of major auditing firms.

Speaking to Power

The focus of this book is the protection of owner-shareholders and other investors who have purchased corporate securities. Protection becomes necessary when chief executives, possessed of unbridled power, become obsessed with greed, and exercise that power over their managerial lieutenants, directors, accountants, attorneys, securities dealers, bankers, financial analysts, and regulators, so that all become complicit in the consequences of "cooking the corporate books." What is surprising, even shocking, is the fact that this financial and ethical debacle involved a breakdown of an elaborate structure of law, professional codes of conduct, and regulatory agencies that had grown up in the wake of the earlier stock market collapse of 1929, and the Great Depression that followed.

Our analysis of the breakdown of that protective structure, and our efforts to strengthen and reinforce it through substantive adjustments to our system of checks and balances, has hopefully enlarged our insight and provided bulwarks against future repetitions of greed run amok. At least, we should have learned that the germ of the disease is in unbridled power, in this case corporate executive power. We should have learned also that the solution lies in encouraging and stimulating a willingness to speak to that power when it moves in wrong directions.

But that is a devilishly difficult outcome to achieve, because power is the ability to inflict pain, and pain is a huge deterrent to challenging power. How then do we stimulate and strengthen those who have been in subordinate managerial positions to speak up, when doing so may result in discharge, demotion, and/or diminished compensation? What about the directors, who have been led astray by a cushy, club-like social atmosphere and pleasant perks accompanied by comfortable compensation arrangements? What about the accountants, attorneys, bankers and analysts who want to protect, or better yet enlarge, the fees to which they are addicted, and which they see as under the control of corporate CEOs? Finally, what about the regulators, governmental and non-governmental, who are presumably the ultimate gatekeepers of lawful, if not ethical, behavior?

One answer is to encourage "whistle-blowers," by offering monetary incentives to those who come forward and report wrongdoing. It is necessary also to provide legal protection against punitive acts of retribution by the malefactors against the "whistle-blowers." Sarbanes-Oxley contains section 806, designed specifically to encourage "whistle-blowers" to speak to power. Unhappily, the enforcement of that section is put under the U.S. Labor Department's Occupational Safety and Health Administration (OSHA). That agency is untrained to deal with complex accounting issues, and its enforcement activity may consequently not be as effective as the situation requires. But, that problem may be resolved over time.

Another answer resides in our system of checks and balances, which is the essence of the American political "experiment," and which represents an assault on unbridled power. This book views the corporate accounting scandals of the late nineties as part of a periodic breakdown in the never-ending struggle against unbridled power, whether political or economic. When power breaks bounds, and becomes an unleashed monster of greed or political absolutism, then our system creates checks and balances to restore restraints. The Sarbanes-Oxley Act is the current manifestation of the system at work.

At the end of the day, the price of corporate integrity is the eternal vigil of shareholders and other investors in corporate securities. When investors keep their own eyes on the financial facts, and are not led astray by the lure of instant wealth from a stock market bubble, the climate of business will be congenial to sound practice. And the fare on our table will be more nutritious than pie in the sky.

Notes

1. *New York Times*, April 13, 2004, p. C3.
2. *New York Times*, April 14, 2004, p. C1.
3. *Business Week*, October 13, 2003, 114.

Appendix I

In Defense of Sarbanes-Oxley

By Paul Volcker and Arthur Levitt Jr.[1]

Two years ago this summer, Congress passed the Sarbanes-Oxley Act, the most far-reaching corporate reform legislation in 60 years, with the support of all but three members of Congress who voted. It was a moment of rare bipartisan action in response to the breakdown in corporate checks and balances that cost investors hundreds of billions of dollars in losses.

Measures to reform the auditing profession and to assure its independence were central elements of the new legislation. Complementing them were strong new corporate governance rules ranging from who can sit on their boards and audit committees to new and clear responsibilities for internal controls and the accuracy of financial reports. These reforms were long overdue, and have made companies more transparent and accountable to shareholders.

Yet now that the personalities behind some of these corporate implosions are either behind bars or on trial, and the stock market has rebounded from its post-scandal sell-off, there are those in corporate America who worry that Sarbanes-Oxley has gone too far.

They say that the requirements are a heavy burden, hampering growth and investment, and putting at risk the health of our economy. They argue that executives are spending more time fulfilling regulatory requirements and less time running their businesses. Joining this chorus is the CEO of the New York Stock Exchange, John Thain, who, while recognizing that the basic thrust of the new legislation is sound, went public at the end of last month with concerns he had about Sarbanes-

Oxley's impact on America's global competitiveness. The implication is that "reform of the reform"—in practice, a scaling back—is urgently needed.

*   *   *

To be sure, the changes in required practices for many companies have required difficult adjustments in thinking and practice, time and money. But interestingly, most corporate executives and board members that we meet tell us that even if they could wave a magic wand and make Sarbanes-Oxley disappear, they would not. And polling data support our impressions: A recent survey of 153 directors by Corporate Board Member magazine found that more than 60% think the effect of the law has been positive for their companies, and more than 70% see it as positive for their boards.

We are under no illusion that complying with Sarbanes-Oxley and other new regulations come for free; financial and managerial effort as well as money is required. But we believe that those costs are justified in light of the benefits—the price necessary to pay for more reliability in accounting, clear accountability to shareholders, and more robust and trusted markets.

When discussing Sarbanes-Oxley's supposed burdens, critics zero in on section 404 of the Act. That section mandates that annual reports contain a statement of management's responsibility to establish and maintain adequate internal controls, assess financial reporting, and disclose any material weakness in a company's internal-controls structure. This is one of the most important parts of the Act and was modeled after similar requirements adopted for all large financial institutions in 1991 by Congress. It ensures that companies are providing the information to investors that they need and deserve in order to make sound investments.

Critics say that it is costing companies too much to set up the systems needed to get these internal controls in place. According to a survey of 321 companies by Financial Executives International, companies with more than $5 billion in revenue expect to spend on average $4.7 million implementing section 404 controls and about $1.5 million annually to maintain this level of compliance. A few of the largest multinational companies even report far higher costs.

There is a reason that the up-front costs are this much: For too long, too many companies have lacked adequate internal controls. Despite legislation existing for over a quarter of a century mandating that companies have adequate internal controls, in recent years investors have had to watch as more than a thousand public companies issued corrections for errors in their financials statements. In 2003 alone, 57 large and small companies reported material weaknesses in their controls once their auditors were terminated. And auditors who used to test all the controls in which they were relying annually, cut back on the level of their tests significantly as they faced pressures to reduce their fees. The investing public had no idea of the impending disaster, and with no one looking, lines were allowed to be crossed.

From our perspective, $5 million down and $1.5 million a year is not too much to pay for a multibillion-dollar international company when compared to how much investors have lost—and stand to lose—if internal controls are not improved. Put it in the context of the tens of millions of dollars paid to investment bankers to advise on a deal, or on legal fees when things go wrong—or think of the $90 billion investors lost just on the collapse of Enron alone. By that calculus, Sarbanes-Oxley clearly meets the cost-benefit test, and is worth every penny.

Another argument made against Sarbanes-Oxley is that it is putting U.S. markets at a competitive disadvantage against other capital markets. Big Board Chairman Thain has pointed out on this page that the number of European companies listing on the NYSE has decreased by more than half since the boom of the late 1990s, and that this year, only one European company has decided to list on that exchange.

We have seen little evidence that companies are not choosing to list on the Big Board because of the supposed burdens of Sarbanes-Oxley. Other exchanges, for instance, have not noticed this phenomenon; NASDAQ, for example, expects six new foreign listings in the second quarter of this year. In addition, a recent survey by Broadgate Capital Advisors and the Value Alliance of 143 foreign companies who issue ADRs in U.S. markets found that only 8% said that Sarbanes-Oxley's requirements would lead them to reconsider U.S. market participation.

More importantly, we must not forget that U.S. markets are the best in the world because they are the best regulated. We should not engage in a race to the bottom. Instead, we should lead the world to the top, and we are. Countries are emulating our reforms—from the new Combined Code in the U.K. to Germany's new Kodex of best practices—and as a result, we are strengthening the global economy, not being defeated by it.

* * *

Finally, critics of Sarbanes-Oxley argue that section 404 requirements and other regulatory obligations are launching an exodus of public companies back into private ownership. Again, we have not seen any hard data demonstrating that this is taking place. But even if it were, this is not necessarily a negative development. Companies that choose to revert to private ownership tend to be small companies, with little trading activity and unable to attract any analyst coverage from Wall Street. In any other time but the overheated markets of the past decade, they would not have gone public in the first place. Our hunch is that Sarbanes-Oxley is but an excuse for a movement into private control that should occur anyway. Furthermore, if a company does see the certification of effective internal controls as a burden, then it should neither be public nor attracting investors' money.

Becoming a public company opens up a world of opportunity for a firm, but with that comes a responsibility to its shareholders. For too many years, too many people in and around our markets were shirking that responsibility, and shareholders suffered through investments made on bad information, restatements and bankruptcies. Sarbanes-Oxley was passed to reinforce the duties that directors, executives, auditors and others have to the investing public. It seeks to bring accountability back into the boardroom and executive suites.

We should not let the relatively quick rebound of the markets induce a collective amnesia toward the real pain and loss that investors suffered, or blind us to the critical role that Sarbanes-Oxley has played in restoring investor confidence and strengthening our free market system. While there are direct money costs involved in compliance, we believe that an investment in good corporate governance, professional integrity and transparency will pay dividends in the form of investor confidence, more efficient markets, and more market participation for years to come.

Note

1. Reprinted from The *Wall Street Journal* c 2004 Dow Jones & Company, Inc. All rights reserved. Mr. Volcker was chairman of the Federal Reserve from 1979-1987. Mr. Levitt was SEC chairman from 1993-2001.

Appendix II

To Save New York, Learn From London

BY SENATOR CHARLES E. SCHUMER AND
MAYOR MICHAEL R. BLOOMBERG

In recent months, there has been a lot of media chatter about the possibility of London taking over New York's position as the world's financial capital. Such speculation, although overblown, has focused our attention on a broader and legitimate concern: Unless we improve our corporate climate, we risk allowing New York to lose its pre-eminence in the global financial-services sector. This would be devastating both for our city and nation.

One of the engines of growth for the U.S. economy, the financial-services industry in New York has long possessed significant comparative advantages over London and all other cities. These advantages include the broadest, most efficient and liquid capital markets in the world, and a concentration of the world's biggest financial firms—which have a much larger presence here than anywhere else. This city dominates global private-equity markets, secondary trading markets, and mergers and acquisitions.

New York has unparalleled quality of life and cultural diversity, which global companies increasingly seek, as well as a dynamic labor market—our unemployment rate is lower than the nation's. Taken together, these advantages explain why New York's financial sector employment numbers are greater than any other city's.

Yet while New York remains the dominant global-exchange center, we have been losing ground as the leader in capital formation. In 2005 only one out of the top 24 IPOs was registered in the U.S., and four were registered in London. London is gaining ground in other areas too, but it is not only London we need to worry about. Next year, more money will be raised through IPOs in Hong Kong than in either London or New York.

We cannot ignore these warning signs. That is why New York has hired a consulting firm, which will issue a report in November identifying the specific variables that are negatively impacting our financial-services industry and recommending an action plan to correct them.

Based on the work completed so far, there are four factors that bear close attention: globalization of the capital markets, overregulation, frivolous litigation, and incompatible accounting standards. The first factor is beyond our control; advances in technology and communication are allowing capital to flow more freely, making it much easier to locate financial activities anywhere in the world. But, we can, and must, do something about the other three factors to maintain and expand our competitive edge.

First, what lessons can we learn from other nations' regulatory systems? Currently, there are more than 10 federal, state and industry regulatory bodies in the U.S. The British have only one such body. Industry experts estimate that the gross financial regulatory costs to U.S. companies are 15 times higher than in Britain. Beyond cost savings, the British enjoy another advantage: While our regulatory bodies are often competing to be the toughest cop on the street, the British regulatory body seems to be more collaborative and solutions-oriented.

With the benefit of hindsight, the Sarbanes-Oxley Act of 2002, which imposed a new regulatory framework on all public companies doing business in the U.S., also needs to be re-examined. Since its passage, auditing expenses for companies doing business in them U.S. have grown far beyond anything Congress had anticipated. Of course, we must not in any way diminish our ability to detect corporate fraud and protect investors. But there appears to be a worrisome trend of corporate leaders focusing inordinate time on compliance minutiae rather than innovative strategies for growth, for fear of facing personal financial penalties from overzealous regulators.

Second, what lessons can we learn from other nations' legal environments? The total value of securities class-action lawsuits in the U.S. has skyrocketed in recent years, to \$9.6 billion in 2005 from \$150 million in 1997. The U.K. and other nations have laws that far more effectively discourage frivolous suits. It may be time to revisit the best way to reduce frivolous lawsuits without eliminating meritorious ones.

Third, what lessons can we learn from other nations' experiences with international accounting standards? Most European and Asian countries have already begun to adopt international accounting standards, which businesses tend to prefer over the American system. Yet we have set no timetable for doing the same.

In the last quarter of the 20th century, we achieved an almost exquisite balance between regulation and entrepreneurial vigor in American financial markets. We learned that too much regulation stifles entrepreneurship, competition and innovation; while too little regulation creates excessive risk to industry, investors and the overall system.

This delicate balance has been upset by technological advances, making it much easier to locate financial services activities anywhere in the world. As a result, foreign markets may be tempted to lower regulatory requirements to achieve a temporary competitive advantage. Though deregulation may help some counties gain more business in the short term, over the long term it could hurt the stability and reliability of the global marketplace.

New York cannot afford to lose its place as the global leader in financial services. We have to carefully redefine this balance of innovation and regulation. That is what we seek to do over the next several months.

Our ability to do that, and to answer these three questions, will determine the future of New York—and, in many ways, the nation. If we do not rise to the challenge, the speculation that New York is losing its preeminence in the global marketplace will become more than just chatter.[1]

Note

1. Reprinted from The *Wall Street Journal*, 2006. Dow Jones & Company. All rights reserved.

Appendix III

Threats to Sarbanes-Oxley: The Outlook

BY ABRAHAM L. GITLOW

Paul Volcker and Arthur Levitt, Jr. warned the American polity of the increasingly intense attacks currently being launched against the Sarbanes-Oxley Act, and the new regulations that are resulting from it. In the main body of *Corruption in Corporate America*, I sought to analyze and explain the corporate scandals that led to its enactment. I noted there that only time would tell us its ultimate outcome. However, it is possible to peer into the future, and to perceive the threats to the law, their likely sources, the channels through which the law's opponents can seek to weaken or threaten its impact, and the groups most likely to fight in its defense.

An Omnibus Look at Sarbanes-Oxley

The main body of *Corruption in Corporate America* noted and discussed the impact of some specific provisions of Sarbanes-Oxley on executives, accountants, attorneys, and others. Here, we become more detailed, and present more complete coverage of the several sections of the Act; especially as they relate to the various groups responsible for managing, counseling, and otherwise influencing the conduct of America's public corporations. Additionally, we will look at the Act's punitive provisions.

Executives

Corporate executives, (principally CEO's, CFO's, and others involved in keeping and reporting financial results), are mainly concerned about sections 302-306 and sections 402-406, of the Act.

Section 302 mandates that the SEC, by rule, require CEOs and CFOs to certify in each annual and quarterly report that: (1) the signing officer has reviewed the report; (2) the report doesn't contain any untrue statement of a material fact, or omit statement of a material fact, the absence of which makes the report misleading; and (3) the report's financial statements fairly represent, in all material respects, the financial condition of the corporation and its operational results.

Section 302 also requires the signing officers: (1) to be responsible for establishing and maintaining internal controls; (2) to design internal controls that are made clear to other relevant corporate officers in the corporation and any subsidiaries; (3) to evaluate the effectiveness of the internal controls within 90 days of the issuance of the report; (4) to present in the report their conclusions of the effectiveness of the internal controls; (5) to disclose to the corporation's auditors and the board's audit committee significant deficiencies in the design or operation of the internal controls, as well as any fraud that involves management or other employees; and (6) to indicate in the report any significant changes in the internal controls, including corrective actions since the date of their evaluation of the controls. These requirements have stimulated considerable complaining about costliness in money, time, and effort.

Section 303 makes it unlawful for corporate officers or directors, or their subordinates, to fraudulently influence, coerce, manipulate or mislead any independent public or certified accountant engaged in auditing the corporation's financial statements. This provision places responsibility for deficiencies more clearly on executives and directors.

Section 304 requires that, in the event an accounting restatement becomes necessary due to noncompliance resulting from misconduct, the CEO and CFO must reimburse the corporation for any bonus or other incentive or equity based compensation received within 12 months of the issuance of the financial report, plus any profits gained from the sale of securities during that 12 month period. However, the SEC may exempt any individuals from this provision, as it deems such exemption to be necessary and appropriate. Here, gains gotten through misconduct must be disgorged, reducing the incentive to bad behavior.

Section 305 amended the Securities Act of 1933 and the Securities Exchange Act of 1934 by substituting the word "unfitness" for "substantial unfitness," thereby making the standard of unfitness easier to apply and prove.

Section 306 prohibits insider trades by executives and directors of issuer (pension fund) equity securities, except exempted securities, during pension fund blackout periods. Any profit gained by such executives and directors is recoverable by the issuer, irrespective of the intent, through court action by the issuer or any owner of such security. However, any recovery action must be taken within two years after a profit is realized. Also, the issuer of the security must notify covered executives and directors of the applicable blackout periods.

Section 402 prohibits public corporations issuing securities (as defined in section 2 of the Sarbanes-Oxley Act) from making personal loans to executives or directors. Limitations on the prohibition apply to home improvement and manufactured home loans, extensions of credit under an open end credit plan or a charge card, or extensions of credit by specified brokers or dealers to any employee to buy, trade, or carry securities, as permitted under rules or regulations of the Board of Governors of the Federal Reserve System.

Section 403 requires disclosure of transactions by corporate executives, directors, and principal stockholders, i.e., beneficial owners of more than 10 percent of any class of any equity security.

Section 404 requires the SEC to prescribe rules mandating that each annual report by a public corporation contain an internal control report, in which management states its responsibility for establishing and maintaining an adequate internal control structure and procedures for financial reporting. The annual report must also contain an assessment of the effectiveness of the internal control structure. Further, management's assessment of the internal controls structure must be certified by the public accounting firm that does the corporation's audit report. Section 404 reinforces section 302, by applying SEC muscle. As noted throughout this book's discussion of Sarbanes-Oxley, section 404 has become the focus of charges of over-regulation, and calls for reform through an easing of its perceived burden on corporate costs and the fear of punishment it inspires in executives, directors, auditors, and attorneys. Section 405 specifies that the foregoing requirement does not apply to investment companies registered under the Investment Company Act of 1940.

Section 406 requires issuers of corporate securities to adopt a code of ethics for senior financial officers, and changes in such codes. The code of ethics involves the establishment of standards of conduct to promote honest and ethical conduct, specifically including the handling of actual or apparent conflicts of interest involving personal and professional relationships, as well as full, fair, accurate, timely, and understandable disclosure of relevant facts in the corporation's periodic reports.

Directors

Many of the requirements that apply to executives apply also to directors, as even a cursory reading of the foregoing reviews of sections 302-306, and sections 402-406 indicate. Other important requirements of boards of directors, while not specified in the Sarbanes-Oxley Act, are authorized by the SEC, and promulgated and policed by non-government organizations (the securities exchanges). They have been extensively discussed in Chapter III of our analysis of the corporate scandals disclosed at the dawn of the new millennium, and deal principally with the independence of corporate boards. They embrace such items as the proportion of independent directors required on a corporate board, and the designation of an independent director as chairman or as a lead director. He/she would have power to call board meetings, minus members of management, with agendas set by such chairman or lead director.

Requirements apply also to board structure, i.e., audit, compensation, and nominating committees. Consisting of independent directors, they are mandated. Note should be made also that the Sarbanes-Oxley Act specifies that the auditor of a covered corporation must report in a timely manner to the audit committee of the board about: (1) all critical accounting policies and practices to be used; (2) all alternative treatments of financial information within generally accepted accounting principles (GAAP) that have been discussed with management, as well as the ramifications of such alternative treatment, and the treatment preferred by the auditor; and (3) other material written communications between the auditor and management (Section 204). Plainly, the thrust of this provision is to overcome any effort by management to make private arrangements with the auditor without the understanding and agreement of the board's audit committee.

A companion provision is contained in section 407. It mandates that at least one member of the audit committee shall be a "financial expert."

Further, the periodic report required of a public corporation, i.e., an issuer of securities sold to the public, must disclose whether the audit committee consists of one such member, and, if not, the reasons for such absence. Section 407 defines a "financial expert" as a person who through education and experience as a public accountant or auditor or principal financial officer of issuer (e.g., comptroller, principal accounting officer, or a position performing similar functions) has: (1) an understanding of GAAP and financial statements; (2) experience in preparing or auditing the financial statements of comparable issuers, as well as the application of GAAP in accounting for estimates, accruals, and reserves; (3) experience with internal auditing controls; and (4) an understanding of audit committee functions. Section 407 also states explicitly that its aim is the protection of investors and the public interest.

Accountants

Surely, one of the most important gate keepers guarding the integrity of corporate accounts is the accountant, through the auditing function. While other sections of the Sarbanes-Oxley Act relate to accountants, sections 101-109 (Title I) and 201-209 (Title II) deal in their entirety with them. Title I, which establishes the Public Company Accounting Oversight Board (PCAOB), sets forth in detail the new body; its composition, duties, powers, and relationships with other agencies, both governmental (SEC) and non-governmental (e.g., the American Institute of Certified Public Accountants, the Financial Accounting Standards Board, and other groups similar to the AICPA and involved in corporate financial records). Title II deals in detail with Auditors Independence. There are other sections of the Act that also relate to the Accounting profession, but they are discussed with the sections in which they are found.

Section 101 of Sarbanes-Oxley establishes the PCAOB, as a non-profit, non-governmental corporate body, subject to the SEC. Its duties are: (1) to register public accounting firms that prepare audit reports for covered corporations (i.e., issuers of securities sold to the public); (2) to establish and/or adopt, by rule, auditing, quality control, ethics, independence, and other standards relating to the preparation of audit reports; (3) to conduct inspections of registered public accounting firms; (4) to conduct investigations and disciplinary proceedings of, and impose appropriate sanctions where justified on, registered public accounting firms and associated persons in accordance with section 105; (5) to perform such other duties or functions as the Board (or the SEC, by rule or order) determines are necessary or appropriate to promote high professional standards among, and improve the quality of audit services offered by, registered public accounting firms and associated persons, or otherwise to carry out the Sarbanes-Oxley Act; (6) to enforce compliance with the Act, the rules of the Board, professional standards, and the securities laws relating to the preparation and issuance of audit reports and the obligations and liabilities of accountants, as well as by registered public accounting firms and associated persons; and (7) to set the budget and manage the operations of the Board and its staff.

Section 101 details the composition of the PCAOB. It includes a provision limiting membership to no more than 2 of the 5 members who are or have been CPAs. And, if one of the 2 is the chairperson of the Board, then he or she may not have been a practicing CPA for at least 5 years prior to appointment to the Board. No doubt this provision reflects concern over a Board chairperson having active ties to a registered or other public accounting firm. Membership on the Board is determined by the SEC, in consultation with the Chairman of the Board of Governors of the Federal Reserve System and the Secretary of the Treasury.

Other provisions of section 101 cover members' terms of service and possible removal for cause, powers of the Board and its rules, and requirement that the Board shall submit an annual report, including its audited financial statements, to the SEC. The SEC, in turn, has to transmit a copy of the report to the Senate's Committee on Banking, Housing, and Urban Affairs, and to the House of Representatives' Committee on Financial Services within 30 days after its receipt of the report.

Section 102 deals with the registration of accounting firms with the Board. It makes such registration mandatory, also making it unlawful for any one other than a registered public accounting firm to prepare or issue any audit report for any covered corporation (i.e., issuer of securities sold to the public). The section goes on to detail the form and contents of applications for registration by accounting firms. Those details are indicative of the range and costliness of Sarbanes-Oxley's provisions that probably underlie some of the complaints causing opposition to the Act, and the pressure for an easing of the alleged burdensomeness of the law.

To illustrate the point, section 102 requires that each applicant specify: (1) the names of all present and prospective covered corporate clients, for whom the accounting firm prepared or expects to prepare or issue audit reports during the current calendar year; (2) the annual fees received from each such client for audit services, as well as for other accounting and non-accounting services (e.g., tax and/or other consulting activity); (3) other current financial information for the most recent completed fiscal year of the firm, as the Board may reasonably request; (4) a statement of the quality control policies of the firm for its accounting and auditing practices; (5) a list of all accountants associated with the firm who participate in or contribute to the preparation of audit reports, stating the license or certification number of each such person, as well as the State license numbers of the firm itself; (6) information relating to criminal, civil, or administrative actions or disciplinary proceedings pending against the firm or any associated person of the firm in connection with any audit report; (7) copies of any periodic or annual disclosure filed by an issuer (i.e., a covered corporation) with the SEC during the immediately preceding calendar year, which discloses accounting disagreements between the issuer and the accounting firm in connection with an audit report; and (8) such other information as the rules of the Board or the SEC shall specify as necessary or appropriate in the public interest or for the protection of investors.

The foregoing segment of section 102 also requires that each application for registration include: (1) a consent executed by the public accounting firm to cooperation and compliance with any request for testimony or the production of documents made by the Board in furtherance of its authority and responsibilities, as well as similar consents from each of the associated persons employed by the accounting firm, as a condition of their continued employment; and (2) a statement that the firm's continuing registration rests on its understanding of this obligation and its cooperation and compliance, as well as the understanding, compliance, and cooperation of its associated persons.

Section 102 ends with a funding concern. It instructs the PCAOB to assess and collect a registration fee and an annual fee from each registered public accounting firm in amounts that are sufficient to recover the costs of processing and reviewing applications and annual reports.

Section 103 deals with auditing, quality control, and independence standards and rules. Perhaps its most important feature is its explicit opening instruction that the PCAOB, in its establishing of the rules relating to these matters, shall, to the extent it determines appropriate, do so through the adoption of *standards proposed by one or more professional groups of accountants or advisory groups covered by it as appropriate*. The thrust of this provision seems designed to keep the PCAOB from becoming a regulatory "loose cannon," by providing for important input from those who are being regulated. Section 104 follows logically on its predecessor sections. Having set standards and rules, the PCAOB is required by section 104 to conduct a continuing program of inspections to assess the degree of compliance of each registered public accounting firm and associated persons with the Sarbanes-Oxley Act. Specific reference is made to the rules of the Board and the SEC, as well as to professional standards; all in connection with the firm's performance of audits, issuance of audit reports, and related matters involving covered public corporations. The body of the section deals with inspection frequency, procedures, conduct of inspections, record retention, review procedures, written reports of Board findings, and SEC reviews of Board determinations (on request by a registered public accounting firm).

Section 105 possesses particular importance, because it sets forth investigatory procedures and document production requirements, plus significant punitive provisions applicable to registered public accounting firms and associated persons. During the investigatory period, for example, non-cooperation by a firm or associated person may result in: (1) suspension or barring any such person, who refuses to testify, produce documents, or otherwise cooperate, from being associated with a registered firm; (2) suspension or revocation of the registration of the firm; and (3) other lesser sanctions as specified in the Board's rules, or considered appropriate by it.

In cases of: (1) intentional or knowing conduct, including reckless conduct, that result in violation of applicable statutory, regulatory, or professional standards; or (2) repeated instances of negligent conduct, each resulting in a violation of the applicable statutory, regulatory, or professional standard, the PCAOB, under section 105, may impose disciplinary or remedial sanctions it deems appropriate. The sanctionable acts or conduct embrace any act or practice, whether by commission or omission, in violation of the Sarbanes-Oxley Act, the rules of the PCAOB, the provisions of the securities laws relating to audit reports and obligations and liabilities of accountants with respect to them, including the SEC rules issued under Sarbanes-Oxley, or professional standards.

The specific sanctions listed under section 105 include: (1) temporary suspension or permanent revocation of registrations; (2) temporary or permanent suspension or bar of a person from further association with any registered public accounting firm; (3) temporary or permanent limitation on the activities, functions, or operations of such person or firm (other than in connection with required additional professional education or training); (4) a civil money payment for each violation equal to no more than $100,000 for a natural person or $2,000,000 for any other person (presumably a legal person, viz. a corporation), and, in any case involving "intentional or knowing conduct" or "repeated instances of negligent conduct," no more than $750,000 for a natural person or $15,000,000 for any other person; (5) censure; (6) required additional professional education or training; or (7) any other appropriate sanction provided for in the rules of PCAOB.

Section 106 deals with foreign public accounting firms doing audit work for any issuer covered by Sarbanes-Oxley and the SEC. The section allows the PCAOB, with the approval of the SEC, as well as the SEC itself, to exempt any foreign public accounting form from the provisions of the Act, or the rules of the Board, or of the SEC issued under the Act.

Section 107 details the powers of the SEC in its oversight of the PCAOB. The section requires Board rules to be approved by the SEC, before they become effective. It states the SEC's power to amend Board rules, and to review disciplinary actions taken by the Board, as well as to enhance, modify, cancel, reduce, or require the remission of a Board imposed sanction. It specifies the power of the SEC to censure or limit the powers of the Board if, after a hearing, it determines that the Board has violated or is unable to comply with any provision of Sarbanes-Oxley, its own rules, or the securities laws; or, without reasonable justification or excuse, has failed to enforce compliance with those provisions by a registered public accounting firm or an associated person. The SEC may also censure or remove individual members of the PCAOB for willful violations of Sarbanes-Oxley, Board rules, or the securities laws; or for willful abuse of the Board member's authority; or, without reasonable justification or excuse, failure to enforce compliance by any registered public accounting firm or any associated person.

Section 108 deals with accounting standards. It authorizes the PCAOB to recognize as "generally accepted" any accounting principles established by a standard setting body that meets certain specified conditions. Of particular interest is the provision in the section requiring the PCAOB to study and report on adopting a principles-based accounting system in place of America's present rules-based system.

Section 109 sets down the details that apply to funding the PCAOB. Annual budgets are required, to be financed by annual accounting support payable by each covered issuer firm, but not to exceed the recoverable budget expenses of the Board or a standard setting body. The fees are to be allocated among issuers on the basis of a formula specifying that: the total amount of the fees shall be multiplied by a fraction (i.e., percentage figure) determined *by dividing the numerator* (i.e., the average monthly equity market capitalization of each issuer for the 12 month period immediately preceding the beginning of the fiscal year to which the budget relates) *by the denominator* (i.e., the average monthly equity market capitalization of all issuers for the 12 month period).

The twin objectives of the Sarbanes-Oxley Act, proclaimed repeatedly throughout its text, are the protection of investors and the public interest. The principal means to these ends are the curbing of the power of corporate executives and the enhancement and stimulation of the independence of the "gatekeepers" of the public weal, who interact with those executives; and who thereby are encouraged and even required to speak to their power, when that power leads them to wrongful paths and errant ways.

Title II, Sections 201-209, entitled "Auditor Independence," is a prime illustration. Section 201 aims squarely at auditor conflicts of interest, by limiting non-audit practice concurrently with the performance of an audit. The performance of these non-audit services are specifically precluded: (1) bookkeeping or other services related to the accounting records or financial statement of the audit client; (2) financial information systems design and implementation; (3) appraisal or valuation services, fairness opinions, or contribution-in-kind reports; (4) actuarial services; (5) internal audit outsourcing services; (6) management functions or human resources; (7) broker or dealer, investment adviser, or investment banking services; (8) legal services and expert services unrelated to the audit; and (9) any other service that the Board determines, by regulations, is not permitted. Other non-audit services by a registered public accounting firm are permitted, if the service is pre-approved by the audit committee of the audit client.

Subject to review by the SEC, the PCAOB may exempt, on a case by case basis, any person, issuer, public accounting firm, or transaction from the prohibitions of section 201 and section 10A(g) of the Securities Exchange Act of 1934, to the extent the exemption is necessary or appropriate in the public interest, and is consistent with protection of investors.

Section 202 specifies these preapproval requirements for non-audit services: (1) the fees paid for the non-audit services do not, in aggregate, exceed 5 percent of the total fees paid by the issuer to the auditor during the fiscal year; (2) the non-audit services were not recognized at the time of the audit to be non-audit in nature; and (3) the non-audit services are promptly brought to the attention of the audit committee of the issuer and approved prior to the completion of the audit. Further, the approval of the non-audit services must be disclosed to investors. Also, the audit committee may delegate to one or more of its independent directors the power to grant preapprovals in its behalf.

Section 203 makes it unlawful for a registered public accounting firm to provide audit services to a client public corporation for more than five *continuous* fiscal years, if the lead audit partner or the partner responsible for reviewing the audit has performed such continuous service. The purpose of the provision seems clear; to avoid the growth of an excessively close relationship between the auditing partner or reviewer and the client.

Section 204 mandates that each registered public accounting firm performing an audit for an issuer (covered public corporation) must provide timely reports to the audit committee. Those reports must contain: (1) all critical accounting policies and practices to be used; (2) all alternative treatments of financial information within GAAP that were discussed with management, as well as the ramifications of the use of those alternative treatments and disclosures, and the treatment preferred by the public accounting firm; plus (3) other material written communications between the public accounting firm and management. Plainly, the aim of section 204 is to avoid any private agreements as to accounting treatment of financial information between auditor and management. Full disclosure by the auditor to the audit committee is required.

Section 205 is devoted to definitions of the terms "registered public accounting firm," "audit committee," and "accountant."

Section 206 deals with the inherent conflict of interest when the CEO, the CFO, controller, chief accounting officer or any person equivalent in position was an employee of the auditing registered public accounting firm in the year immediately preceding the initiation of the audit and participated in the audit. The section forbids the accounting firm from doing the audit in such a case.

Section 207 requires the Comptroller General of the United States to conduct a study of a potential rule mandating rotation of registered public accounting firms after some specified period of years. The report is to be submitted to the Senate Committee on Banking, Housing, and Urban Affairs and the House Committee on Financial Services, within one year of the date of enactment of Sarbanes-Oxley.

Section 208 deals with SEC authority, requiring that agency to issue final regulations relative to section 10A of the Securities Exchange Act of 1934, as added to by title II of Sarbanes-Oxley. The section also makes it unlawful for any registered public accounting firm to perform any audit work for any issuer, if that firm or an associated person engages in any act prohibited by section 10A of the Securities Exchange Act of 1934, as added to by Sarbanes-Oxley or rule or regulation of the SEC or of the PCAOB.

Section 209 deals with non-registered public accounting firms, encouraging State regulatory bodies to make independent determinations of the applicability of relevant standards to such accounting firms. In so doing, the State authorities should consider the size and nature of the accounting firms and their clients, without presuming that the standards of Sarbanes-Oxley are applicable to small and medium size non-registered public accounting firms.

Section 404, which deals with internal controls and became the most controversial section of Sarbanes-Oxley, had a major impact on the power of auditors relative to management and directors, as well as on the financial rewards of the profession. It is discussed in detail below that discussed modification of the impact of the law.

Attorneys

Section 307 of Sarbanes-Oxley, which was discussed at some length in Chapter V of this book, requires the SEC to issue rules setting forth minimum standards of professional conduct for attorneys appearing and practicing before it in behalf of issuer corporations. The rules, while they may be more extensive, must: (1) require covered attorneys to report evidence of a material violation of securities law or breach of fiduciary duty or similar violation by the company or an agent to the CEO, or chief legal counsel, or equivalent of said company; and (2) in the absence of an appropriate response to the evidence (including remedial measures or sanctions that are appropriate), to report the evidence to the audit committee, or another committee of the board comprised completely of independent directors, or to the entire board. A more extensive rule might require attorneys, in the absence of appropriate responses by the foregoing corporate officers and board, to report the evidence to the SEC itself. But, such a rule might be considered a violation of the legal profession's code of professional conduct mandating confidentiality, and could elicit strong opposition by the profession.

Financial Analysts and Investment Banks

Title V of the Sarbanes-Oxley Act consists of a single section 501. It aims at financial analyst conflicts of interest. The main thrust of the section is to create a Chinese wall between analysts and the investment banks that have often been their employers. Where such conflicts of interest continue to exist, the section requires full disclosure by the analyst. The enforcement agency is the SEC, or, on its authorization and direction, a registered securities association or national securities exchange.

The SEC or the authorized non-governmental securities association is directed to adopt rules designed to address conflicts of interest that can arise when securities analysts recommend equity securities in research reports and public appearances. The aim is to improve research objectivity, and to provide investors with more useful and reliable information. The rules should:

1. Foster research objectivity and investor confidence by: (a) restricting prepublication clearance or approval of research reports by employees of brokers or dealers who are engaged in investment banking activities, or others not so directly engaged, excepting legal or compliance staff; (b) limit the supervision and compensatory evaluation of analysts to broker or dealer officials who are not engaged in investment banking; and (c) require that brokers or dealers, or their employees, who are involved with investment banking, may not, directly or indirectly, threaten or retaliate against any analyst employed by them or their affiliates, as a result of an adverse, negative, or otherwise unfavorable research report that may impact poorly on the relationship between the broker or dealer with the subject corporation;

2. Define blackout periods during which brokers or dealers participating in a public offering of securities as underwriters or dealers do not distribute or publish research reports about the subject securities to the issuer or others;

3. Establish structural and institutional safeguards within broker or dealer firms to assure that analysts are separated by appropriate informational partitions from the review, pressure, or oversight of investment bankers who might potentially bias their judgment or supervision; and

4. Address other issues that the SEC or the exchanges determine to be appropriate.

The rules adopted by the SEC or the securities exchanges shall also require disclosure of any conflicts of interest by each analyst, broker, or dealer. The disclosure must be in public appearances and in each research report. It must also include: (1) the extent to which the analyst has debt or equity investments in securities that are the subject of a research report; (2) whether any compensation has been received by the broker or dealer, or any affiliate, including the analyst, from the issuer, with certain exemptions deemed appropriate and necessary by the SEC regarding future potential transactions; (3) whether the issuer has been a client of the broker or dealer handling the issue during the preceding year, and, if so, the types of services provided to the issuer; (4) whether the analyst received compensation relating to the research report that was based on the investment banking revenues of the registered broker or dealer; and (5) any other disclosures of conflicts of interest that are material to investors, analysts, or brokers or dealers, as the SEC or the securities exchanges deem appropriate.

It is probably appropriate to note here that section 705 of the Sarbanes-Oxley Act called for a study of possible investment bank involvement in public company manipulation of earnings data that falsely portrayed their true financial condition. The study was to be done by the Comptroller General of the United States (i.e., the General Accounting Office), and made specific reference to the Enron and Global Crossing cases. The results of the study were to be reported to the Congress, as the basis for possible regulatory or legislative action.

Studies and Reports

Apart from section 705, discussed above, Title VII (Sections 701-704) of Sarbanes-Oxley calls for a series of special studies and reports to be done by the Comptroller General of the United States (i.e., the General Accounting Office) or the SEC. Section 701 instructs the GAO to study the consolidation of public accounting firms since 1989, with attention to its impact on the profession's capability to provide audit services to large national and global businesses, as well as its future impact on capital formation and the securities markets. The study is to look also at possible problems arising from less competition among public accounting firms and impacting on business; such as higher costs, lessened quality of service, impairment of auditor independence or lack of choice, and whether Federal or State regulations impede competition among public accounting firms.

Section 702 calls for an SEC study and report of credit rating agencies. The study is instructed to examine: (1) the role of credit rating agencies in evaluating issuers of securities; (2) the importance of that role to investors and the functioning of the capital markets; (3) any impediments to the accurate appraisal by credit rating agencies of the financial resources and risks of issuers of securities; (4) any barriers to entry into the credit rating business, and any measures required to remove such barriers; (5) any measures required to improve dissemination of information as to the financial resources and risks of issuers when credit rating agencies announce credit ratings; and (6) any conflicts of interest in the operation of credit rating agencies and measures to prevent such conflicts or ameliorate their consequences.

Section 703 calls for a study and report, by the SEC, of primary violators of Federal securities laws who have not been sanctioned, disciplined, or otherwise penalized, as well as those who have been found to have aided or abetted a violation. The target study group embraced securities professionals, defined as public accountants, public accounting firms, investment bankers, investment advisers, brokers, dealers, attorneys, and others practicing before the SEC. The study and report was to describe the violations that had been committed, including: (1) the specific provision of the Federal securities laws violated; (2) the specific sanctions and penalties imposed on the primary violators, and the aiders and abettors, as well as the monetary penalties assessed and collected; (3) the occurrence of multiple violations by the same person or persons; (4) whether disciplinary sanctions were imposed on each such violator; and (5) the amount of disgorgement, restitution, or any other fines or payments assessed and collected by the SEC from the primary violators, aiders, and abettors. The study period was to cover the calendar years 1998, 1999, 2000, and 2001.

Section 704 instructed the SEC to review and analyze all its enforcement actions involving violations of reporting requirements imposed under the securities laws, as well as restatements of financial statements, over the five year period preceding the date of enactment of the Sarbanes-Oxley Act. The review and analysis results are to be reported to the House Committee on Financial Services and the Senate Committee on Banking, Housing, and Urban Affairs.

Punitive Provisions of Sarbanes-Oxley

The remainder of the Act, embracing Title VI and Titles VIII-XI (with the exception of a brief single section Title X), deals with its punitive provisions. Title VI deals with SEC resources and authority to regulate appearance and practice before it, and to specify the qualifications required of associated persons of brokers and dealers. The Title also includes the sums appropriated by the Congress for fiscal year 2003 for the SEC ($776,000,000). Finally, it provides authority for Federal courts to bar persons from participating in offerings of penny stocks.

Section 602 of the Title is of particular interest, since it provides that the SEC may censure any person, or deny, temporarily or permanently, to any person the privilege of appearing or practicing before it in any way, if that person has been found: (1) not to possess the requisite qualifications to represent others; (2) to lack character or integrity, or to have engaged in unethical or improper professional conduct; or (3) to have willfully violated, or willfully aided and abetted the violation of, any provision of the securities laws or the rules and regulations issued under those laws.

Another provision of section 602, specific to registered public accounting firms or associated persons, defines the term "improper professional conduct." The provision defines such conduct as: (1) intentional or knowing conduct, including reckless conduct, that results in a violation of applicable professional standards, and (2) negligent conduct, i.e., a single instance of highly unreasonable conduct that results in a violation of applicable professional standards in circumstances in which the accounting firm or associated person knows or should know, that heightened scrutiny is warranted; or repeated instances of such conduct that indicate incompetence to practice before the SEC.

Here, as elsewhere throughout the Sarbanes-Oxley Act, the inclusion of words such as willful, knowing, intentional, unreasonable, should know, and improper are important. They are undoubtedly intended to guard against overly zealous guardians of the law who may be carried away and use the enforcement and punitive powers they possess to "improperly" and "unreasonably" invade civil liberties and the "prudent" administration of the law. At the same time, they provide fertile ground for well heeled defendants to engage in expensive and extended litigation. But that is probably the price necessary to the preservation of due process and the just enforcement of the law.

With the exception of Title X, which states the sense of the U.S. Senate that the Federal income tax return of a corporation should be signed by its CEO, the rest of the Sarbanes-Oxley Act (Titles VIII-XI) deals with its punitive provisions.

Title VIII (Sections 802-807) is concerned with corporate and criminal fraud accountability. Section 802 specifies the penalties for destruction, alteration, or falsification of records in Federal investigations and bankruptcy. The committing of such an act, or even contemplation or relationship to such an act, is subject to a fine or imprisonment of not more than 20 years, or both. Section 803 makes debts nondischargeable if incurred in violation of the securities fraud laws. Section 804 sets the statute of limitations for securities fraud. It is set at not later than two years after the discovery of the facts constituting a violation; or 5 years after such violation; whichever comes first. Section 805 calls for the U.S. Sentencing Commission to review and amend sentencing guidelines for obstruction of justice and extensive criminal fraud, to ensure that they are "sufficient to deter and punish that activity." Section 806 is a whistle blower protection provision, covering employees of publicly traded companies who expose fraud. The section prohibits discrimination against the whistle blower, permits the filing of a complaint by the whistle blower with the Secretary of Labor or the bringing of an action by him/her in an appropriate Federal district court. Such legal action may seek relief for the whistle blower, to make him/her whole, and should include compensatory damages (i.e., reinstatement in a position equivalent to the employee's former one, back pay with interest, and compensation for any special damages, i.e., litigation costs, attorney fees, etc. The Labor Department has assigned its responsibility to the Occupational Safety and Health Administration (OSHA), which may prove inadequate, because OSHA is not trained to handle complex accounting issues. Section 807 sets down criminal penalties for defrauding shareholders of publicly traded companies. Anyone who knowingly commits, or attempts to commit, such a scheme shall be fined or imprisoned for not more than 25 years, or both.

Title IX (Sections 902-906) enhances the penalties for white collar crime. Section 902 extends the existing penalties for committing criminal fraud offenses to those who attempt and conspire to commit them, although they have not yet actually committed the criminal fraud. Section 903 extends the period of imprisonment from 5 to 20 years in cases of mail and wire fraud. In cases of violations of ERISA (the Employee Retirement Income Security Act of 1974), the monetary penalties are expanded by section 904, by increasing the sums from $5,000 to $100,000, and from $100,000 to $500,000, respectively, and the jail time from one year to ten years. Section 905 instructs the U.S. Sentencing Commission to review and amend the Federal Sentencing Guidelines to implement the provisions of the Sarbanes-Oxley Act in order to deter, prevent, and punish white collar crimes covered by the Act. Section 906 deals with failure of corporate officers to certify financial reports. If the failure is not willful, the penalties are not more than $1,000,000 or imprisonment for not more than ten years, or both. If the failure is willful, than the monetary penalty is increased to not more than $5,000,000, or not more than twenty years, or both.

Title XI embraces sections 1102-1107. Section 1102 provides that, in cases of tampering with a record or otherwise impeding an official proceeding, miscreants are to be fined or imprisoned for not more than twenty years, or both. Section 1103 authorizes the SEC to petition a Federal district court for a temporary order (freeze) to compel a publicly traded company to place in escrow, with interest and subject to court supervision and limited to 45 days, any extraordinary compensation to any of its directors, officers, partners, controlling persons, agents or employees. The SEC may seek such an injunction whenever it appears to the SEC that such a payment will be made. The injunction may be extended, for good cause, for an additional 45 days, but not to exceed a total of 90 days. Section 1104 requests the U.S. Sentencing Commission to review the sentencing guidelines applicable to securities and accounting fraud and related offenses, and to consider the promulgation of new sentencing guidelines or amendments, so as to enhance existing penalties for officers or directors of publicly traded companies who commit fraud and related offenses. Section 1105 authorizes the SEC to prohibit service as officers or directors of publicly traded companies persons who have violated the relevant provisions of the Securities Exchange Act of 1934

(Section 10b or 15b). Similar authority is applied to the Securities Act of 1933, sections 17a (1) or 15d. Section 1106 increases the penalties specified in the Securities Exchange Act of 1934 from $1,000,000 to $5,000,000, from $2,500,000 to $25,000,000, and from not more than ten years to not more than twenty years. Finally, section 1107 provides that anyone who knowingly, and with the intent to retaliate, takes any harmful action against an informant who provides truthful information about the commission, or possible commission, of a Federal offense shall be fined or imprisoned for not more than ten years, or both.

Costliness of Sarbanes-Oxley

The major complaint against Sarbanes-Oxley is its costliness, i.e., the direct monetary expenditures by covered public corporations to meet its new and enhanced regulatory requirements. The particular portion of the law which is the major target of this attack is section 404. That section mandates the SEC to require that each annual corporate report contain an assessment of the corporation's internal control structure and procedures for financial reporting. The annual report must also state specifically management's responsibility for establishing and maintaining the system of internal control. Section 404 contains a key word that indicates the degree of quality that must be met by the internal control structure. The word is "*adequate.*" And adequacy must be assessed and reported on by the registered public accounting firm doing the corporation's audit.

The adequacy requirement, taken in the context of the punitive provisions of Sarbanes-Oxley, has undoubtedly concentrated the attention of management, auditors, and the board of directors' audit committee, on satisfying the standard. There is consequently a preparedness, even if unwilling, to spend money to achieve adequacy. Unhappily, that standard is known to have been achieved beyond doubt only in the absence of a discovery of malfeasance. Presumably, discovery of malfeasance is proof positive of a failure of adequacy in the internal controls. But, is that truly the case? In the end, human failures, i.e., a rogue employee in a key position may be able to conceal chicanery and abort the effectiveness of the controls. In case of such a failure, does the auditor's attestation of management's assessment of adequacy in the control structure hold harmless the management and the directors from punitive sanctions? These are the issues that can involve great expense in litigation procedures in money, time, and effort.

Paul Volcker and Arthur Levitt, Jr. considered the costliness issue in their defense of Sarbanes-Oxley, pointing specifically to section 404. They cited a survey of 321 companies by Financial Executives International. The companies studied had annual revenues of over $5 billion. They expected to spend $4.7 million each to implement section 404 controls, and an additional $1.5 million annually to maintain the control structure. The expenditures by the largest global corporations were expected to be far higher. Later data, cited by *Business Week*, indicated that companies doing $4 billion or more annually were spending an average of $35 million to comply. But Volcker and Levitt are convinced that existing controls were inadequate, as evidenced by the fact that in 2003 alone, 57 companies, both large and small, reported material weaknesses in their controls, following the termination of their former auditors. Later data indicated that, in the period January-November 2004, 550 companies reported control weaknesses. That number varies widely from the 200 reported by the SEC, of 2,500 filing internal control reports as of March 31, 2005.[1] Volcker and Levitt concluded that the requirements of Sarbanes-Oxley are a necessary and tolerable burden to be borne for the protection of the investing public. They observed that the money cost paled in comparison with the losses sustained by investors and employees when corporations fail, or suffer severe loses due to inadequate internal controls, or the expenditures in the litigation that occurs when things turn bad.

The costliness of section 404 compliance, great as it was, was matched by the volume of complaints about that cost. The situation was not helped by significant variation in the estimates of the cost. Matt Kelly, in an article in *Compliance Week*, reported one estimate that the average cost of 404 compliance in fiscal 2004 was $14.3 million for a company with annual sales of $1 billion or more, a 45 percent increase from 2003.[2] A concurrent Financial Executives International survey of 217 big companies estimated the cost of section 404 compliance at $ 1 million per $1 billion in revenue.[3] But, a CRA International survey reported that the average cost for companies with revenue of more than $700 million fell 44 percent, to $4.8 million, in the second year of compliance reporting.[4] The *Wall Street Journal*, based on an analysis of data compiled by Standard and Poor's, reported that average audit fees in fiscal 2004, by market cap size, amounted to $7.4 million for S&P 500 firms, $2.2 million for S&P mid-cap 400 firms, and $1 million for S&P small-cap firms; up substantially from prior fiscal years.[5] Of course, the four sets of numbers may not be comparable, but they are confusing in the absence of detailed data.

Confusion existed also with respect to the outlook for future compliance costs. Many observers expected that with the passage of time costs would be reduced. A learning curve would appear. Firms would adopt automated compliance procedures for section 404 requirements. Experience would be a factor, and firms would become more efficient in additional ways. Again, available data was unclear, because it was mixed. The S&P data just cited indicated increasing costs, across all sizes of firms. Matt Kelly, cited above, noted that there was some resistance to the cost of implementing automated systems, especially among small and medium size firms. Yet, he observed in the same article that the effect of that resistance might be offset by the fact that section 404 risk assessment and documentation tasks were now complete, and that would be a cost reducing factor. Also, as automated technology systems were implemented costs should be reduced, although they rose in the short-term because of the expensiveness of the technology.

By mid-2006, the cost issue was clearly coming to a head. On July 11, 2006, the SEC announced that it anticipated proposing a rule that would curb costs. "The commission published a 'concept release,' setting forth numerous questions regarding both how the carrying out of the law had proceeded and what should be done now. It asked for comments on those questions over the next two months."[6] A number of suggestions had already accumulated about how section 404's impact might be moderated. Most involved differentiating the requirements by size of company, with the rigorousness of the requirements varying directly with the size of the firm. One suggestion, by Robert Greifeld, President and CEO of NASDAQ, involved an exemption from section 404 for smaller companies with less than $128 million in market capitalization and annual revenues below $125 million, partial exemption for firms with a market cap between $128 million and $787 million and revenues below $250 million annually. Larger companies would have to comply completely with section 404 internal controls. Other suggestions were similar in nature, but less liberal in offering complete exemption for the smallest firms, while some would ease the impact on smaller companies by allowing less rigorous requirements for evaluating their internal controls, perhaps by easing or eliminating the requirement for external auditor examination and sign-off.[7] A quite different approach was suggested by Robert C. Pozen. Rather than focusing on size of firm, he focused on the "materiality" of the financial data, i.e., whether the information required was significant to a company's overall financial situation. This concept of materiality differed significantly, in Pozen's judgment, from the one contained in PCAOB rule number 2, which judged materiality as a "reasonable assurance" that the internal controls were effective. Pozen thought the reasonable assurance standard invited consideration of hypothetical situations where there is a "reasonable likelihood" that wrongdoing could or would occur. This possibility would lead auditors, in turn, to engage in detailed and expensive examinations of a firm's internal controls, rather than simply evaluating the overall design of the control system.[8] Despite all these differences in opinion, some commentators believed full compliance to be the only road leading to maximum protection for investors. In any case, the significant easing of the impact of section 404 in December 2006, with its emphasis on materiality and risk assessment, should lessen the costliness of compliance.

Volcker and Levitt wrote also about another alleged cost of Sarbanes-Oxley; namely, that it might put the American capital markets at a competitive disadvantage against other capital markets. They were skeptical of a claim by the chairman of the New York Stock Exchange that the number of European companies listing on the NYSE decreased by more than half since the late 1990s, and that only one such firm listed on the NYSE in 2004, because of Sarbanes-Oxley. They discussed the allegation that Sarbanes-Oxley was the cause of the diminution, pointing out that other American exchanges had not had the same experience. Their confidence rested also on their firm belief that the American markets remained the best in the world, because they are still the best regulated, and the proof is that other countries seek to emulate our reforms (e.g., England and Germany). But, *Business Week* reported a significant drop in IPOs of companies seeking to go public in US markets as against foreign ones in 2005. According to that report, 9 out of 10 global IPOs in 2000 were listed on US exchanges, but, in 2005, only 1 out of the 25 top global IPOs were listed on an American exchange.[9] A further factor could be the increasing ability of foreign exchanges to raise substantial amounts of capital. We noted earlier the increased activity in mergers of exchanges internationally (Euronext, Deutsche Borse, London Stock Exchange, NYSE Group, NASDQ, etc.). In this context, rigorous implementation of the strictest possible interpretation of section 404 might well hinder the future growth and strength of the American exchanges. That concern led Senator Schumer and Mayor Bloomberg to argue for an easing of the burden of section 404 (Appendix II), An interesting and seemingly significant piece of evidence involves a presumed premium gotten by foreign firms that list on NYSE Group or NASDAQ; i.e., a higher market value for their stock than would otherwise be the case (due to greater confidence in the quality required of their financial reports). The *Wall Street Journal* reported such a premium appeared to exist prior to 2002 (when the Sarbanes-Oxley Act was passed), but was significantly reduced thereafter. That fact would appear to influence the present reluctance of foreign firms to do IPOs on American exchanges.[10] In any event, the SEC signaled a major change in its attitude toward foreign firms delisting (leaving) from an American exchange, when it announced that it would reconsider its existing rule (permitting delisting only if fewer than 10 percent of their securities were owned by Americans and less than 5 percent of their trading volume was done in the U.S.). In place of that rule, the SEC indicated it would consider one based only on trading volume.[11] Floyd Norris, of the *New York Times*, disagreed strongly with the SEC's action, writing "when fraud engulfs an overseas company that was allowed to stop complying with American rules despite having thousands of American investors, the public may ask whether that was a wise decision.[12]

There is a further aspect to the burden imposed on business by Sarbanes-Oxley. It is the growth of a regulatory bureaucracy emboldened and stimulated by the strictures of the law and the regulatory zeal unleashed by the spirit of the time, to cause a serious diversion of time, energy, and thought from managing and directing the future course of business to meeting excessive regulatory requirements. It is feared that, by seeking an excessive level of regulatory protection, the requirements may harm the productive power of American industry, and the competitiveness of its capital markets. Achieving balance between protection and productivity is a neat judgmental exercise. At this moment in time, concern over the costs of protection is gaining strength. Hopefully, our system of checks and balances will prove adequate to correct the imbalance.

Modifying the Impact of Sarbanes-Oxley

What are the ways to weaken the impact of Sarbanes-Oxley? The legislative way is perhaps the most potent. Indeed, the quarter century preceding passage of that law was notable for deregulation. Beginning with President Jimmy Carter's deregulation of the airline and trucking industries, and President Bill Clinton's dramatic announcement that the Age of Big Government was over, powerful pressures were at work in the legislative and executive branches of the government to reduce regulation, which was widely regarded as stifling initiative, enterprise, and economic growth. The explosive growth of the nineties seemed to validate that line of reasoning.

The bubble of optimism collapsed with the implosion of Enron, the associated crash of the securities markets, and the accompanying recession. The role of the corporate accounting scandals in that scenario resulted in a reversion to regulation as protector of the public interest. Sarbanes-Oxley was the legislative response, and, while its impact is still growing in extent and depth of penetration into American corporate business, so too is opposition. It is consequently not surprising that lobbyists in behalf of regulated businesses and professions are busily engaged in seeking the weakening of the law's provisions. This pressure is being exerted directly on the Congress and, directly and indirectly, on the regulatory agencies (both governmental and non-governmental).

The powerful desire of legislators to be re-elected and move up the ladder of political office, plus the ever growing expensiveness of contemporary political campaigns, tends to suborn their independence and surrender them to dependence on campaign contributions channeled through lobbyists. The quid pro quo is lending a sympathetic ear and more or less eager support to the pleas of lobbyists and their sponsors. Today's professional politician is not likely to reject support, minus considerable soul searching. This path to change involves our legislative bodies, who can respond to political pressure by revisions of Sarbanes-Oxley, or the enactment of entirely new laws. A corollary path to modification of Sarbanes-Oxley lies in the power of the SEC to change its impact through new regulatory rules or interpretations of specific provisions of the law; specifically section 404. The point is illustrated by the SEC's announcement in November 2006 that it would divulge such changes in December 2006, and by its request to the Public Company Oversight Accounting Board to issue rules that would ease the impact of section 404, especially for small and mid-level corporations.[13] And, in December, an easing of the auditing standards for small businesses was effected by specifying materiality as a basic factor in evaluating the adequacy of internal controls, i.e., the SEC asked the PCAOB to implement the change.

The change emphasized an evaluation of risk in determining the minuteness and frequency required for the auditor to assess a firm's internal controls. Of course, the costliness of audits should be significantly reduced for smaller firms, but they did not get a blanket exemption from section 404. It is of interest that, for large corporations, section 404 appears to have clearly benefited investors, i.e., while financial restatements for all public companies rose by 12 percent in 2006, they declined by 25 percent among large firms.[14]

Another way to weaken the impact of Sarbanes-Oxley is by extended and expensive litigation. The government's power is overwhelming against an ordinary business. But, a wealthy, powerful corporation, like Microsoft, is well positioned to make a real fight, and to tie up a government agency in litigation that strains the agency's budgetary and personnel resources. The same observation holds for a trade or professional association that is well financed by an industry or body of professional people. It is worth repeating the caveat that words that qualify the law, like unreasonable, adequate, willful, knowing, etc., lend themselves to lengthy litigation, especially in the context of our emphasis on due process and the adversarial nature of the judicial system.

Note must be taken also of special ad hoc study groups that are set up to analyze the impact of laws and policies on business and the economy. The formation of such a group was announced on September 12, 2006. Known as the Committee on Capital Markets Regulation, studied the impact of Sarbanes-Oxley on America's capital markets; as well as possible changes in the laws dealing with civil and criminal liability for companies and auditors, and directors; the role of State governments (especially State Attorney Generals), the impact and costliness of section 404; and shareholder rights. Early rumors of the directions taken by the Committee indicated particular concern over the potential liability of accounting firms performing audits performed in accordance with the requirements of section 404; a concern that was related to the destruction of the Arthur Andersen accounting firm, which left only four major accounting firms doing the overwhelming majority of audits for America's public corporations. Another proposal would counter the efforts of the Justice Department to require firms under investigation to withhold payment of legal fees of executives suspected of violations of the law. The Committee had no official status, but its membership of well known academics, business leaders, and research related organizations gave it status, as did the public praise of Henry M. Paulson, Jr., U.S. Treasury

Secretary. The Committee's Executive Director was Harvard law professor Hal S. Scott, who was joined by two co-chairmen (R. Glenn Hubbard, dean of Columbia University's Business school, and John L. Thornton, board chairman of the Brookings Institution). The three men chose the other members of the Committee. Its first report was made public on November 30, 2006, and was likely to be influential.

Hubbard and Thornton, in a piece in the *Wall Street Journal*, emphasized their concern over the possible negative impact of Sarbanes-Oxley on the international competitiveness of America's capital markets.[15] They followed with a lengthy summary of the November 30 report of the Committee's recommendations, published in the *Wall Street Journal* on that day.[16] The summary made clear the Committee's desire to avoid losing Sarbane-Oxley reforms that contributed to shareholder protection and enhanced the transparency of America's capital markets. But, its primary thrust was strongly in favor of changes that would reduce their costliness, notably through "reducing excessive risk aversion of corporate managers, auditors and directors." Translated into less elegant language, the intent is to lessen the fear of the named parties that they would be as subject to criminal and/or civil prosecution and penalties as is now the case. The underlying concern is that executives, directors, auditors and other gatekeepers are now so frightened of severe punishments that they go to uinproductive and unnecessary lengths to achieve protection, and, in so doing, harm the efficiency and innovativeness of American industry, and the competitiveness of our capital markets.

The Hubbard-Thornton Committee Report focused on six major areas for reform: (1) more cost effective implementation of section 404 of Sarbanes-Oxley; (2) reform of the U.S. litigation and enforcement system; (3) strengthening of shareholder rights; (4) curbing the harmfulness of excessive gatekeeper litigation; (5) enlargement of the role of economic analysis, to improve the effectiveness of regulation; and (6) a presidential directive to the Working Group on Financial Markets, to "evaluate . . . key legal and regulatory issues and formalize a process of cost-benefit analysis for capital markets regulation." Within that framework, these especially notable recommendations were made: (1) revise (ease) the "materiality" standards applied under section 404, i.e., Auditing Standard No.2; (2) clarify and permit greater auditor judgment in assessing management's internal control system; (3) allow multiyear cycling of auditor reviews of internal controls; and "reshaping" of section 404 for small firms; (4) remove non-U.S. companies from the requirements of section 404, where their home country requirements are equivalent to ours; (5) modification (easing) of our litigation system and better balance in or criminal enforcement system, e.g. criminal enforcement against an entire company should be a last resort and applied only in cases where the entire firm has become a criminal enterprise; (6) reversal of the Justice Department's Thompson Memorandum, in particular its pressure to withhold payment of legal fees for employees charged with transgressions in the course of their work for the employer, and its equally severe pressure for the waiving of attorney-client privilege in such cases; (7) modification of board adoptions of poison pills and staggered terms for directors, to enhance board sensitivity to shareholder interests; (8) curbing excessive litigation against gatekeepers, most notably directors and auditors, that reduces the effectiveness and efficiency of their input in corporate decisions , e.g. a cap on auditor liability, and upholding the reliance of independent directors on an audited financial statement, or an auditor's comfort latter; and (9) encouragement of the SEC to enlarge its use of economic cost-benefit analysis in making and enforcing rules and regulations (more economists and fewer lawyers?).[17]

Senator Charles Schumer and Mayor Michael Bloomberg had strongly pressed similar concerns in an earlier piece published in the *Wall Street Journal* (reproduced in Appendix II).[18] A second study group was formed by the United States Chamber of Commerce, and was originally headed by Robert K. Steel, who has since left to become Undersecretary of the Treasury for Domestic Finance, and its final reports will also attract significant attention. Also, the six largest accounting firms in the world issued a joint report ("Serving Global Capital Markets and the Global Economy") which called for measures that would limit their liability in lawsuits by disgruntled, angry investors.[19] Ben Stein, writing in the *New York Times* decried the efforts of these study groups, seeing in them attempts to weaken unduly the thrust of the Sarbanes-Oxley law.[20]

Finally, there is the media, that powerful instrument to sway public opinion. Full page ads in influential newspapers, similar ads on TV, efforts to direct the content of presumably non-political entertainment programs, the influence of avowedly ideological radio talk shows, so-called documentary movies like Michael Moore's "Fahrenheit 9/11"; as well as op-ed pieces by prominent personalities may attempt to build a public mood adverse to the impact of increased and increasing governmental regulation. A particularly potent op-ed piece deserves attention. It appeared on the editorial page of the *Wall Street Journal*, and warrants special note because of the prominence of its authors—Senator Charles Schumer, Democrat of New York and Michael Bloomberg, moderate Republican Mayor of New York City. Senator Schumer, in particular, is a leading Democrat, who might be expected to be a strong supporter of rigorous governmental regulation, rather than proposing the reverse. Yet, in their op-ed piece, that is precisely what the Senator and the Mayor were proposing. Expressing great concern that New York City's famed capital markets would lose their position as world leaders, with severe economic consequences for the city and the nation, they called for actions that would: (1) simplify America's regulatory system; with particular attention to the impact of the Sarbanes-Oxley Act (presumably section 404), while not weakening the ability to discover corporate fraud; (2) reduce the burden of securities class action lawsuits; and (3) contrast America's accounting standards with those of foreign countries, with an eye to the former's burdensomeness, while not undermining protection of investor interests (a neat balancing trick).[21]

That is the battleground, and the contending parties are engaged. An ultimate outcome that seals the issue in favor of one side forever is not likely; rather the future will see ebb and flow as regulation, with its benefits and costs, are subjected to changing conditions and public moods, as they manifest themselves through our system of checks and balances.

Protecting the Public Interest:
The Defenders of Sarbanes-Oxley

We conclude with a look at the defenders of Sarbanes-Oxley. The regulatory agencies, both governmental (e.g., SEC) and non-governmental (e.g., NYSE, AMEX, NASDAQs, plus State Attorneys General (e.g., Eliot Spitzer in New York State) appear to be most prominent. They have been energized by the passage of Sarbanes-Oxley, and the sense of public outrage that resulted from the corporate accounting scandals. Regulations have multiplied, budgets enlarged, research and enforcement personnel increased, with regulatory, investigative, and prosecutorial muscularity invigorated. Although it has taken some four years for the most prominent cases and individuals to be prosecuted and brought to a guilty verdict, the wheels of justice have continued to move forward. As of November 2006, Martha Stewart; Kenneth Lay, Jeffrey Skilling, and Andrew Fastow of Enron; John and Timothy Rigas of Adelphia; Kozlowski and Swartz of Tyco; Bernard Ebbers of World Com, and Walter Forbes of Cendant, as well others have all been found guilty and punished with severe financial penalties and prison terms. Kenneth Lay died before final sentencing, perhaps partly from the aggravation and stress of 5 years of bitter, expensive litigation. Bernard Ebbers lost his appeal of a 25 year prison sentence as being too severe, because it was tantamount to a life sentence, and the judge showed more sympathy for the unfortunate victims of Ebbers' misdeeds than he did for the perpetrator. Numbers of other former executives are in process. Still more individuals and corporations have negotiated settlements involving large fines and significant sanctions. The regulators are presently very active. But, Mark Belnick of Tyco has been found not guilty and exonerated, while Frank Quattrone's conviction was overturned on appeal, and the Grasso-Langone case, involving the NYSE, is not a legal slam dunk. How long the zeal of regulators and prosecutors, like Eliot Spitzer, will continue, plus public and legislative support for it, remains to be seen.

Large institutional investors, like Calpers and other major pension funds, are acting vigorously in exerting shareholder pressure on boards of directors and corporate management. However resistant those groups may be to the pressure, their stubbornness carries the risk of their possible replacement by more compliant people. The main body of *Corruption in Corporate America* discusses institutional investors at some length, but it is worth repeating the caveat made there, i.e., institutional investors may have internal conflicts of interest, which may muddy the clarity with which they pursue the best interests of their investors.

The media can be a potent actor in defending Sarbanes-Oxley. Investigative journalism can uncover and publicize corporate malfeasance, and marshal public opinion that compels regulatory and legislative action. It seems evident that, in the economic bubble of the nineties, the media reported and enhanced the public persona of CEOs and deal makers, converting many of them into celebrities with an aura of stardom. That aura easily convinced many of them that they were above the law. They became somewhat contemptuous of lowly regulators. That worm has turned, and those former celebrities are now depicted in negative news photos, manacled and doing a "perp walk." The mighty have fallen, but, once again the chastening after effect will be revealed with the passage of time.

The average investor is also a defender of Sarbanes-Oxley, but only to the degree that he/she is active in behalf of his/her interest. If the individual investor is supine, passive, and/or ignorant of financial realities, then corporate malefactors have fertile ground for their chicanery. Caveat emptor applies. The individual investor must become informed about the investments being made, and alert to the performance of managers and directors of the firms being invested in. Of course, opponents of zealous regulation and enforcement claim that the heavy hand of regulation is actually an unnecessary evil in a free market economy, because the individual investor can always sell shares in a poor company and walk away. And, when numbers of individuals do that, the share value collapses, and the bad managers and directors suffer. But, that is glib, because it does not recognize the damage that is done by managerial cheats, who can escape harm for significant periods of time, and even accumulate ill-gotten, golden nest eggs to sustain themselves lavishly after they have been uncovered and fired.

Finally, we should note the importance of the concerned citizen, who, while not an investor in public corporations, may well suffer in an economic downturn caused by accounting scandals, a market collapse, and significant losses of employment and income. Such a citizen, through the power of the ballot box, can stimulate legislative action and regulation.

Together, these groups can constitute a powerful, combined defense for corrective legislation, like the Sarbanes-Oxley Act.

Notes

1. *New York Times*, April 17, 2005, p. 5.
2. *Compliance Week*, "404 Compliance in Year Two Isn't Getting Cheaper," July 12, 2005.
3. *New York Times*, July 15, 2005, p. 5.
4. *New York Times*, December 18, 2005, pp. C1, C5.
5. *Wall Street Journal*, October 17, 2005, see table in article.
6. *New York Times*, July 12, 2006, p. C3.
7. *Wall Street Journal*, April 13, 2006, p. A12.
8. *Wall Street Journal*, April 5, 2006, p. A20.
9. *Business Week*, May 22, 2006, pp. 33-34.
10. *Wall Street Journal*, November 28, 2006, pp. C1, C14.
11. *New York Times*, December 7, 2006, p. C6.
12. *New York Times*, December 15, 2006, pp. C1, C10.
13. *Wall Street Journal*, November 10, 2006, pp. A1, A14; *Wall Street Journal*, November 17, 2006, p. C3.

14. *New York Times*, December 11, 2006, pp. C1, C2.

15. *New York Times*, September 13, 2006, p. C3; *Wall Street Journal*, October 30, 2006, p. A12.

16. *Wall Street Journal*, November 30, 2006, p. A16.

17. *Wall Street Journal*, November 30, 2006, p. A16; *Wall Street Journal*, December 1, 2006, p. C3; *New York Times*, November 30, 2006, pp. C1, C5.

18. *Wall Street Journal*, November 1, 2006, p. A18.

19. *New York Times*, November 8, 2006, p. C3; *Wall Street Journal*, November 8, 2006, p. A22.

20. *New York Times*, October 29, 2006, pp. 1, 23; section 3, p. 3.

21. *Wall Street Journal*, November 1, 2006, p. A18.

Index

About the Author

A braham L. Gitlow is Dean Emeritus and Professor of Economics Emeritus of New York University's Stern School of Business. He served as dean for 20 years, and became a member of the faculty in 1947. He is currently an honorary director of the Bank Leumi (USA), having served as a director from 1980 to 1994. He served also as a director of Macmillan, Welbilt, Leslie Fay, and other public and private corporations. His experience with government organizations included service as president of Ramapo Central School District No. 2. He has been a consultant to Western Electric, Westinghouse, and other corporations and trade association groups. He is the author of twelve books and numerous articles in professional journals. His most recent books are: *Being the Boss: The Importance of Leadership* and *Power and Reflections on Higher Education: A Dean's View.*